AN HISTORICAL APPROACH TO MUSICAL FORM

By

IAN SPINK, M.A., B.Mus.

Senior Lecturer in Music, University of Sydney

LONDON

G. BELL AND SONS LTD

COPYRIGHT © 1967 BY
G. BELL AND SONS LTD

Published by
G. Bell and Sons Ltd
York House
Portugal Street
London, W.C.2

Printed in Great Britain by
William Clowes and Sons, Limited, London and Beccles

Contents

Contents

Author's Note
and Acknowledgements

Needless to say, I hope this book will prove illuminating to a wider range of readers than those students in the early years of a music course at a University or Conservatorium of Music whom I had in mind while writing it. I hope, too, that school music teachers (and intending teachers) will read it and derive some benefit from it, and that others will find that it offers something more than notes on a concert programme or record cover provide. In order to avoid being held up by explanations of technical terms, I have assumed a certain pre-knowledge in this direction on the part of the reader. Even so, it is hoped that the immediate context will explain unfamiliar terms and expressions. The titles of musical works are generally given in the form which English-speaking musicians most commonly use in referring to them, however inconsistent this may be. Nicknames, whether composer-sanctioned or not, have been preferred to a more elaborate identification, though number, key and/or opus number have usually been supplied at least once. Composers' Christian names and dates are given at the first important mention of the composer in question; similarly, as an aid to historical orientation, the dates (of completion or first performance) of works cited. These have been limited as far as possible to those scores which are likely to be generally accessible (and frequently performed), but in the case of works dating from before 1750 or so, references are confined, for the most part, to examples contained in certain fairly widely circulating anthologies, such as the *Historical Anthology of Music*

(*HAM*) by Archibald T. Davison and Willi Apel (2 vols., 1946, 1950; Britain: Oxford University Press; U.S.A.: Harvard), *Masterpieces of Music Before 1750 (MM)* by Carl Parrish and John F. Ohl (1951; Britain: Faber & Faber; U.S.A.: W. W. Norton), *A Treasury of Early Music (TM)* by Carl Parrish (1958; Britain: Faber & Faber; U.S.A.: W. W. Norton), and *Geschichte der Musik in Beispielen (GMB)* by Arnold Schering (1931; Breitkopf & Härtel).

The absence of a bibliography is justified on the ground that in a general work such as this a vast number of books have some bearing, while (as far as I know) there are none which, so to speak, run parallel. So far as further reading is concerned, the appropriate volumes of the 'Norton' and 'New Oxford' Histories of Music may be recommended. Individual points may be verified or pursued further there, or in *Man and his Music* by Alec Harman and Wilfrid Mellers (1962, Barrie & Rockliff) and the excellent *Pelican History of Music* (so far 2 vols., 1960, 1963) edited by Alec Robertson and Denis Stevens. 'Grove's Dictionary' is useful, but perhaps not so valuable—all things considered—as Willi Apel's *Harvard Dictionary of Music* (1944, Harvard University Press; in Britain: Heinemann) or even the *Collins Music Encyclopedia* by J. A. Westrup and F. Ll. Harrison (1959, Collins).

I would like to thank most sincerely my colleagues Mrs. Doreen Bridges and Professor Donald Peart for reading my manuscript, and for making numerous helpful suggestions many of which I have adopted, and especially Dr. William Lovelock, of Brisbane, who has been particularly generous in this respect. Thanks are also due to Miss Marianne Rosenberg and Mr John Jennings who helped to correct typescript and proofs.

Ian Spink

Department of Music,
University of Sydney,
Sydney, N.S.W.

Introduction

Surely we learn more about the true nature of a thing if we are able to watch it grow and develop: a moment's thought will show that this is so, whether we are biologists, social historians or musicians. After all, what sort of understanding of the French Revolution can we gain from the events of 1789 alone ? The study of changing forms gives us a perspective which helps us to distinguish what is essential from what is accidental. In other words, it increases our understanding, not just our knowledge. So far as music is concerned the range of our perception is widened, and our insight into the conscious and unconscious creative processes of the composer throughout the history of music is deepened. This book is justified if it does that.

The study of changing and developing forms also leads to a truer appreciation of what form is. One of the most limiting attitudes in music is that which regards fugue or sonata form—or indeed any form—as an immutable fixture, as if the rules had been engraved on stone and handed down with the rest of the Law on Mount Sinai. Forms are not formulae.

Form is shape and everything has a shape, even—if we think again—things we normally describe as shapeless. Physical shapes exist in space; musical shapes exist in time. And whereas the materials of, say, sculpture may be wood or stone, the material of music is sound, or to be more precise—musical sound. The arrangement of this material gives us the form, that is, the mode in which the composer's impulse is realized through his material. The nature of this impulse or 'idea' behind the music is often hidden from us; from the composer too. But however abstract, like a finite idea, it demands (or at least, is best served by) a logical mode of expression. Indeed, there is something syllogistic about musical form. The general idea that 'all men should be free' and the particular idea that 'I am a man' leads to the conclusion that 'I should be free'. Here an idea has been developed in the form of a three-stage argument and brought to a logical conclusion. The form of the argument resulted from the logical manipulation of its contents, and the same form will result from a similar treatment of different contents; thus 'vegetables are good for you, carrots are vegetables, therefore carrots are good for you'.

If we examine these syllogisms, or any others we may care to construct, we shall see that for the conclusion to be logical a certain relationship must exist between the first two stages of the argument. Without going into these precisely we may describe the whole process, loosely, as one in which new but congruous subject matter is introduced at the second stage and assimilated in the third. Otherwise the form of the syllogism is no guarantee of the logic of the argument. The same may be said of musical composition, for all music consists of a succession of ideas more or less congruously relating to what has gone before. The more congruous the relationship, the more the element of repetition is apparent; the less congruous the relationship, the more the element of contrast is apparent. These twin tendencies are always present, balancing each other, and they apply not only to the melodic or thematic aspect of music, but to rhythm, tempo, dynamics and timbre as well. Separately and together these are areas in which repetition and contrast can operate. But in reality, repetition and contrast are not two but one, since each may be understood as the absence of the other. There is thus at the heart of a viable form the idea of unity, although the ways in which this unity, or cohesion, manifests itself throughout the history of music have differed. A piece of Gregorian chant is a musical entity because, among other things, its melodic members are balanced against each other and within themselves. Mediaeval polyphony coheres because of the continuous thread of the *cantus firmus* running through the texture, while renaissance and baroque counterpoint extends the *cantus firmus* principle to all strands of the musical texture—the subject of a fugue is, after all, a type of *cantus firmus*—achieving integration through an interlocking, overlapping stratification of voices. The unifying element in classical music is tonality, which makes its effect directly through adherence to a single tonic throughout a piece, or reflected indirectly in the relationship of the dominant and other keys. It is not until the 19th century that themes become the principal structural component, as the cyclic procedures of Liszt, and Wagner's use of leitmotives exemplify. Serialism, if not the *reductio ad absurdum* of this thematic preoccupation, is at least a logical extension of it into the 20th century.

But these developments were evolutionary not spontaneous. Monophony did not just stop and polyphony start; in the 14th century, for example, Machaut wrote monophonic chansons and elaborate polyphonic motets. Polyphony did not just stop and tonality begin; Bach's fugues are proof of this. Nor did tonality give way all of a sudden to thematicism; Wagner's 'Ring' shows both principles operating side by side. Yet each evolutionary cycle at its peak nourished within it the seeds of its own destruction; the new development that was to supersede the old. Thus, while polyphony was at its height, tonality was emerging as a by-product; and when tonality in its turn had established itself as the main cohesive force, the thematic principle began to develop. Schoenberg himself demonstrated how note-row composition grew from 19th-century thematicism, and at the present time, post-Webern serialism harbours yet another parasite (which may or may not consume its host), the aleatory, or random principle.

This is the course of evolution which this book traces. Repetition schemes, *cantus-firmus* technique, imitation, tonality, thematicism and serialism are the underlying and successive unifying ideas which we can discover in Western music of the past thirteen hundred years. Associated with each are the forms in which they find realization; melodic repetition in the *formes fixes* of the troubadours and trouvères, *cantus firmus* in *organum*, *clausula*, the 14th-century motet and 15th-century cyclic Mass; imitation in Mass, motet and madrigal of the 16th century and the 17th-century fugue; tonality in the 18th-century symphony, sonata and concerto; thematicism in the 19th-century symphony, symphonic poem and in the Wagnerian music-drama. As far as possible the structural principles and the forms which embody them are treated together, though naturally they do not always coincide. For example, 16th-century Mass settings often illustrate *cantus firmus* techniques and imitation together (but the polyphonic Mass has been treated within the general context of the *cantus firmus*), while the 19th-century symphony illustrates both tonal and thematic aspects of unity, but has been considered along with the latter. The major divisions of the book have been made according to the structural principles enumerated above; the minor divisions according to the forms which resulted. Within an overall historical treatment this plan seems the best way to display the development of both the structural principles and their resultant forms parallel to each other.

One thing I have learned in writing this book is that there is no such thing as the simple truth. So it is just as well to add a warning that, in addition to downright mistakes that may have slipped in, human frailty being what it is, half-truths masquerading as generalities will be found here as in every other book whose range is wide and size is small. If, in addition to the stated objects of the book being to some extent achieved, there are fewer half-truths here than in other books on form, I shall be satisfied. My belief is that the historical approach makes this more likely.

I

Repetition and refrain

I : 1 Song and Dance Forms
in the Middle Ages

The oldest music of our culture that anyone is likely to hear, or
come across these days, is the traditional chant of the Christian
Church. A few examples of ancient Greek music have survived;
but even so, no body of music exists comparable in both age and
quantity with plainsong. It was moulded and formed by many
influences, the earliest stemming from the eastern Mediterranean,
but by the time of Pope Gregory the Great (c. 540–604) its early
formative period was over. It is true that new styles and forms of
plainsong were to appear in the following centuries, but they did
so within an established tradition, that of Gregorian chant.

It was the same Gregory who gave further impetus to the spread
of Christianity beyond the Mediterranean shore of southern
Europe. As his missionaries travelled north they took the chant
with them, and in spreading their religion they spread their music.
The common musical culture of Western Europe dates from this
time.

What of secular music? It is doubtful if the folk-songs of Western Europe as they survive today can tell us very much about the
music of the people of such a distant age; the influences of the
last four hundred years or so are all too clear. The music of the
troubadours, though it is 'art music', is more likely to do so, and
so also may Gregorian chant, which undoubtedly absorbed secular influences. Both do, in fact, illustrate certain primitive features;
features which we can find today in the music of pre-literate
peoples still surviving in various out-of-the-way parts of the
world. The comparative study of their music has given us reason

to suppose that music passes through a similar development among races who are remote from each other geographically and ethnically. In other words, primitive music is to some extent the same the world over: it is in the later stages of civilization that differences become more pronounced. This after all, is Darwinism transplanted from the animal kingdom.

Most primitive music is essentially monophonic and vocal. Much of it consists of short motives or phrases repeated over and over again, and the melodic range of these motives is often narrow, sometimes only a single step above or below a tonic. (For the moment 'tonic' can be defined as the most frequently occurring note in a piece, or the note on which the phrase comes to rest —the 'final'.) A further stage is represented by longer phrases, varied repetitions and an increased melodic range. It is noticeable that as the ambit expands there is a tendency for a secondary tonal centre to be established, often at a distance of a fourth or fifth from the tonic. The tonic may even cease to be the most frequently occurring note, but will still be recognizable as the last note of the phrase or song as a whole. This polarity of 'tonic' and its rival 'dominant' (as it might as well be called) is the very seed from which the tonic-dominant relationship of tonal music springs.

The narrow range and melodic repetitiveness of the most primitive music may be illustrated by a melody of the Vedda of Ceylon (Ex. 1), and the earliest stage of cadential differentiation into 'open' (i.e. incomplete) and 'closed' (i.e. complete) cadences in a Fuegian chant from the tip of South America (Ex. 2). Compare this with the fourth Gregorian psalm-tone, and we have a convincing demonstration of the primitiveness of one aspect of Gregorian chant (Ex. 3).

Psalms were the earliest songs of the Church and the 'tones' to which they were sung are examples of primitive melodic formu-

Ex.1   Vedda chant

etc.

Ex.2   Fuegian chant

Ex.3   Gregorian psalm tone (4g)

Glo-ri - a Pat-ri et Fi-li-o,   et in Spi-ri-tu-i San-cto

lae of short duration and limited ambit repeated over and over again.[1]

They must have been the prototypes of many kinds of chant, since most of the sung portions in the early liturgy were taken from the psalms. 'Gradual' chants in particular show this origin—perhaps because they are among the oldest extant—and though the primitive formulae upon which they were based are now obscured through elaborate ornamentation, one still notices the rising intonation, the syllabic recitation and the cadence of the original 'tone'. The Gradual *Haec dies*[2] may be analysed in terms of these formulae.

But however fundamental the inflected psalm-tone, it is not the only ingredient of plainsong. As in primitive music, we must also recognize the existence of ecstatic melody. Curt Sachs has used the term 'pathogenic' to describe melodies which are an uninhibited expression of emotion, as distinct from those which are 'logogenic' or 'word-born'. We have an example of pathogenic melody in the Alleluia chants,[3] with their long vocalizations on the final vowel, the *jubilus*, 'which', as Pope Damasus said, 'neither through words, nor syllables, nor letters, nor speech, makes it possible to express and understand how much man should praise God'. It is music expressing the inexpressible.

[1] See *MM* i, *HAM* ii.   [2] *HAM* 12.   [3] *HAM* 13 and *MM* 2.

We may postulate, then, two original types of chant; the recitation formula and the vocalization. In the course of time each borrowed from the other, in turn providing models for further melodies and materials from which to build new chants. Thus one can recognize chants that are adaptations of older ones and still others which are 'centonized', that is, pieced together from various sources into a kind of patchwork quilt. In doing this, the composers preserved the traditional character of the chant. However remote the psalm-tone origins might be, phrases were still moulded to its rise and fall. We find this arch-shape at all levels, from the lengthy period down to its smallest member, and it is this 'wave-motion' that is the principal dynamic force in Gregorian chant. As the melodic line rises and falls, the tension arising between it and its tonic fluctuates, producing a forward motion that, once started, cannot stop until it comes to rest on the final 'tonic'.

When it comes to joining portions of chant together, the possession of a comon 'tonic' is the most important cohesive element. For a common 'tonic' means more besides sharing the same final. The classification into modes that the chant underwent towards the 10th century attempted to force a not very well understood Greek system on music which had grown up outside the orbit of non-Christian Greece. The first and last notes of the chant and its melodic ambit were singled out as the principal factors determining which of the eight modes it belonged to, but in doing so theorists were recognizing certain almost secondary features of an older Byzantine classification more closely bound up with the development of the chant—the eight *echoi*. This system grouped the chant melodies into eight families (or, more correctly, four— an authentic and plagal version of each), characterized by certain common melodic formulae and progressions, as well as by initial and final notes. Thus modal classification based on finals implies much more. It arranges the chant according to melody type and it follows that chants in the same mode will bear some sort of family relationship to each other. Certain quite lengthy chants achieve unity in this way, through modality and all that it implies, without resorting to melodic repetition as such.

Nevertheless, the device of repetition is very common. We have already come across direct repetition in the singing of psalms, and similar instances are also to be found in certain early chants of the 'Ordinary of the Mass' (the sung portions of the Mass which do not change from day to day, comprising Kyrie, Gloria, Credo, Sanctus and Benedictus, and Agnus chants); 'Gloria XV' for example, or 'Mass XVIII' in the *Liber Usualis*. Alternate or indirect repetition schemes are also characteristic of certain parts of the Ordinary, particularly the three-fold Agnus and the nine-fold Kyrie which naturally lend themselves to *ABA* treatment. But it is in the music for the 'Proper of the Mass' (the sung portions which change from day to day, comprising Introit, Gradual, Alleluia or Tract, Offertory and Communion chants) that alternation schemes came into their own. All except the Tract were originally alternation schemes in which a choral Antiphon or Respond was sung before, between and after the verses of a psalm, though nowadays in the Roman rite only the Introit and Alleluia (and certain other portions of the 'Requiem' Mass) retain an *ABA* structure.

The basic forms of Gregorian chant had been laid down by the 7th century. Over the next two or three hundred years some were to undergo further modifications, the most important result of which was the emergence of the Sequence in the 9th century. The Sequence began simply enough with the addition of non-liturgical words—tropes—to certain plainsong melismas, particularly in the Kyrie and Alleluia chants. For example, instead of singing the words *Kyrie eleison* to the chant now known as 'Kyrie IV', the words *Omnipotens genitor, Deus omnium creator* were divided one syllable to a note where previously the word *Kyrie* had been sung on a melisma.[1] All the florid Kyrie chants were troped in this way at some period, and are still referred to by the first words of their trope, e.g. *Kyrie Cunctipotens*.

The origins of the Sequence were similar. We have seen that the Alleluia chant ends with a long melisma, or *jubilus*, and this lent itself to troping. A certain monk of St. Gall in Switzerland,

Notker (d. 912, nicknamed Balbulus, the Stammerer) was one of the first writers of Sequences. He said that by adding words to the *jubilus* he could remember the notes of the chant more easily. This relation of Sequence to Alleluia is sometimes discernible, for example in Notker's *Christus hunc diem*,[1] but rarely in later Sequences. Wipo's *Victimae paschali laudes* (11th century) is an independent composition, as are the other sequences still sung today, *Lauda Sion*, *Dies Irae* and *Stabat Mater*, though the *Veni Sancte Spiritus* takes its first phrase from the opening of the preceding Alleluia. The typical form of the Sequence consists of a single line of verse, followed by a series of couplets ending with another single line, a plan which the music follows closely by setting both lines of the couplet to the same tune. Thus a musical (and poetic) scheme *A BB CC DD ... Z* results. By the time of Adam of St. Victor (d. 1192) the texts are rhymed and metrical, and often lack the odd single line at the beginning and the end (see *Jubilemus Salvatori*).[2] Thus the Sequence came to resemble the Hymn, which, however, was strophic.

Another type of liturgical interpolation which had even more far-reaching effects was that typified by the *Quem quaeritis* trope.[3] The words, meaning 'Whom seek ye?' are those of the Angel addressed to Mary Magdalen and the women on their visit to the empty sepulchre early on Easter morning, and in the 10th century they were elaborated into a short musical play about the Resurrection leading into the Introit of the Easter Mass. *Infantem vidimus*[4] is a later specimen of liturgical drama, this time for the Feast of the Epiphany. It is from such beginnings that the mediaeval drama had its origins. The 12th-century 'Play of Daniel', though very extended musically, is directly in this tradition, which was to lead to the miracle and mystery plays.

The music of these liturgical dramas drew on Gregorian chant, either taking over complete chants or adapting chant formulas. But original composition played an increasing part, and in the 'Play of Daniel' we find the word '*conductus*' applied to various

---

[1] *HAM* 16a.   [2] *HAM* 16c.   [3] *GMB* 8.   [4] *TM* 5.

processional pieces. This term seems to have been generally applied in the 12th and 13th centuries to Latin songs, both sacred and secular. One such *conductus*, the 'Song of the Ass'[1]—not from the 'Play of Daniel'—was sung in a liturgical play as the Virgin Mary rode into Beauvais Cathedral on an ass. The words and music have an unmistakable secular feeling, and the repetitive elements are obvious. Melodically the first and fourth lines are very similar to each other, while the whole song revolves round the notes of the major tonic triad. In *Christo psallat*[2] the repetitions are arranged in a special way so that the following melodic scheme results—*AAABAB*—which corresponds with the earliest *rondeau* form. These are examples of the monophonic *conductus*, but in the 13th century, the polyphonic *conductus* was to become one of the principal musical forms and lend its distinctive style to all types of composition. Though polyphonic, it was written in a simple note against note style with the same text in all parts and a freely composed tenor. As Franco of Cologne said, 'He who wishes to write a conductus ought first to invent as beautiful melody as he can . . . using it as a tenor is used in writing discant.' The example *De castitatis thalamo*[3] shows in its tenor, the lower voice, something of the same freshness and spontaneity that is characteristic of the monophonic variety. It is an example of a species of *conductus* having a tail (*cauda*), a cadenza-like prolongation of the final syllable, sometimes also found at the beginning, as here.

Outside the liturgical and non-liturgical music of the Church, the earliest songs about which we have more than a hazy notion are those of the goliards. The goliards (10th–13th centuries) were wandering scholars, a roistering mob from all accounts, despite the fact that they were in minor ecclesiastical orders. The most famous collection of their songs is the 13th-century *Carmina Burana*, but there are earlier songs of which we have a good idea how the music went, such as the 10th- or 11th-century *O admirabile Veneris idolum* (Ex. 4).

In the neumatic notation of the period neither the rhythm nor the pitch of the notes is clear from the manuscript. Probably the

[1] *HAM* 17a. [2] *HAM* 17b. [3] *MM* 11.

Ex.4

rhythm followed the scansion of the words, but in most cases only a hint of the pitch of the notes, not an exact indication, was given. But in the case of the song just mentioned, a version exists in an early type of 'sol-fa' notation, so we know the notes exactly. The most striking thing about it is the 'timelessness' of its idiom. We feel that it might have been written at any time during the last eight or nine hundred years, and probably find it hard to realize that it is as old as it is. Leaving aside considerations of rhythm and tonality, one reason for its appeal lies in its formal balance; the repetitions of the opening strain *A*, answered by something new; the repeated phrases of *B*; the sequential repetitions of *C* with its charmingly irregular ending. These are formal features which we notice again and again throughout the centuries, particularly in association with the metrical rhythms and regular phrasing of popular songs and dances. We shall come across the opening repeat and sometimes a reference to it in the last line almost immediately in the trouvère *ballade* and the minnesinger *bar*.

The jongleurs, like the goliards, were also wanderers. In their repertoires they carried epics telling of the deeds of such heroes as Roland and Charlemagne. The *Chansons de Geste* ('Songs of Deeds') were of great length, though they were broken up into shorter sections each dwelling upon a particular episode in the story. Musically, they illustrate a most primitive form; that of repetition of the same piece of music over and over for each line of verse, with (perhaps) a prolonged cadence of greater finality at the end of each section. Only one such melody seems to have survived, quoted many years later in Adam de la Hale's *Robin et Marion* (*c.* 1280), yet it may typify not only the music of the *Chanson de Geste*, but in some respects provide a relic of traditional bardic practice stretching back to pre-Christian times. The *lai* of the trouvères and the *leich* of the minnesingers show the same idea at a later stage of development,[1] but influenced by the couplet structure of the Sequence.

More sophisticated repetition schemes are characteristic of the troubadours, trouvères and minnesingers, who, unlike the goliards and jongleurs, were not wanderers. Usually they were of aristocratic birth, though two of the most famous, the troubadour Bernart de Ventadorn (d. 1195) and the 13th-century trouvère Adam de la Hale, were both of humble origin. Their chansons were of several literary types, often in one of the *formes fixes* such as *rondeau*, *virelai* and *ballade*, in which the treatment of the refrain is the distinguishing feature. The *virelai* is characterized by a refrain at the beginning and end of the song, and between each of its several stanzas. In a *rondeau* the first half of the refrain makes an appearance in the middle of the poem (only a single stanza long) with the full refrain sung at the beginning and at the end. So far as the music is concerned the arrangement is not quite so simple as this, for in the *rondeau*, the opening refrain contains all the musical material which is later portioned out according to the following scheme (capitals indicate the refrain); *AB a A ab AB*. As an example see *Vos n'aler* by Guillaume d'Amiens.[2] The *virelai* on the other hand presented only half the musical material in the opening refrain, the other half following in the verse section. *Virelais* such as *C'est la fin*[3] and *Or la truix*[4] may be represented by the following scheme: *A bba A*.

The *virelai* form was adapted in the Italian *lauda* and the Spanish *cantiga*, though the character of both was more popular and devotional than the songs of the troubadours and trouvères. *Laude* frequently took the form of the *ballata* (not to be confused

[1] *HAM* 19i.   [2] *HAM* 19e.   [3] *HAM* 19f.   [4] *MM* 4.

with the French *ballade*); the *cantigas* that of the *villancico*, and as with the *virelai* a feature of both was the repetition of a refrain between verses, and at the beginning and end of the poem. The *A bba A* structure of *A tutta gente*, a *ballata*, is clear;[1] so too in *Mais nos faz*, a *villancico*.[2]

The commonest *forme fixe* was that of the *ballade*, usually of three stanzas, called by the troubadours, '*canzo*', and '*bar*' by the minnesingers. Here the repetitive element is a purely musical consideration, for the refrain (if present) was merely the last line, or lines, of the stanza, whereas the musical repetitions occurred at the beginning. These repetitions, not being dictated by the form of the verse, are thus all the more significant as an expression of a natural musical tendency which leads, eventually, to the repeated exposition of sonata form. Most typically, the music of the first two lines of the stanza was repeated for the third and fourth; these two *pedes* or *stollen* (as the Italians and Germans called them respectively) comprised the first section. From then on the verse was set to new music (this concluding portion was called *cauda*, or in German *abgesang*) though reference was often made to material from the first section, particularly at the final cadence which frequently repeated the cadence of the first section. The term 'rounded chanson' is applied in this case and it is especially common in minnesinger songs.[3]

Although the *formes fixes* originated in the monophonic songs of the troubadours and trouvères, they persisted to the end of the 15th century in the polyphonic chansons of composers such as Adam de la Hale, Guillaume de Machaut (d. 1377), Guillaume Dufay (d. 1474) and Johannes Ockeghem (late 15th century). For example, *Tant con je vivrai* by Adam de la Hale[4] is a three-part *rondeau*; *Plus dure* by Guillaume de Machaut[5] is a two-part *virelai*; *Mon chier amy* by Dufay[6] is a three-part *ballade*; and *Ma bouche rit* by Ockeghem[7] is a three-part *virelai*—all of which reproduce the repetition schemes of the earlier monophonic forms and are clearly accompanied songs with the principal interest in

---

[1] *HAM* 21b.   [2] *HAM* 22b.
[3] See *HAM* 18b; 20b, d; 36a; *TM* 6 and *MM* 5.   [4] *HAM* 36b.
[5] *HAM* 46b.   [6] *HAM* 67.   [7] *HAM* 75.

the top part, with instrumental tenor and countertenor supporting. The mastersingers even persevered with the monophonic bar-form right into the 16th century, as for example in Hans Sachs' *Gesangweise*.[1]

Italian composers of the 14th century wrote *ballate* and madrigals, the former stemming (as we have seen) from the *virelai*, the latter (possibly) from the *ballade*. However, the first part of the madrigal was frequently repeated more than once, and the last section (called *ritornello*) usually changed into some form of triple-time. The refrain form of the *virelai* is clearly evident in such *ballate* as *Io son un pellegrin* by Giovanni da Florentia,[2] and *Amor c'al tuo suggetto*[3] and *Chi più le vuol sapere*[4] by Francesco Landini (1325–1397); and the *ballade*-like repetitions of the first section in such madrigals as *Non al suo amante* by Jacopo da Bologna[5] and *Nel mezzo* by Giovanni da Florentia.[6] The later polyphonic *villancico*, and the 15th-century English carol are also related to the *virelai*, whose alternation of verse and refrain they illustrate. Regarding the carol, the modern association with Christmas, or, for that matter, any other religious festival is not necessarily the case. Indeed, the famous 'Agincourt Song' is a carol.[7]

No refrain or scheme of repetitions characterizes the 14th-century Italian *caccia*; usually a hunting song in which the pursuit of the hunted by the hunter was symbolized by the exact pursuit of one voice by another some distance behind. This, of course, is a species of canon, and the two canonic voices are normally supported by an independent tenor part. A good example is *Tosto che l'alba* by Ghirardello da Firenze,[8] or Giovanni da Florentia's *Con brachi assai*.[9] Like the madrigal, the *caccia* has a triple-time *ritornello* at the end. An earlier type of canonic composition was the *rota*, favoured by English composers and illustrated by perhaps the most famous piece of mediaeval music, 'Sumer is icumen in'.[10] In many respects this work appears to be an isolated phenomenon,

[1] *TM* 22.   [2] *HAM* 51.   [3] *HAM* 53.   [4] *MM* 14.
[5] *HAM* 49.   [6] *HAM* 50.   [7] *GMB* 32b.   [8] *HAM* 52.
[9] *TM* 16.   [10] *HAM* 42.

and even now, after intensive research, it still presents something of a problem. But its musical origins are probably more bound up with sacred than secular music, so we shall postpone discussion of it until later.

Much of the music we have been considering would seem to have been eminently suitable for dancing. The *ballade* and *chanson balladé* (another name for *virelai*) could not have got their names had they not been danced at some stage, since the word 'ballade' obviously stems from '*ballare*', to dance. One such dance song, the *carole* (a round dance possibly related to the *virelai*) is interesting in that it probably provides the origin of the English word 'carol'. Certain instrumental pieces from the 13th century called *danses royales*[1] are of a type known as the *estampie*, an instrumental form of couplet construction (rather like the Sequence and *lai*) but with 'first time bars' ('open' cadences) leading back to the repeat and 'second time bars' ('close' cadences) rounding off the section. The troubadour song *Kalenda maya*[2] is supposed to have been written by Raimbault de Vaqueiras (d. 1207) to the tune of an *estampie* which he heard played by some jongleurs. A continued relationship with the dance is evident from the titles of some 14th-century *estampies*, such as *La Rotta* and *Saltarello*.[3] But it is interesting to observe that others have descriptive titles such as *Lamento di Tristan*, rather like those of the French clavecinistes three hundred years later, which may indicate a similar development away from functional dance music to a more sophisticated type of musical representation in stylized dance forms.

There can be no mistaking the important role melodic repetition has played in the music so far discussed. Essentially, repetition is a unifying factor whatever scheme is employed. It is rather like rhyme in poetry, which, while the poem moves onward, links up with what has gone before and outlines the architecture of the verse. And as with poetic rhyme we find two basic principles underlying musical repetition; that of immediate or direct repetition, as in the psalm-tones, the Sequence, the *lai*, the *estampie*; and various types of alternate or indirect repetition, in the *virelai* and

---

[1] *HAM* 40.   [2] *HAM* 18d.   [3] *HAM* 59a, b

rondeau, for example. There are, of course, other factors which make for cohesion. Modality is one, so—in one way or another—is rhythm. However, it is repetition which delineates the overall structure, and defines its proportions.

II

'Cantus firmus' and the development of imitation

II : 1 'Tenor' construction from organum to cyclic Mass

We have seen how repetition schemes were carried over into polyphonic music in the 13th and 14th centuries; in the polyphonic chansons of Machaut, for example. However, the fundamental principle underlying the construction of polyphonic music was not the use of a repetition-scheme but of the *cantus firmus*; that is, a pre-existing melody (the *cantus prius factus*) held by the lowest part, the tenor (*tenere* means 'to hold'), above which a second part (the *duplum*), and perhaps another (the *triplum*) were added in counterpoint. Throughout the mediaeval period the *cantus prius factus* was almost invariably a piece of Gregorian chant. Mediaeval sacred music never really freed itself of the *cantus firmus*, which in many ways symbolized the continuing tradition and authority of the Church asserting itself in music. The only mediaeval form of sacred music which was not so tied was the *conductus*, and we have seen (p. 9) that this has a claim to be considered a secular form despite its religious associations.

Cantus firmus construction is at the root of all contrapuntal structure, and finds its final and freest application in the fugue. Its earliest form, called *organum*, was both strict and simple, though several types may be distinguished. In 'parallel *organum*' one or more voices moves in fourths or fifths with the *cantus firmus* in note-against-note style. This is the earliest kind of part music that was written down, and examples are to be found dating from the 9th century (for example the setting of *Sit gloria Domini*).[1]

[1] *HAM* 25b, 1.

Sometimes the two voices begin and end in unison, opening out to fourths and fifths in the middle of the phrase, and in doing so may pass through the intervals of a second and a third. This marks the beginning of 'free *organum*' (see *Rex cæli Domine*)[1] in which, typically, the movement is still note against note, though mixing parallel with contrary motion involves seconds, thirds, sixths and sevenths, as well as the normal fourth, fifth and octave consonances. Among 11th-century examples of free *organum* is *Alleluia, Angelus Domini*,[2] which gives us an idea not only of how the music was composed but the manner of its performance. For *organa* cannot be considered independently, but rather in the context of the liturgy. The Alleluia is a type of responsorial chant in which solo 'verses' and choral 'responses' alternate. In this case it is the 'solo' sections which are in *organum*, while the chorus or *schola* sings the plainsong response in unison, an arrangement which applies generally throughout the middle ages. Polyphony was written for soloists, and plainsong was sung by the *schola*, thus introducing episodes of dynamic and textural contrasts within the liturgical framework.

The next stage in the development of *organum* is exemplified in music surviving from the early 12th-century schools of St. Martial at Limoges, and St. James at Compostela. Here we have a species of *organum* in which several notes in the added part are intended to be sung against a single note in the *cantus firmus*. This is known as 'melismatic *organum*', the melismas probably being sung in free rhythm. The Gradual *Viderunt omnes*[3] has its solo sections treated in melismatic *organum*, and in one place has more than a dozen notes in the added part to one in the tenor.

Once note for note movement was no longer the rule it became necessary to devise some means of synchronizing the two parts so that they could move together in time. In the 13th century certain arbitrary triple-time rhythmic patterns governed the added parts. These patterns or modes were repeated over and over again, and were as follows:

[1] *HAM* 25b, 2, and *MM* 6. [2] *HAM* 26c. [3] *HAM* 27a.

Mode 1	(trochaic)	♩ ♪		♩ ♪	etc.,
Mode 2	(iambic)	♪ ♩		♪ ♩	etc.,
Mode 3	(dactylic)	♩.		♪ ♩	etc.,
Mode 4	(anapaestic)	♪ ♩		♩.	etc.,
Mode 5	(spondaic)	♩.		♩.	etc.,
Mode 6	(tribrachic)	♩ ♩ ♩		♩ ♩ ♩	etc.

Of these the most commonly encountered are the first, second and third in the added parts, and the third and fifth in the tenor (when it was measured). However, the result of this rhythmic repetition is not quite so monotonous as one might at first expect; for variety was introduced by varying the *ordo* (the number of repetitions of the rhythm within a phrase), by changing the mode, and by introducing certain ornamental figures which broke the mode temporarily. The earlier works of the 'School of Notre Dame' at Paris—represented by the *organa* of Leonin (second half of the 12th century)—show the change from melismatic to measured *organum*, even with rhythmic tenors in places, while in the next generation Perotin demonstrates consolidation of the rhythmic style in *clausulae* and increase in sonority in three and four part *organa*. A comparison of the two-part *Haec dies*[1] with the three-part organum on the same *cantus firmus*[2] shows something of the difference in style between Leonin and Perotin. But in both it is the rhythm of the upper parts which impels the music forward and through its very repetitiveness imposes a unity to which the long notes of the tenor contribute. Indeed, these tenor notes are so long that they function as drones or pedals and thus establish a sort of tonality over long stretches.

The *organa* of the Notre Dame School are the greatest and the latest examples of this impressive but cumbersome form. No doubt the enormous time scale involved in their performance, due to the long tenor notes, made this music impracticable from the liturgical point of view, and the development of the *clausula* would seem to confirm that one of the main objections to *organa* was their length. *Clausulae* are, in fact, sections of *organum* with rhythmic tenors derived from plainsong melismas. They were

---

[1] *HAM* 29.   [2] *HAM* 31.

introduced as substitutes for the organal setting of the same *cantus firmus*; thus, in *Haec dies*[1] we find *clausulae* inserted at the '*Domino*', '*Quo [niam]*' and '*In saeculum*' sections, presumably for the sake of brevity since the tenor is disposed of much more quickly in this measured 'discant' style. When *clausulae* became detached from their settings within *organa*, sometimes even before this happened, the added parts acquired words (*mots*) of their own, and the form thus became the 'motet'. This process of emancipation is admirably demonstrated in the *organum* '*Benedicamus domino*', the *clausula* on the '*Domino*' melisma, and the motets based on the same tenor.[2] Particularly interesting is the change-over from *clausula* '*Domino*' to the motet *Pucelete/Je languis/Domino*, the two lower parts of which are identical with those of the *clausula*.[3] In becoming a motet, all that happened to the original *clausula* was that the *duplum* gained a text (thus becoming the *motetus*), and a *triplum* (with its own text) was added.

The two marks of the Parisian motet in the 13th century were (*a*) its polytextuality and (*b*) its tenor chant-melisma which presumably was played on an instrument. Hybrid forms with the *conductus* do exist however. *Deo confitemini/Domino*[4] is a motet in which the two added voices sing the same text, and *On parole/A paris/Frèse nouvele*[5] is a motet without a chant tenor, though it adopts the usual practice of repeating the same tenor segment several times in the course of the piece. Sometimes too, the parts are not independent, but exchange phrases from one to the other in a manner not dissimilar to the round or *rondellus*. In *Alle, psallite/Alleluya*[6] a *duplum* and *triplum* exchange phrases thus:

triplum	AB	CD	EF	G
duplum	BA	DC	FE	H
tenor	ww	xx	yy	z

This exchange of parts (*stimmtausch* as it is called in German—an English equivalent would be 'part-swopping') is fairly frequent in the work of the Notre Dame School, and indeed canonic writing

[1] *HAM* 29.   [2] *HAM* 28b—g.   [3] *HAM* 28h.   [4] *HAM* 32c.
[5] *HAM* 33b.   [6] *HAM* 33a.

(of which this is a type) is not unknown at this time. The motet *En non Diu/Quant voi/Eius in oriente*[1] has examples of both 'part-swopping' (compare bb. 1–4 with bb. 21–24) and canon (see bb. 5–8). The practice probably originated in England, where it survived into the 14th century and beyond (see *Alleluia psallat*)[2] and undoubtedly the most famous example of this device is to be found in the *rota* 'Sumer is icumen in'.[3] Its date of composition is certainly post-Perotin (probably late 13th century), yet it is a remarkable piece for all that. The two-voiced *pes* is pure *stimm-tausch*, while the application of this idea to the other four parts is disguised by canonically delayed entries. Compare the scheme of *Alle, psallite/Alleluia* above with 'Sumer is icumen in':

$$A \; B \; C \; D \; E \; F \; G \; H \; I \; J \; K \; L$$
$$A \; B \; C \; D \; E \; F \; G \; H \; I \; J \; K$$
$$A \; B \; C \; D \; E \; F \; G \; H \; I \; J$$
$$A \; B \; C \; D \; E \; F \; G \; H \; I$$

$$pes \begin{cases} x \; y \; x \; y \; x \; y \; x \; y \; x \; y \; x \; y \\ y \; x \; y \; x \; y \; x \; y \; x \; y \; x \; y \; x \end{cases}$$

The types of composition we have been discussing in this section belong to the phase of musical development known as the *Ars antiqua*. We have seen the *clausula* emerge as a substitute for certain sections of *organa* in which a melismatic chant tenor was measured in modal rhythm rather than in the long notes characteristic of *organa*. And from the *clausula* we have seen the motet develop into an independent form, through the addition of text(s) to the upper part(s). Side by side with the motet we have the *conductus* differentiated by its single text, its note-for-note chordal style, and the absence of a *cantus firmus* (cf. pp. 8–9).

In contrast, the music of the 14th-century *Ars nova*, is marked by strong secular trends which we see reflected in the works of the most famous composer of the time, Guillaume de Machaut, whose *ballades, virelais, rondeaux*, etc., outnumber his motets by five to one. Even so, most of the motets have secular texts though they

[1] *MM* 10.   [2] *HAM* 57.   [3] *HAM* 42.

still preserve the plainsong tenor, now treated in a manner known as 'isorhythm'. Isorhythm is the repetition of a *cantus firmus* segment (the *color*) in a certain rhythmic pattern (the *talea*) throughout a piece. Its development from 13th-century tenors in modal rhythm can be traced easily in the following stages. The motet *Huic main/Hec dies*[1] has a strictly modal tenor (fifth mode), whereas the tenor of *Deo confitemini/Domino*[2] has a slightly more complicated rhythmic pattern that is not modal. Here the *color* is the twenty-six note *'Domino'* melisma from the *Haec dies* Gradual verse *Confitemini Domino*[3] played through twice, with a five-note *talea* superimposed. An analysis of the tenor of Machaut's motet *S'il estoit nulz*[4] shows a more complex interplay of *color* and *talea*. The *color* is the chant fragment *Et gaudebit cor vestrum* (29 notes in all) and is played twice through. The *talea* is stated three times completely (a fourth statement is begun) during the first run-through, and three times again in the second, though in a slightly modified form. (Repetitions of the *color* are usually subjected to some modification such as diminution of note values in some degree.) A closer look reveals that not only is the tenor isorhythmic, but so too are lengthy stretches of the upper parts. Compare the rhythm of the phrases beginning *'je me devroie'*, *'ne vost laissier'*, *'en resgardant'*, *'de ardans desirs'*, *'sanz le secours'* and *'et courtoisie'* in the *triplum*; the same rhythm is to be found in each, though continued longer in some than in others.

The phenomenon of isorhythm is of immense interest structurally. Like the rhythmic modes, only in a more complicated way, it furnishes us with an example of rhythm functioning by itself instead of as a subordinate to melody. Not only is it a means of keeping the music going; it gives coherence and establishes rhythmic relationships in the upper parts which are recognizable in much the same way as melodic repetitions. It is not until the middle of the 20th century that we meet a similar sort of rhythmic procedure in the works of Olivier Messiaen and his pupils, where a series of note durations (comparable to the *talea*) is rotated without consideration of the melodic consequences.

[1] *HAM* 32a.   [2] *HAM* 32c.   [3] *HAM* 12.   [4] *HAM* 44.

Isorhythmic treatment of the tenor is chiefly characteristic of the *Ars nova* motet, though examples are to be found in secular forms, as in Landini's madrigal *Sy dolce non sono*.[1] Generally though, French polyphonic secular forms of the period observed repetition schemes similar to the *formes fixes* of the troubadours. But well into the 15th century the motet clung to its chant tenors, its isorhythm and polytextuality. At best it was an impressive rather than an endearing style; but it endured.

Machaut's 14th-century *Messe de Notre Dame* uses both motet and *conductus* styles. The longer movements, the Gloria and the Credo are in syllabic homophony which allows the text to be disposed of fairly quickly, while the shorter movements—Kyrie, Sanctus, and Agnus[2]—are isorhythmic (often in all four parts) and more thoroughly polyphonic, their tenors being derived from Mass-chants. Although this work is often described as the first cyclic setting of the Mass, it does not seem to be quite the integrated whole that is often claimed. Stylistically it bears the marks of a compilation of two well-differentiated 'Mass-pairs'; Gloria-Credo in *conductus* style, Sanctus-Agnus in motet style (with tenor based on appropriate chants from Mass XVII), and Kyrie (tenor from Kyrie *Cunctipotens*) and *Deo gratias* (tenor from the Sanctus of Mass VIII) added to complete the Mass. Some scholars have professed to discover a motive which unites the several movements, and it is true that the top-part of the opening of the *Christe eleison*—particularly the descending scale figure—does recur at times, especially in the Gloria and Credo, which are related stylistically in any case (Ex. 5).

Ex.5

Chri - - - - [ste]

[1] *HAM* 54.   [2] *MM* 13.

But whether it is anything more than a characteristic ornamental feature of the composer's style is open to doubt, while in its original and most distinctive shape it cannot be said to permeate the structure of the rest of the Mass. Nevertheless, we have here two recognizable Mass-pairs by the same composer, at the least, and this in itself is remarkable for the time. It is not until the 15th century that the idea of polyphonic settings of the Ordinary of the Mass took hold, at first in pairs of related movements, Gloria-Credo and Sanctus-Agnus, then in the complete liturgical sequence.

The Mass as a form in several musically related sections, consistent in style with each other and inter-related thematically, was a concept that was still strange at the beginning of the 15th century. The longer texts of the Gloria and Credo naturally tended to be set in a syllabic style deriving from the *conductus*—the so-called 'treble-dominated' style,[1] which in itself was a factor that drew the two sections together. Certain Gloria-Credo pairs by Johannes Ciconia and Lionel Power (d. 1445) actually show evidence of motivic relationships between the two movements. Conversely, the comparatively brief texts of the Sanctus and Agnus naturally lent themselves to a more complex polyphonic treatment, this again being a factor which drew them together. The Sanctus from a Sanctus-Agnus pair by Power[2] shows the style of polyphony which was often adopted in these pairs, though in this case the chant-based tenor is not isorhythmic. Such pairs, related either through common motives, or common chants used as a tenor *cantus firmus* (or 'paraphrased' in the treble part), are the origins of the cyclic Mass. Power seems to have been one of the first composers, if not the first, to carry the idea a stage further, and relate all the movements of a Mass in one of these ways. His Mass based on the hymn *Alma redemptoris mater* treats the chant isorhythmically in the tenor in each movement, while his contemporary from Liège, Arnold de Lantins, was probably the first to relate all movements of the Mass through the use of a recurrent motive or 'motto'.

The most frequent device used to relate the Mass-movements

[1] See *GMB* 29, *HAM* 55, 56.   [2] *HAM* 63.

in the second half of the 15th century was the use of a common *cantus firmus* throughout. It was either a portion of chant, part of a secular song, or arbitrarily invented (usually with some significance attaching to its 'sol-fa' syllables). The technique varied from placing the *cantus firmus* in long notes in the tenor—the more old-fashioned method—to a free paraphrase which might be shared by all voices. The first Kyrie of Dufay's Mass *Se la face ay pale*[1] illustrates the earlier technique, using as a *cantus firmus* the tenor of his chanson from which the Mass takes its name. Characteristically the tenor has no influence on the other parts which imitate neither each other, nor the *cantus firmus*. The same composer's Mass on *L'homme armé* (one of the earliest of the many on this celebrated tune) shows a similar treatment in the Kyrie[2] and a canonic elaboration in the final Agnus where the *cantus firmus* is sung, first backwards in long notes, then forward in notes of half value.

The absence of imitation and derived material in parts other than the tenor is still noticeable in a Mass based on the same melody by the most important composer of the next generation, Johannes Ockeghem.[3] At this period, round about 1470, imitation was still quite rare in sacred music, though rather more common in secular chansons. But composers frequently adopted strict imitation in various types of canon, and sometimes wrote Masses which were entirely canonic, as in the *Missa Prolationum* by Ockeghem, the Sanctus of which[4] has the soprano and tenor following the alto and bass in canon, four voices from two at the sixth above, all voices with a different time-signature.

With Josquin des Près (d. 1521) the idea of imitation and the derivation of thematic material from a *cantus firmus* is clearly established. We find this in the Mass *Pange Lingua* where the familiar plainsong hymn (Ex. 6(i)) is paraphrased and broken up into fragments from which derive imitative points. In the Kyrie, for example, each of the six lines of the chant gives rise to a set of imitations; the first and second in the first Kyrie, the third and fourth in the Christe, the fifth and sixth in the second Kyrie (Ex. 6(ii)).

[1] *MM* 15.   [2] *HAM* 66.   [3] *HAM* 73a, b.   [4] *MM* 17.

Ex.6

(i)

(ii)

The sharing of the *cantus firmus* between voices, its ornamentation and adaptation, and its germinating function with regard to thematic material are all characteristic of the 16th-century 'paraphrase Mass' (for example, Palestrina's *Aeterna Christi munera*).

Composers often went further than borrowing a single melody for the *cantus firmus*. They would frequently adapt and re-write already existing chansons or motets so that the words of the Mass could be fitted to them: the borrowed material might not even be their own composition. Masses composed in this way are called 'parody Masses', and they may be said to differ from the stricter *cantus firmus* or 'tenor Mass', in that at times they may use the whole texture of their model, not just a single part. The idea is foreshadowed in isolated Mass-movements before 1500, but cyclic parody technique begins early in the 16th century and later becomes the most common type. A simple example of parody technique may be illustrated by comparing certain sections of Victoria's Mass *O quam gloriosum* with his motet of the same name (Ex. 7).

Ex.7

(i) *from* 'O Quam Gloriosum'

se - quun - tur Ag - - - num,

(ii)

Kyrie *of* 'Missa O Quam Gloriosum'

. Ky - ri - e . e - . - lei - son

(iii)

from Gloria of 'Missa O Quam Gloriosum'

Tu so — lus Al — tis — si — mus

Of the 105 or so Masses by Giovanni Pierluigi da Palestrina (d. 1594), half (52) are parody Masses, while 42 are based on a *cantus firmus* (35 paraphrasing it, and 7 confining it to the tenor in the old-fashioned way), 5 are canonic and 6 'freely' composed.

Freely composed Masses usually employ a musical motto-theme or 'head-motive' not necessarily in the top part, which recurs throughout the Mass at the beginning of movements, and sometimes at other places. An example is the Mass *Sine nomine* by Jacob Obrecht (1450–1055)[1] in the first Kyrie and the second Agnus of which (and elsewhere) we may note the use of a head-motive—compare the top part at the opening of both sections. The most famous example of this sort of Mass is Palestrina's *Missa Papae Marcelli*[2] in which the bass parts in the openings of the movements are related as follows (Ex 8):

Ex. 8
(i)

Ky — rie e — lei — — — son

Pa — trem om — ni — po — ten — tem

[1] *HAM* 77.   [2] Agnus in *HAM* 140.

Head-motive technique is also found in settings of the English liturgy, called 'Services'. In the 'Great Service' of William Byrd (1543–1623) the openings of the evening canticles, the Magnificat and Nunc Dimittis, are very similar—in fact, they parody each other; so too in the Venite and Benedictus of Morning Prayer, not only in their openings but also in their final Amens. Several movements of the 'Short Service' of Orlando Gibbons (1583–1625) are related through the use of a head-motive, also in the 'First Service' of Thomas Tomkins (1572–1656), which again has the Amen of the Venite, Creed and Nunc Dimittis corresponding.

The unifying tendencies of these various techniques are obvious. We can see that purely musical considerations are at work, and that thematicism is the most important cohesive principle. In fact, the cyclic Mass adumbrates many of the formal ideas (such as thematic recall and metamorphosis) to which 19th-century composers were dedicated, though they can hardly have inherited these ideas directly.

II : 2 Sacred and secular forms of vocal polyphony

In the Renaissance the term 'motet' acquired a more general application than it had in the *Ars nova*. Johannes Tinctoris (*c.* 1475) defined it as 'a song of moderate length on any subject, but usually religious'. Isorhythm and polytextuality survived well into the 15th century, in motets by John Dunstable (d. 1453) and Dufay, for instance, but did not last into the 16th century except as special effects. At first the renaissance motet borrowed the *cantus-firmus* technique of the Mass, usually using a chant appropriate to the text being set. The tenor of Obrecht's motet *O beate Basili* presents such a *cantus firmus* (with alto in canon a fifth above) in a simple form; so also the bass part of his *O vos omnes*.[1] We can find examples of *cantus-firmus* treatment in motets throughout the 16th century, for example *Victimae paschali laudes*[2] by Adrian Willaert (d. 1562) which gives out the chant in long notes, first in the *sextus* part, then in the *quintus*, while the other voices weave counterpoints around it. But on the whole, thorough-going *cantus firmi* in long notes are quite rare, except in polyphonic settings of plainsong hymns and Lutheran chorales.[3] (Chorale tunes so treated were either melodies of religious songs existing from pre-Reformation times, adaptations of traditional chants or newly composed melodies to Lutheran hymn-texts, or else secular songs provided with sacred words—*contrafacta*.)

On the other hand, imitative techniques, often with subjects derived from the chant are normal. It is in the motets of Jacob Obrecht that we find imitation emerging as an important

[1] *HAM* 76.   [2] *HAM* 113.   [3] *TM* 24.

33

structural feature, though this device had been quite common in secular music for a generation or more. By Josquin's time (i.e. early 16th century), imitation is usual rather than exceptional, and in his *Ave Maria*[1] we may notice how motives are derived from the plainchant in a manner which recalls the paraphrase technique of the Mass. The same derivatory process is employed in the 'chor-ale-motet' using a Lutheran chorale instead.[2]

Paraphrase technique is found in motets throughout the century freely applied, but more often the motet (like its secular counter-parts the chanson, and later, the madrigal) was a freely composed work making use of a variety of structural elements, of which all-pervading imitation was the most important. Except in cases where certain words or phrases (*alleluia* for example) recur several times in the course of a work, or where liturgical performance requires repetition, as in responsories—note the responsorial *ABCB* form of *O vos omnes* by Tomás Luis de Victoria (1548–1611)[3]—refrain-forms are rare. The typical motet is through-composed, usually consisting of a continuous series of imitative points dovetailed into each other; each point setting a phrase of the text, with passages in chordal style introduced for the sake of occasional variety. In Palestrina's *Sicut cervus*,[4] for example, there is virtually no homophonic writing, but the texture of *Tristis est anima mea* by Orlando Lassus (1532–1594)[5] is rather more varied.

Sometimes variety was also achieved by contrasting high and low groups of voices, or reduced forces with the full choir. This sort of writing is found early on in Ockeghem and Josquin, usually as an alternation of paired voices—see the sections beginning '*via errantium*' and '*in te spero*' in Josquin's *Tu pauperum refugium*[6]—and, transmitted and developed by Willaert, it was one of the origins of what was to become the polychoral style of certain Venetian composers, notably Andrea (d. 1586) and Gio-vanni Gabrieli (1555–1612), and of composers such as Hans Leo Hassler (1564–1612)[7] and Heinrich Schütz (1585–1672)[8] who came under their influence. At St. Mark's in Venice, choirs of voices and instruments were divided between the galleries on each

---

[1] *MM* 19.   [2] *GMB* 108–110.   [3] *HAM* 149.   [4] *HAM* 141.

[5] *MM* 23.   [6] *HAM* 90.   [7] *TM* 28.   [8] *HAM* 202.

side of the church—*cori spezzati* ('spaced-out choirs')—which gave opportunity for contrasting high choir against low, loud against soft, tutti against solo, and instruments against voices. The resultant texture, harmonically conceived though highly diversified, was characteristic of the style of the 'church-concerto' or *concerto ecclesiastico*. With Giovanni Gabrieli space itself became an element in the separation and unification of musical texture. His motet *In ecclesiis*[1] may be regarded quite apart from its purely musical qualities as a spatial sound-mosaic, in which contrasting colour-choirs are handled so that out of diversity unity results. The same idea lies partly behind the *decani* and *cantoris* division of English cathedral choirs, though on a much more modest scale.

The variegated texture of a motet such as *In ecclesiis* finds some sort of parallel in the English 'verse anthem' of the end of the 16th century and the beginning of the 17th century. The English 'full anthem' corresponds in almost every way to the 16th-century motet, apart from the use of English instead of Latin: we can see the same polyphonic texture and interlocking points in works such as 'Hear the voice and prayer of thy servants' by Thomas Tallis (d. 1585),[2] Gibbons' 'Hosanna to the Son of David' or Tomkins' 'When David heard'.[3] But, perhaps because it heeded the reformers' desire for audibility of the words, or (more likely) because it represented a type of performance already established in the secular field, one which was suitable for domestic use, the verse anthem alternated solo sections (setting the 'verse' in an elaborate polyphonic style for one or two solo voices with instrumental consort—viols perhaps, or organ) with chorus or 'full' sections in a simpler style. Byrd's anthem 'Christ rising'[4] has the verses set for two soloists with four-part accompaniment, with full sections for voices and viols concluding each verse. Perhaps the most famous verse anthem is Gibbons' five-part 'This is the record of John'[5] for countertenor and instrumental consort. In this, as in other verse anthems, the fact that the verse is solo does not imply a subordinate role of the accompaniment. The

[1] *HAM* 157.   [2] *TM* 27.   [3] *HAM* 169.   [4] *HAM* 151.
[5] *HAM* 172.

polyphonic texture of the verse is quite homogeneous; instruments and voices use the same subjects for imitation and are not widely differentiated in style. The most obvious difference is the practical one that rests are more common and phrases shorter in the voice than in the viol parts. In general, however, the music—in the contemporary phrase—is 'apt for voice or viol'.

In considering the structural characteristics of polyphonic music we can hardly fail to recognize the paramount importance of the *cantus firmus*, whether we understand the term as a true *cantus prius factus* given to the tenor in long notes, as in the 'tenor Mass', or as a series of short imitative motives freely invented by the composer (but nevertheless invented before the rest of the material and in this sense pre-existing) and shared between all the parts, as in the motet. It is this which provides the foundation upon which the other voices are laid, overlapping and interlocking to form a continuity of sound. Intermeshing imitation is obviously one of the major cohesive features of polyphonic music. Movement is thus maintained through the main points of harmonic and structural inertia, the cadences.

However, underlying the polyphonic weave, there is a force which binds the texture in another sense, viz. the modality of the piece. By the 16th century, theorists had expanded the modal system from eight to twelve modes; six authentic modes starting on D, E, F, G, A and C respectively, and their related plagal forms, starting a fourth lower on A, B, C, D, E and G, but with the same final (i.e. 'tonic') as the corresponding authentic mode. As we have seen (p. 6), the system of modes had originally been formulated with reference to monophonic music and was not strictly relevant to part-music, where voices had different ranges and finals. Even so, there were still aspects of the theory which could be applied. For with the tenor (or treble) in one mode, let us say the authentic G mode, bass (and alto) would fall naturally into the plagal form starting on D but with G as the tonic. If, on the other hand, the tenor (or treble) was in the plagal G mode, bass (and alto) would fall naturally in the authentic C mode, both with C as their final. Any note (except B) could thus be the final of two modes, and it is in terms of this authentic-plagal ambivalence that we may regard 16th-century modality, and consider its cohesive effect. Lacking the strong internal and external relationships that characterize the later tonal system (though these were emerging in the tonally committed cadences which resulted from the *musica ficta* practice of sharpening cadential leading notes), 16th-century modality is a wider, less exclusive concept than key, amounting almost to two 'keys' in one. Yet undoubtedly it exerted the same sort of cohesive effect as did tonality at a later period, and it is rare for the movements of a Mass or the sections of a motet not to show this modal compatibility. If we study the cadences of a piece of polyphonic music, we notice how they cling to the prevailing modality, and (because points and cadences interlock) how the imitations answer plagal for authentic and vice versa.

From the outset, the renaissance motet was, as we have seen, less reliant on such purely structural devices as *cantus firmus* and parody technique than settings of the Mass. In fact, the partial renouncing of the tenor *cantus firmus* by the motet parallels almost exactly the abandonment of the *formes fixes* by the chanson; both coming instead to depend for cohesion on the physical continuity of texture achieved through imitation, and consistency of mood and mode. It is true that the use of a refrain is still very common in the chanson after 1500 (as is the use of chant-derived material in the motet) but not in the stereotyped way that had been typical of the Middle Ages. Even so, *Royne du ciel* by Loyset Compère (d. 1518)[1] is in the form of a *rondeau*, and the early 16th-century *frottola* and *villancico* still retained the opening and closing refrain that related them to the *virelai*.[2] But in the early years of the 16th century the polyphonic chanson and motet approached each other in form and texture, so that in many cases a casual glance reveals only a difference of language and subject matter rather than profound stylistic differences.

Literally thousands of chansons were written by French composers during the first half of the 16th century. Some are polyphonic, others homophonic, some are strophic, others

[1] *HAM* 79.   [2] See *HAM* 95, 97 and 98.

through-composed, while others use simple repetition schemes. Some are serious, some are gay, and others elaborately programmatic—such as the descriptive *L'alouette* by Clément Janequin,[1] not to mention his famous *Bataille de Marignan*. Most common are those of a lightly polyphonic texture, rhythmic and with easy imitations in typical chanson-rhythm ♩ ♩ ♩ or ♪ ♩ ♩ ♩. See, for example, *Pour ung plaisir* by Thomas Crequillon[2] with its *ballade* structure, or *Allon, gay, gay* by Guillaume Costeley (d. 1606)[3] with its homophonic refrain heard five times in all, the last time in the major key. So popular were the chansons published by Pierre Attaignant in the years from 1539 to 1549 that arrangements were frequently made for instruments or organ, giving rise to the *canzona* (= chanson) and eventually to the fugue and the sonata. We shall follow these developments later.

The chanson and its Italian counterpart the *frottola* were the forerunners of the madrigal. The earliest use of the term 'madrigal' in the 16th century as designating a musical form was in 1530. (The 16th-century madrigal is musically quite unrelated to the 14th-century variety.) The exact meaning of the word is uncertain, but in effect it signifies a more elevated type of verse and music than the *frottola*; usually a single verse through-composed to which was brought a more learned, motet-like style of composition. We can see the influence of both *frottola* and chanson in two madrigals published in 1539, one by Costanzo Festa (d. 1545), *Quando ritrova*,[4] in which the influence of the *frottola* predominates (not in form but in simplicity of texture); the other by Jacob Arcadelt, *Voi ve n'andat'al cielo*[5] which seems to favour the chanson in its more sophisticated polyphony, and chanson-like rhythms and imitations. But the madrigal was to develop in a very different direction. With the Italian madrigal it is impossible to separate verse and music, as could happen with the chanson; the words are 'mistress of the harmony'—to quote Monteverdi. In seeking to exploit to their fullest the emotional contrasts of madrigal verse, musical continuity and homogeneity tended to be less regarded. Cipriano de Rore (1516–1565) was one of the

[1] *HAM* 107.   [2] *MM* 20.   [3] *HAM* 147.   [4] *HAM* 129.
[5] *HAM* 130.

first madrigal composers to strive for expressiveness at the expense of abstract constructional principles, and in this he was followed by Luca Marenzio (1553–1599), whose skill and taste enabled him to hold the two in balance, Carlo Gesualdo (d. 1613), who was prepared to sacrifice almost everything for emotional effect, and Claudio Monteverdi (1567–1643), who allowed his search for greater expressive resources to lead him away from the established madrigal style altogether. Thus Marenzio's *S'io parto*[1] illustrates the varied texture of the late 16th-century madrigal, yet retains a considerable measure of polyphonic continuity and tonal consistency; Gesualdo's *Moro lasso*[2] juxtaposes smooth counterpoint with agitated descriptive writing, diatonic progressions with atonal chromaticisms; and Monteverdi's *Lasciatemi morire* is both madrigal (published as such in 1614) and operatic monody from *Arianna* (1608).[3]

The beginnings of these tendencies may be observed in de Rore's madrigal *Da le belle contrade*[4] printed in 1569. The poem, hence the music, divides naturally into three parts:

(i) the dawn, a pair of lovers in each other's arms,
(ii) the complaint of the woman as her lover is about to leave,
(iii) their final embraces.

So far as the music is concerned the first section (bb. 1–21) is neutral in tone and conventional in structure, combining polyphonic and homophonic writing in typical madrigal style, beginning and ending in F major, and including an expressive 'madrigalism' (bb. 6–8)—a rising figure to suggest the rising sun. The complaint (bb. 21–56) is much more highly charged, introducing many foreign chords and moving well outside the mode. See especially the phrase beginning *'Ahi crud'amor'* and note the madrigalism at *'sospir ardente'* (b. 25)—a rest in all parts to represent the 'ardent sigh'—also the voice left alone to sing *'sola mi lasci'* (b. 33). The third section is like the first in that it returns to a more conventional style of writing, and is in F major throughout. The contrapuntal elaboration is no doubt intended to suggest the

[1] *MM 27.*   [2] *TM 33.*   [3] *GMB 177.*   [4] *HAM 131.*

idea of the lovers' arms entwined 'in so many coils that ivy or acanthus never made more'.

The fact that this madrigal as a whole forms a kind of ternary structure is due to a literary rather than to an independent musical design. So far as the style is concerned it is by no means an extreme example, though the middle section is remarkable, anticipating as it does the more advanced writing of Gesualdo and Monteverdi. However, it would be futile to pretend that this one example typifies the thousands of madrigals written in Italy in the 16th century. A fairly consistent distinction is made, however, between the more serious and highly wrought madrigal proper, and madrigals in lighter chordal style known as *canzonette*. This latter type includes varieties known as the *balletto*, often with 'fa-la' refrain (see *L'acceso* by Giovanni Gastoldi (d. 1622)[1]) as well as the *mascherata*, *villanella* or *villanesca* (sometimes described as *'alla Napolitana'*)—works in which lively syncopated rhythms and local dialects are frequently used for humorous effect.[2] Strophic settings and repeated sections are found in these *canzonetta*-types. Simple binary form is especially common in contrast to the through-composed madrigal, or the motet-like *madrigale spirituale* with its religious (but vernacular) text.

At the end of the 16th century English and German composers came strongly under the influence of the Italian madrigal and *canzonetta*, which ousted to some extent the indigenous English part-song and German *lied*. These were the native equivalents of the *frottola* and chanson, and the best English examples from early in the century (some by Henry VIII himself) are chordal and attractively melodic (see 'Adieu, adieu' by William Cornysh (d. 1523)[3]). But later, the influence of the chanson may be noted, despite the melancholy tinge of the words, in the simply worked out 'points' of such songs as Robert Johnson's 'Defiled is my name' and Richard Edwards' 'In going to my naked bed'. The tradition of the tuneful part-song managed to survive the tremendous vogue for the Italianate madrigal following the publication of *Musica Transalpina* in 1588, as may be seen in certain collections 'apt for voices or viols' such as Gibbons' so-called 'Madrigals

[1] *HAM* 158.   [2] See *GMB* 101, 140.   [3] *HAM* 86.

and Mottets' (1612). His 'Silver Swan' is not really a madrigal in the Italian sense, but in the direct line of English part-songs. One could view certain of the more serious lute-songs of the early 17th century as belonging to the same tradition, though the influence of the *canzonetta* is clear in the more light-hearted ones. Others, such as 'If my complaints' by John Dowland (1563-1626) belong to a class of vocal adaptations of instrumental dance music—in this case 'Captain Piper's Galliard'.

But a piece such as 'My bonny lass' by Thomas Morley (1557- c. 1602) [1] is clearly modelled on Gastoldi, while Marenzio provides the inspiration for the serious madrigals of John Wilbye (1574-1638) and Thomas Weelkes (d. 1623). However, the typical English madrigal, even of the Italianate variety, was on the whole less high-pitched emotionally, less literary and more purely musical than the Italian madrigal. Even so, it set out to do the same things; above all to represent through expressive harmony and descriptive writing the meanings of the poem. Compare, for example, John Bennet's handling of the same two madrigalisms in his madrigal 'Thyrsis, sleepest thou?'[2] that we drew attention to in de Rore's *Da le belle contrade*; the 'sighs' in bar 43, and the phrase 'let me alone' in bar 46. In general though, English madrigalists went in for less extravagant effects, and had greater respect for a continuous and integrated texture than the Italians.

In Germany, too, the tradition of the polyphonic *lied* came under strong Italian influence at the end of the 16th century. In the earlier part of the century the *lied* had frequently combined rustic heartiness with strict *cantus firmus* technique, often using a folk-song as tenor. Heinrich Isaac (d. 1517) in *Zwischen Berg*[3] treats the song in canon between bass and tenor, and like the tenor of *Oho, so geb' der Mann ein'n Pfenning* by Ludwig Senfl (d. 1543)[4] it gives rise to anticipatory imitations in the opening bars. The term '*tenorlied*' has been applied to these songs for obvious reasons, and we have noted the same procedure in contemporary chorale settings. Sometimes the tenor is the only part supplied with words, suggesting instrumental accompaniment. This may even be reflected in the actual style of part-writing, as in *Mein's*

[1] *HAM* 159.   [2] *MM* 28.   [3] *HAM* 87.   [4] *TM* 32.

traurens ist by Paul Hofhaimer (1459–1537),[1] where the tenor is clearly differentiated from the other voices. This song, like many others of its type is in bar-form.

Italian traits show strongly in the madrigals and canzonets of a later composer such as Hassler (though without sacrificing musical propriety in the furtherance of emotionalism). An Italian composer setting the sense of his *Ach schatz*[2] would have wallowed in its pathos, no doubt, and perhaps never arrived at the same clearcut binary structure.

It is in the late Italian madrigal that we notice certain formally disruptive influences at work. The chromaticisms of de Rore, and those who followed him—Marenzio, Gesualdo, Monteverdi—tended to destroy the cohesive effect of modality, while the introduction of homophonic passages into polyphonic texture, either for variety or reasons of expression, naturally had a disintegrating effect. Round about 1600 the madrigals and motets of the most advanced composers had developed such a discontinuity of texture that some remedy was needed to avoid complete fragmentation. (The same sort of situation is to be observed in the music of Anton Webern and his followers in the 20th century, and we shall see how they sought to avert complete disintegration through a kind of systematic rotation of musical components called 'serialism'.) Monteverdi and his school found a partial answer in the use of chordal 'fill-in' accompaniments for instruments such as the harpsichord, capable of realizing the harmonic implications of the lowest part, the *basso continuo*; not without profound changes of tremendous importance for the future. To some extent, however, the continuo merely recognized a fact which had become apparent, namely, that the bass part (which had begun life as a *contratenor* of more or less equal range with the tenor in the 14th century and—as *contratenor bassus*—slipped below the tenor in the middle of the 15th century) had acquired an harmonic function, and in doing so had supplanted the tenor as the most important part from the structural point of view. From this it was but a short step to the concept of harmony as bass-derived; a concept which was to last throughout the tonal period.

[1] *HAM* 93.   [2] *HAM* 165.

II : 3 Instrumental adaptation and development of polyphonic forms

A great deal of instrumental music written in the 16th century was based on vocal models if not actually directly transcribed from them. The practice of adapting vocal pieces, secular and religious, for organ with ornamental *coloratura* had existed in Germany at least since the middle of the 15th century. In his early 16th-century settings for organ of the hymn *Salve Regina*[1] and the religious song *Maria Zart*,[2] Arnolt Schlick furnishes us with two important instrumental applications of *cantus firmus* technique, the organ hymn and chorale prelude respectively. In the first case the *cantus firmus* is given to the tenor, mainly in long notes, whereas the melody of *Maria Zart* is in the top part, gently ornamented and supplied with breaks between the lines, in which one may sometimes notice an anticipatory imitation in the middle part (bb. 10–12, bb. 20–24). Of somewhat later date are the organ hymns of John Redford (d. 1547)[3] and Girolamo Cavazzoni.[4] The latter composer was among those to set sections, or verses, of Mass-chants for organ, intending the resulting pieces to alternate with verses sung by the choir. This arrangement is known as the 'organ-Mass', and Cavazzoni's *Intavolatura* (1543) contains three: the Kyrie and Gloria of the *Missa Apostolorum* (otherwise '*Cunctipotens*') with the plainsong treated as a *cantus firmus* in the top part.[5] The same *alternatim* treatment of organ and choir is continued in the organ Masses of Girolamo Frescobaldi (1583–1643), Samuel Scheidt (1587–1654) and François Couperin (1668–1733), and

[1] *HAM* 100.   [2] *HAM* 101.   [3] *HAM* 120.   [4] *GMB* 103.
[5] *HAM* 117.

43

applied to psalms and canticles such as the Magnificat. Hence we find verses (*versets, versetti, versillos* etc.), based on the psalm-tones by the Spanish composer Antonio de Cabezón (1510–1566),[1] the French composer Jean Titelouze (1563–1633), and many others.

With Scheidt the chorale prelude, as such, strikes out on its own, leaving behind the rather conservative long-note *cantus-firmus* style of the organ hymn. Scheidt and Michael Praetorius (1571–1621) have left some impressive 'fantasias' on chorale tunes in which each line of the chorale is used as a basis for imitation. The tradition was largely confined to the Protestant north of Germany during the 17th century, Johann Pachelbel (1653–1706) being the only southerner in the company of Heinrich Scheider-mann (d. 1663), Dietrich Buxtehude (1637–1707) and Georg Böhm (1661–1733). During this period, several distinct types developed, some tending towards the stricter *cantus-firmus* treatment of the organ hymn, others to the freer fantasia.

They may be grouped into two main types; those which treat the whole chorale more or less continuously and those which treat it partially or intermittently. The first category includes chorale preludes in which the melody, usually in the top part, is quite simply presented.[2] This is the most common type in Bach's *Orgelbüchlein* (from which the following examples are all drawn unless otherwise stated), and is characterized by a more or less elaborate accompaniment based on certain motives and figures, sometimes—but not always—derived from the chorale (see *Dies sind die heil'gen zehn Gebot*) and at other times intended to illustrate some aspect of the text, such as the ascending movement and pedal leaps in the Easter chorale *Erstanden ist der heil'ge Christ*. In other examples the melody is elaborately and expressively orna-mented. This type is often associated with Böhm, but Bach uses it in such preludes as *Das alte Jahr vergangen ist* and *O Mensch bewein' dein' Sünde gross*. Sometimes the chorale is treated in canon; a device which Bach employs nine times in the *Orgel-büchlein* (for example, *In dulci jubilo* is a canon 4 in 2) and in a variety of ways in the canonic 'chorale-partita' *Vom Himmel hoch*

[1] *HAM* 133.   [2] *MM* 47.

(1747). In the chorale-partita the melody is set differently verse by verse (see also *Christ ist erstanden*). This form may derive from Scheidt's verse-settings and ultimately from the organ hymn, but frequently it shows a secular influence carried over no doubt by such composers as Pachelbel and Böhm from their keyboard variation-suites on popular songs.

The second category of chorale preludes includes the 'chorale-motet', the 'chorale-fugue' and the 'chorale with interludes'. The first treats each line of the chorale as a subject for imitation, usually in diminution. After anticipatory imitations the line is— as a rule—given out in long notes in one part or another, followed by anticipatory imitations of the next line. The texture is thus a series of interlocking entries based on successive lines of the chorale, and is clearly analogous with the chorale-motet for voices (see p. 34). Scheidt's 'chorale-fantasias' are of this type, as are many of Pachelbel's chorale preludes.[1] Bach favoured it in his longer settings, as for example in the famous *Wenn wir in höchsten Nöthen sind*, the last of the 'Eighteen Chorales'. In the chorale-fugue the first line of the melody is treated as a fugue, usually without reference to subsequent lines. Pachelbel, again, is an exponent of this type, and Bach uses it frequently, not in the *Orgelbüchlein*, but in his collections of more extended settings; see the 'Giant'—*Wir glauben all' an einen Gott, Schöpfer*—No. 9 in Part III of the *Clavier-übung* (1739). Also belonging to this group is the chorale with interludes, sometimes called '*cantus-firmus* chorale', in which the melody is given out in long notes and the lines of the chorale spaced out. The setting is usually so homogeneous and closely integrated within itself that it sometimes seems as if the chorale is an afterthought. Certainly the anticipation of lines that one finds in the chorale-motet is foreign to this style. The opening chorus of the 'St. Matthew Passion' (and the closing chorus of Part I) are examples; so are many of the longer preludes such as *Komm heiliger Geist*—No. 1 of the 'Eighteen Chorales'. Finally, the 'chorale-fantasia' deals freely with the chorale (or parts of it) in one or more of the ways already described. It is thus different from the fantasia type of Scheidt, and is actually the least favoured

[1] *GMB* 243.

category of all by Bach, to whom the description *Fantasia super* ... did not necessarily imply this type of improvisatory treatment. As an example *In dir ist Freude* may be mentioned: a fantasia on various lines of the chorale freely treated as regards order.

The forty-six chorale preludes of the *Orgelbüchlein* are as perfect a consummation of their tradition as Bach's '48 Preludes and Fugues'. The fugue, as we have said, also had its origin in instrumental adaptations of vocal forms, in particular the chanson. The canzona copied the style of the chanson (including the typical chanson rhythm ♩ ♪ ♪) and in the beginning was often nothing more than an instrumental transcription of a particular chanson for lute, keyed instrument, or consort of instruments. The earliest specimens date from the turn of the 15th century, and as an example of the process Thomas Crequillon's *Pour ung plaisir*[1] in its chanson version (printed 1543) should be compared with Andrea Gabrieli's organ arrangement published in his *Canzoni alla francese* (1605).[2] In essentials the organ version is identical except for ornamental passages which decorate Crequillon's rather plain counterpoint. Not all canzonas are so closely modelled on their originals, however. Cavazzoni's reworking of Josquin's *Faulte d'argent*[3] is much freer and contains a great deal of original material, while others are original pieces for instruments.

The word *fuga* means 'imitation', and the canzona, being imitative was sometimes—especially in Germany—called *fuga*. In fact, Bernard Schmid in his *Tabulatur Buch* (1607) refers to 'Fugues, or as the Italians call them, *canzoni alla francese*'. A related form was the ricercar, though at first the term ricercar—'fantasia' also—indicated a type of idiomatic music for lute or keyed instrument, as for example, the ricercars in Petrucci's early 16th-century lutebooks[4] and Luis de Milan's fantasias in his *Libro de musica* (1535).[5] But later ricercars for organ, such as those by Cavazzoni,[6] or those for instruments by Willaert[7] clearly approximate to the style of the motet. Since the word implies discovery, either of the

---

[1] *MM* 20.   [2] *MM* 21.   [3] Compare *HAM* 91 with 118.
[4] *HAM* 99.   [5] *HAM* 121.   [6] *HAM* 116.   [7] *HAM* 115.

potential of an instrument or a theme, it is applicable to both types.

The stylistic distinction between canzona and ricercar is frequently blurred, and no thoroughly consistent differentiation can be maintained beyond the general one, that the ricercar is the more densely contrapuntal, the more polyphonically engrossed in its subject matter. Together with the fantasia and capriccio (and the Spanish *tiento*) they illustrate the following tendencies:

(i)   the working out of a single theme at some length in a more or less homogeneous movement[1];

(ii) the working out of a single theme in a number of more or less clearly defined sections, the theme undergoing transformation from section to section—the 'variation canzona'[2];

(iii) the working out of several themes in successive sections— the 'chain' or 'quilt canzona'.[3]

In the course of the 17th century these three types were to lead to the fugue, (i) and (ii), and the sonata, (iii). Postponing consideration of the latter development until the next chapter, we shall follow the canzona and its related forms to their culmination in the Bach fugue. The point we have already reached is best exemplified by the canzonas and ricercars of Frescobaldi, and the monumental fantasias of Jan Pieterszoon Sweelinck (1562–1621). Sweelinck favoured the monothematic type of fantasia, (i) above, treating his themes at great length by means of augmentation, diminution, stretto and a succession of countersubjects—that is, counterpoints to the main theme—taken up, used in combination and discarded in turn.[4] To him the fantasia was a single, cumulative structure moving powerfully towards its end; as it did so rising towards a climax of rapid figurations, diminutions and strettos of the subject. Thus, despite the English influence which is often alleged, it differs from the contemporary English fantasia,

[1] See *HAM* 175, *MM* 34.   [2] See *HAM* 191.
[3] See *MM* 26, *HAM* 194.   [4] *GMB* 158.

or 'fancy', for keyboard or viol consort, which is not normally monothematic.

Through Sweelinck's pupils, Scheidt and Scheidemann, his approach to the fugue—actually called 'fugue' in Scheidt's *Tabulatura Nova* (1624)—was carried on and was to exert considerable influence on the North German organists. In fact, the gap between Scheidemann and Bach is bridged by one man, Jan Adam Reinken (1623–1722), a pupil of the former who lived long enough to be admired by the latter.

Nevertheless, the influence of Frescobaldi was, if anything, dominant in Germany, where in the north his pupil Franz Tunder (1614–1667) was Buxtehude's predecessor at Lübeck from 1641, and in the south where his pupils Johann Kaspar Kerll (1627–1693) and Johann Jacob Froberger (d. 1667) were at Munich and Vienna. Like his master, Froberger favoured the sectional variation form for his fugues which he called 'fantasia', 'ricercar', 'canzona', or 'capriccio', not yet recognizing the term 'fugue' as meaning anything more than imitation. No clear formal distinction is apparent between these four types of composition, though the general style of the fantasias and ricercars is more sober than that of the canzonas and capriccios. All these titles are to be found applied to fugal works in the 17th century, and for the most part the variation scheme predominates, with sections in duple, triple and sometimes compound-time treating different forms of the subject, though rarely at any other pitch than that of its original authentic or plagal version. Even in Buxtehude's so-called 'Preludes and Fugues', the fugues are in most cases imitative episodes within a free rhapsodical texture and based on transformations of a single theme—the variation idea again. A typical example is the E minor Prelude and Fugue[1] which contains two related fugues in 4/4 and 3/4 respectively, sandwiched between sections of toccata-like writing. In fact, this sort of variegated structure probably owes less to the pre-fugal ricercar and canzona than to the keyboard toccata, which almost from the first had contained imitative sections side by side with freer ones that explored the virtuoso possibilities of the instrument; see *Toccata*

[1] GMB 249.

Quinta by Claudio Merulo (1533–1604).[1] Froberger's *Toccata II*[2] exactly anticipates the form of the Buxtehude 'Prelude and Fugue' just mentioned.

But despite the influence of Sweelinck's and Frescobaldi's pupils, the fugue as a single, monothematic, homogeneous movement seems to have emerged neither in the north nor in the south, but in the middle of Germany, at the hands of a modest but attractive school of composers which included the Nurembergers Johann Krieger (1651–1735) and Pachelbel. In the latter's 'Magnificat fugue'[3] episodes between the entries are still short, but in each case sequential use is made of a quaver pattern borrowed from the end of the theme and combined with a counterpoint in longer notes suspended against it. This results in a harmonic progression based on the 'circle of fifths'; the roots of successive chords falling a fifth (see bb. 11–12, 14–16 and 18–22). This sort of thing became a cliché in late Baroque fugal episodes—in fact, generally. It signifies nothing less than the establishment of the classical tonal system whose strongest and most typical harmonic progression, the perfect cadence, is but a segment of the circle of fifths.

With a clearly defined sense of tonality and of tonal relationships, composers could be more enterprising in the modulations they pursued in their fugues, and we find Reinken about 1670 advocating, in effect, that the modulatory scheme of a fugue should include cadences in the dominant and relative keys. By Bach's time, and especially with Bach, middle entries of the theme in related keys are common, though still by no means the rule.

Apart from this greater tonal range and the superlative quality and expressive potential of Bach's themes, his fugues differ most from those of his contemporaries and predecessors in their integral use of subordinate material, the counter-subjects and episodic motives particularly. Although he still uses the names and forms of the past—toccata, fantasia, even on a few occasions canzona, ricercar and capriccio—Bach generally regarded the fugue as self-contained, continuous in texture, and conforming to a fairly

[1] *TM* 29, bb. 29–39.   [2] *HAM* 217.
[3] *HAM* 251, one of 94 similar pieces.

consistent general outline, though we have only to look at the fugues in the 'Well-tempered Clavier' (otherwise known as 'the 48') to see the tremendous variety in detail which is possible. Nevertheless, three stages are usually discernible in a Bach fugue. The first, which we may call the exposition or enunciation, is taken up with the entry of the voices (normally from three to five) with the theme one after another. The theme is presented in two forms alternately: first the subject then the answer, which can still be regarded as authentic and plagal versions of the same theme. In practice this usually means that the answer follows the subject a fifth higher or a fourth lower, but, as Tovey says, it should be thought of as being 'as far as possible *on* the dominant, not *in* the dominant'. Thus the subject of the C major fugue (I/1) is answered exactly a fifth higher, that is, transposed from its authentic to its plagal form (Ex. 9). In terms of tonality we may say that it is not so much a G major tonic in its own right as a G major dominant in the key of C. Subjects like this which can be transposed exactly without disturbing the mode produce 'real' answers, but frequently this is not possible. For example, an initial leap up of a fifth or down of a fourth from the tonic, or a subject starting on the fifth above or the fourth below the tonic, would give a real answer conflicting with the mode. Similarly, on the rare occasions when a subject modulates to the dominant, a real answer would modulate to the dominant of the dominant—too far to be tolerable in the early stages of a fugue. To prevent this happening some modification is made to the subject, in the first case by answering authentic tonic with plagal tonic and vice versa, in the second by returning the dominant modulation in the subject to the tonic in the answer—which is the same idea expressed in terms of modulation that was previously expressed in terms of melody. Answers modified in either of these two ways are called 'tonal' answers (Ex. 10 shows both in I/7's answer), and it will be gathered that the practice was a continuation of principles established in the 16th century aimed at preserving the modality of a theme when transposed into a different vocal register (see p. 36), but applied in the baroque period to maintain the tonality of a subject throughout the first stage of the fugue.

Ex. 9

(i)

Authentic Subject

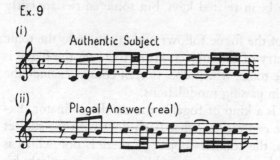

(ii)

Plagal Answer (real)

Ex. 10

(i)

(ii)

Normally, the first stage of a fugue is completed once all the
voices have entered, but it may be extended through the introduction of one or more additional or 'redundant' entries, that is,
further entries of the subject or answer at their original pitch.
There are many examples in 'the 48'. Not to go beyond the C
sharp major fugue (I/3), note the redundant answer starting at bar
10, in the top part. Redundant entries occurring in two or more
voices may be taken as constituting a partial or, if all voices
participate, a complete counter-exposition—a second exposition
(see for example the E major fugue, I/9, bb. 6–10).

The second stage of the fugue now begins during which, within the limits of the style, virtually anything may happen. In
general terms the usual procedure is to alternate entries of
the subject or answer with modulating episodes, though the C
major fugue (I/1) has no episodes at all! The entries of the

theme will usually be in related keys, but tonic entries are fairly common.

The final stage of the fugue follows with a return to the tonic key and a tonic entry of the subject. From there on the fugue is firmly based on the tonic, which does not, of course, exclude the possibility of certain passing modulations.

The above plan is a kind of fugal common denominator. Except perhaps in the exposition, what Bach does with the subject and its companion, the counter-subject (if there is one which is used regularly), or how he constructs his episodes, is entirely his own affair. He may or may not use stretto, augmentation, diminution or inverse motion, or any combination of these. Normally they appear (if they do appear) towards the end of a fugue, in the second or third stage. For example, the C minor fugue (II/2) introduces the subject in its original form in stretto with itself in augmentation, and inverse motion at b. 14—that is, half-way through (Ex. 11); on the other hand, the next fugue, in C sharp

Ex. 11

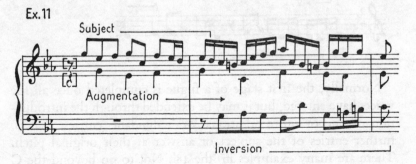

major (II/3) begins with stretto of the subject right-way up and upside down! It should be stressed, however, that devices such as these do not make a fugue. In this respect Bach is much more abstemious than Beethoven, who could hardly resist the whole gamut of devices in his later fugues.

Sometimes a fugue is based on more than one theme. The technique of invertible counterpoint involves one or more counter-subjects which may accompany the theme at each entry, sometimes above and sometimes below it (see I/21). Occasionally theme and counter-subject are announced together at the very beginning; a type of 'double fugue' which Bach rarely adopts (however, see the fugue of the Passacaglia and Fugue in C minor), but which Handel and Italianate composers use quite frequently. (The first and third of Handel's six *Grandes Fugues* are examples.) Bach prefers another sort in which the second subject, or the third, is introduced after the exposition of the first either in combination, or by itself, to be combined with the first subject at a later stage. For example, in the C sharp minor fugue (I/4) the second subject is introduced in combination with the first starting at b. 35, and the third in combination with both the others starting at b. 49. But in the F sharp minor fugue (II/14), the second subject is exposed by itself (bb. 20–22) and not treated in combination until bb. 28–31; similarly the third subject enters at b. 36, and it is not until b. 51 that the first subject is recalled, and still later that all three are combined (bb. 55–57, 60–62, and finally 66–68).

It must be expected that every fugue will be different in details. Let us compare two adjacent fugues—the last two—from 'the 48', noting both the similarities and the differences. We will make the comparison stage by stage.

STAGE ONE (Exposition)

B major (II/23): The theme is introduced by the four voices in the order bass, tenor, alto, soprano, and there is a redundant entry of the subject in the bass (b. 19). The counter-subject is regular, that is, it accompanies the theme on each appearance, and the answer is real. Between the end of the answer and the beginning of the subject there is a short one bar link (b. 9 and b. 18) necessitated by the fact that the end of the answer will not lead satisfactorily into the beginning of the subject without some such join. For no very good reason, apparently, the word 'codetta' is sometimes applied to such a link, sometimes the word 'episode'. Neither is very satisfactory, though episode is perhaps better, but this term can best be reserved for longer stretches of linking material such as we find leading up to the first cadence (bb. 23–27).

B minor (II/24): The three voices are introduced in the order alto, soprano and bass. The answer is tonal (only the first note is altered, being the fifth above the tonic) and the regular counter-subject gives rise to a three bar link (bb. 12–15) between answer and subject. There is no clear cadence to mark the end of the first stage; but an indirect cadence in the tonic (b. 21) signifies the commencement of a canonic episode, soprano following the bass at the 12th above (bb. 21–26) modulating to the dominant.

STAGE TWO (Modulatory middle section)

B major: The redundant entry in the bass already mentioned is now seen to have been the first entry in a counter-exposition with which is combined the exposition of a new theme in flowing quavers starting at b. 28. The actual pitches of the first theme up to b. 45 are still those of the exposition, but at times the new counterpoints lead into G sharp and D sharp minor. The ambiguous tonality of both subjects is exploited in later entries, due to the two subjects being invertible at the twelfth as well as the octave. Most of the longer episodes are in three parts (e.g. bb. 63–75) and continue the quaver movement of the second theme.

B minor: The episodes here are for the most part sequential and based on the circle of fifths. Successive entries of the theme are in F sharp minor (bb. 26–32), D major (35–41), A major (44–50) and F sharp minor again (54–60), with a new counter-subject of oscillating semiquavers used regularly and as a source for episodic material. The opening of the theme returns in the tonic (b. 69), but as it will not work in stretto beyond the third bar, it drops out in favour of the subdominant version (E minor) that entered a bar behind.

STAGE THREE (Final Section)

B major: The return to the tonic is marked by an entry of the subject in the bass (b. 75), then of the answer in the tenor (b. 85) combined with the second subject (b. 86), and finally of the subject in the soprano (b. 93).

B minor: Another sequential episode (b. 76–81) leads to a complete tonic entry in the soprano (b. 81), and still more sequences end in a final suggestion of the subject—only the first five notes—in stretto between alto and bass.

Two fugues could hardly be more different. The B major is a magnificent double fugue on one of Bach's austere ricercar-like subjects; the B minor a slighter, more lively affair altogether. Yet clearly their principles of construction are the same, and their link with the past recognizable.

As we shall see, fugues are also found in sonatas and *concerti grossi*, usually as the first and second allegro movements (i.e. normally the second and fourth movements) and as the second section of the 'French' overture. In fact, of the twelve *concerti grossi* in Handel's Op. 6, only the eighth has no fugue. Of the remaining eleven, seven have a fugal second movement, and the other four have fugues either as the fourth or (in one case) the fifth movement. In works such as these we find fugue and concerto forms coming together usually with the episodes being treated 'solo' and the entries of the subject 'tutti'. One of the most felicitous examples of such fugal-concerto movements is the last movement of the fourth Brandenburg concerto of Bach, where, following the exposition in G major, the middle entries are treated as ritornellos in D major, E minor and C major before returning to the tonic, with solo-episodes in between. It provides a convincing illustration of a fact that will become more obvious later, that nearly every late-baroque 'Allegro', be it fugue, two-part invention, sonata or concerto movement, even a dance in binary form, can be reduced to a series of modulations leading away from and back to the tonic with cadences *en route* in related keys. This modulatory scheme is actually the basis of their form, and with differing shades of emphasis it underlies all tonal music up to the middle of the 19th century.

III

Tonality and the development of the 'sonata principle'

III : 1   Instrumental forms of the baroque period

Even as early as the 14th century we may observe a tendency for instrumental dances to come in pairs, and, what is more, for the second dance to be a variation on the first. (See the *Lamento di Tristan*[1] with its 'after-dance' entitled *La Rotta*.) By the 16th century it was common for the second dance to be treated as a rhythmic variation, usually changing what was in slow or moderate duple-time into quick triple-time—hence the name *proportz* or *tripla* for the after-dance (*nachtanz*). Such a pair were the pavan and galliard, each commonly in three sections, or strains, marked to be repeated. The *Pavane d'Angleterre* and its *Gaillarde* by the 16th-century composer Claude Gervaise[2] show the typical form and inter-relationship, though by no means all pavans are in three strains, and not all galliards are variations on the preceding pavan. William Byrd's pavan and galliard 'The Earle of Salisbury' for example, are each in two strains, and thematically unrelated.

It was the expansion of such pairs into longer sequences of dances that provided at least one of the origins of the suite—in particular those suites which observed the variation principle. But the idea was taken up in two different ways. German composers in the early 17th century developed the suite as a sequence of contrasted dances, applying the principle of rhythmic variation from one dance to the next. Examples of these variation suites are to be found in the *Banchetto Musicale* (1617) by Johann Hermann Schein (1586–1630) and Paul Peuerl's *Neue Paduan, Intrada, Däntz und Gagliarda* (1611),[3] which contains suites of dances in the order

[1] *HAM* 59, also *GMB* 28.   [2] *HAM* 137.   [3] *GMB* 157.

specified in the title. Each movement begins with the same motive treated differently according to the style of the dance.

In Italy the most popular dance-pair in the latter part of the 16th century was the *passamezzo* and *saltarello*, and here again the second dance was a variation on the first. Later the *corrente* became the most popular 'after-dance', frequently following a piece called simply *balletto*. However, Italian composers developed the idea of the suite somewhat differently from the Germans, favouring sets of variations (called *partite*) on strophic basses derived either from popular songs such as the *romanesca*,[1] and *ruggiero*, or from dances like the *folia*, *bergamasca*, *passamezzo* ('*antico*'[2] and '*moderno*'), the *passacaglia* and *ciaccona* or chaconne. Although these ground-bass forms are not analogous to each other in every respect, in general they represent stereotyped harmonic progressions which are treated with different figuration at each repetition, as is done to-day in the 'blues'. Emphasis on the intervals of the fourth and fifth in these basses encouraged as well as reflected the tendency to-wards tonic-dominant tonal orientation. Bach has provided us with three superlative applications of the strophic bass principle in the C minor organ Passacaglia, the D minor Chaconne for solo violin, and the 'Goldberg' variations, for harpsichord. In the latter, the bass derives from an aria which begins and ends the work. Within this frame are thirty 'strophic' variations, grouped in two sets of fifteen (the second set beginning with a variation in the style of a French overture) and further divided into ten groups of three—each group (except the last) ending with a canon at intervals increasing progressively from the unison to the ninth.

But exactly how the allemande–courante–sarabande sequence of dance movements which is basic to the 'French' suite of the second half of the 17th century arose is difficult to say. Within most collections of dance music for lute or clavecin the pieces were arranged according to key, and within each key according to type, i.e. all the allemandes together, all the courantes together, and so on. With common keys such as C major this could result in 'suites' of twenty movements or more, and possibly a selection was made in performance, one from each type as seemed fitting.

[1] See *HAM* 124, 192.   [2] *HAM* 154, *TM* 35.

However the basic order became established—and it may be that alphabetical arrangement played some part—we find it clearly followed by Froberger in his suites and the dances reduced to a manageable number.[1] Froberger is perhaps the central figure in the development of the suite. He was strongly influenced by the raking *arpeggiando* style of French lute and clavecin music, and carried this influence through to the next generation of German composers such as Pachelbel and Böhm. The manuscripts of his suites indicate that he usually placed the gigue before the sarabande, although they were printed many years after his death the other way round in order to conform to a later taste—the form in which Bach would have known them. As with the dance-pair we find that Froberger often relates the allemande to the courante[2] —that is, the rhythmically subtle French courante with its interplay of 3/2 and 6/4, not the livelier 'running' Italian *corrente* or *coranto* in simple triple-time—a variational device which is occasionally exploited by Johann Kuhnau (1660–1722), Bach's predecessor at Leipzig, and at least as late as Johann Mattheson (1681–1764), and Handel (see Suite No. 4 in E minor).

Towards the end of the 17th century the allemande–courante–sarabande–gigue sequence became enlarged by the addition of sundry optional movements: the 'galant' dances, the 'gallantries' (called *galanterien* in German) inserted before or after the gigue. Bach puts them before the gigue in his French and English suites and in the Partitas. The introductory movement, which he and many other composers often placed before the allemande, could be any one of a number of forms. Bach himself uses most of them in his Partitas, a different one to each of the six, thus: *Praeludium, Sinfonia, Fantasia, Ouverture, Praeambulum,* and *Toccata*. Similarly, Bach's *galanterian* may be taken as a representative selection— *air, anglaise, bourrée, burlesca, caprice, gavotte, loure, minuet, passepied, polonaise, rondeau, rigaudon,* and *scherzo*.

Outside Germany, the form of the suite remained less rigid. The first 'suite' of *Pièces de clavecin* (1670) by Jacques Champion de Chambonnières comprises an allemande, a courante with its 'double' (i.e. ornamental variation) followed by two more

---

[1] *MM* 35.   [2] *GMB* 205.

courantes, a sarabande and a galliard, while the second contains only an allemande, two courantes and a sarabande. On the other hand the G minor suite by Jean Henry d'Anglebert (d. 1691) from his *Pièces de clavecin* (1689) contains twenty-two items,[1] some of which are arrangements of theatre tunes. Purcell's posthumous keyboard 'Lessons' (1696) also contain a number of keyboard arrangements from his stage music. Rather later, the great François Couperin in his *Ordres* (harpsichord suites published between 1713 and 1730) sometimes disregards the basic sequence completely, at other times follows it fairly closely. Like other French composers, Couperin furnishes most of his dance movements with titles, sometimes obviously descriptive, but at other times fanciful and even enigmatic. *La Galante*,[2] for example, is a gigue; on the other hand neither *Le Rossignol en amour* nor *Sœur Monique*[3] are formal dances. The latter illustrates the form of the *rondeau* in which episodic 'couplets' in different keys alternate with a recurrent refrain in the tonic. There is no direct link with the mediaeval *forme fixe* of this name, but the French clavecinistes were particularly fond of the scheme. They habitually wrote their 'chaconnes' thus,[4] instead of using the ground-bass form that Purcell (for all the French influence in his music) and other composers adopted.

With the exception of these *rondeaux*, and of course, the opening preludes, the movements of the suite were invariably in binary form. Occasionally we find a pair of gavottes, bourrées or minuets together, in which case the first dance is repeated after the second, giving a ternary arrangement *ABA* (each of Bach's 'English Suites' provides an example). The second dance, called *alternativo* or *trio*, sometimes contrasts with the first by substituting the tonic minor key for the tonic major, or vice versa; otherwise, all the movements of a suite are in the same key. The *alternativo* to a gavotte is usually a *musette*, a rustic dance characterized by its drone bass in imitation of the bagpipe-like instrument whose name it bears.

All these forms were to play a part in the development of the

---

[1] 3 in *HAM* 232.   [2] *MM* 40.   [3] *HAM* 265.
[4] See Chambonnières' Chaconne *HAM* 212.

sonata and symphony, for out of binary came sonata form, from the *rondeau* came the rondo, and the minuet and trio led eventually to the scherzo.

Binary form already had a long history in Bach's time, going back at least as far as the bar-form of the mediaeval *ballade*. In the 17th century it comprises, essentially, two mutually dependent sections or strains, the first moving away from the tonic key, and ending in an 'open' cadence, the second returning and ending with a 'close' cadence. The open cadence, is normally in the dominant key (or, if the tonic key is minor, in the relative major) and is thus inconclusive with respect to the original key: the close cadence is in the tonic, and is thus conclusive—though a short coda may follow as happens at the end of the allemande in Bach's E major French Suite. Three clear stages in the development of binary form can be traced, though it is not so easy to relate each stage to a definite period. The first may be called 'symmetrical-binary', good examples of which are provided by the movements of Froberger's suite in E minor.[1] The allemande and courante both begin in the tonic and end their first division on the chord of B— the dominant. (It will be noted that there is a modulation to the dominant in the allemande, but only a half-close on the dominant chord in the courante.) In the sarabande and the gigue the modulation is to the relative major. The second division of each dance reverses the process, taking roughly the same number of bars to do so—hence the term 'symmetrical'. Secondary characteristics of the form at this stage are, (i) that there is often no thematic relation between the two halves of the dance, merely a stylistic and rhythmic consistency, (ii) that there may or may not be some sort of correspondence between the cadences, as there is in the allemande and gigue of the Froberger suite. In the next stage, the second half of the movement is extended by modulations so that it becomes appreciably longer than the first half—hence the term 'asymmetrical-binary' can be applied. The first strain of Couperin's *La Galante*[2] is eight bars long; the second, fourteen, cadencing in C sharp minor and passing through A major and B major sequentially on the way back to E major. This type of binary form

[1] MM 35.   [2] MM 40.

is more likely to show a thematic relationship between the two divisions, as well as corresponding cadences.

The final stage is marked by a tendency to cadence in the tonic key towards the end of the second division, which is then rounded off by recalling the original thematic material (or perhaps only a hint of it) in a kind of recapitulation ending on a cadence in the tonic corresponding to that which ended the first section in the dominant. This process has been described as 'rounded-binary', and all three stages may be expressed diagrammatically as follows:

type of binary	A		B	
'symmetrical'	I $\quad$ V :a ⟶ 'open' : $\quad$ cadence		V $\quad$ I :a ⟶ 'close' : $\quad$ cadence	
'asymmetrical'	I $\quad$ V :a ⟶ 'open' : $\quad$ cadence		V (possibly via VI to) $\quad$ I :a—modulations ⟶ 'close' : $\quad$ cadence	
'rounded'	I $\quad$ V :a ⟶ 'open' : $\quad$ cadence		V (possibly via VI to) I $\quad\quad$ I :a—modulations ⟶ a ⟶ 'close' : $\quad$ cadence	

Rounded-binary is fairly commonly encountered in the suites of Bach and his contemporaries. It is interesting to observe the three stages of binary form illustrated in the first three movements of the E flat French Suite. The allemande is symmetrical (10:10) with a certain amount of corresponding thematic and cadential material. The courante is asymmetrical (16:20), the second division extended by modulations to related keys. The sarabande illustrates the rounded binary principle, the second division being twice as long as the first (8:9+7) but returning to the tonic seven bars before the end with the original thematic material divided between the right and left hand. Of the remaining movements of the suite the gavotte is asymmetrical (8:14), the minuet symmetrical (8:8), the air neatly rounded (6:10+6). The final gigue too is rounded (26:27+7), the subject returning upside down in the tonic key seven bars from the end.

Parallel with the development of the suite and embodying similar ideas of variety in movement is the baroque sonata. But whereas the suite came about through the grouping together of separate movements, the reverse is true of the sonata. It arose through the fragmentation of what was originally a single movement form, the canzona.

We have already seen how the canzona arose as an instrumental adaptation of the chanson (see p. 46), and how, towards the end of the 16th century it showed a tendency to differentiate into sections, giving rise to the 'quilt' or 'chain' canzona. The word meant literally 'song', but a song to play rather than to sing, hence the term *canzona per sonare* (*sonare*= to sound, i.e. to play). Gradually during the first half of the 17th century the canzona intended for instrumental group came to be known simply as 'sonata' (i.e. 'played'). The keyboard canzona, however, was still called *canzona per organo* or *per cembalo*, or for short, simply 'canzona'. These two types developed in their own way; the *canzona per organo* treating each 'link' of the chain in contrapuntal style, the *canzona per sonare* exploiting stylistic contrasts of metre and tempo, and particularly of texture, from section to section.

Even as late as the sonata *La Buscha* (1671) by Giovanni Legrenzi (1626–1690)[1] we get echoes of the canzonas of his fellow (but long dead) Venetian, Giovanni Gabrieli. The opening movement is imitative and based on a typical canzona motive. The ensuing Adagio is homophonic, very short, and serves as a link to a quicker, highly syncopated movement in triple time in which antiphonal contrast of wind and string instruments is an important feature. Another short Adagio then leads into a final Allegro, which is again imitative and antiphonal in treatment. Although this sonata does not provide an example, Legrenzi in common with many other composers is particularly fond of repeating material from the beginning of his sonatas at the end.[2] In some cases this idea is carried further by repeating sections from the first half in reverse order in the second half; a sort of unwinding process which results in an arch-shaped structure (or 'bow', hence the German term *bogenform*) with the centre section as the head-stone.

[1] *HAM* 220.   [2] See *HAM* 191, *GMB* 184.

Towards 1650 the sectional structure of the canzona settled into the movement structure of the sonata. The sections became longer and fewer, and more clearly differentiated from each other. In a sonata by Giovanni Battista Fontana (d. 1630)[1] there are seven sections in a total of 116 bars. A generation or so later, the sonata *La Pellicana*[2] by Maurizio Cazzati (d. 1677), of about the same length, shows four more or less clearly defined movements. In general, however, the sonata was still a 'patchwork' scheme in which contrasts of fast and slow, polyphony and homophony, duple and triple time, resulted in a highly discontinuous texture. (This is true as late as 1680 in the viol-fantasies of Henry Purcell.) The quick movements tended to be imitative, the slow ones often little more than links, and movements in triple time sometimes took on a dance-like character.

In so far as this tells us anything at all about the sonata in the middle of the 17th century, it tells us almost as much about the concerto and *sinfonia*; for these three terms were virtually interchangeable. What they came to mean later will be considered in due course, but in the meantime two other terms must be explained—*da chiesa* and *da camera*. Instrumental music was almost as important in church as was choral music; indeed, in some places there was more or less continuous music both choral and instrumental from the beginning of Mass to the end. The designation *canzona per l'epistola*[3] indicates that the canzona was to be played during the reading of the Epistle, similarly, *ricercar dopo il credo*[4] that it was to be played after the Creed. The sonata in its turn was used in the same way, hence the description *da chiesa* (*chiesa*=church). Later in the 17th century the term *sonata da camera* came into use, denoting generally a set of dances of variable order and number more suited to chamber than church performance (*camera*=chamber). The *Sonate da camera* (*c.* 1670) of Johann Rosenmüller (d. 1684) are, in fact, suites of dances preceded by *sinfonie*[5] and in the sonatas of Giovanni Battista Vitali (d. 1692) and Arcangelo Corelli (1653–1713), the church and chamber styles are clearly distinguished. The movements of

[1] *HAM* 198.   [2] *HAM* 219.   [3] *MM* 26.   [4] *MM* 34.
[5] *GMB* 220.

Corelli's chamber sonatas tend to follow the usual suite sequence with omissions and sometimes additions; that in E minor (Op. 5 no. 8)[1] consisting of *Preludio, Allemanda, Sarabanda* and *Giga*—all binary movements. And although binary elements are not lacking in the church sonatas, there is, comparatively speaking, a definite contrapuntal bias to their style. The overall four-movement pattern of alternating slow and quick movements that we find in Corelli's church sonata in E minor (Op. 3 no. 7)[2] may be taken as generally typical of the church sonata at the end of the century.[3]

The favourite combination of instruments in both chamber and church sonatas was two violins and cello, though alternative instruments were often specified. Sonatas for this combination are called 'trio sonatas' despite the need for at least four players, the extra one realizing the figured bass on the harpsichord. Likewise the 'solo sonata' needed three players! The trio sonata combination was ideal since it was easy and effective to compose for in the contrapuntal style. It was usually the second movement that was written in this manner, often on a canzona-type fugue subject treated fairly freely with numerous sequential episodes. (Purcell still calls this movement 'canzona' in his sonatas.) The opening slow movement was often little more than an introduction, sometimes ending on a half-close and leading straight into the fugal Allegro, the weightiest movement. This in its turn was usually followed by a slow movement, the only one likely to be in a different key and frequently in triple time. Accented second beats often betray the influence of the sarabande, and binary form is common though the double bar may be absent. The last movement is often explicitly binary, or it may be a fugue (or both), perhaps in the style of a gigue.

It will be seen from this that dance elements from the chamber sonata to some extent invaded the church sonata, especially after 1700. In Germany, the strong organ tradition made the church sonata largely redundant as church music in any case. Bach clearly distinguishes the forms in his six sonatas for violin alone by calling those in church style 'sonatas' and those in chamber style 'partitas', and alternating them thus: *Sonata I, Partita I, Sonata II,*

[1] *HAM* 253.   [2] *MM* 39.   [3] See *HAM* 263, also *GMB* 241.

Partita II, etc. The fourth sonata of the set, (that is, the second partita) is the one which ends with the famous Chaconne, preceded by the regular movements of the suite—allemande, courante, sarabande and gigue. In contrast, the sonata which is placed before this partita comprises four movements marked simply *Grave, Fuga, Andante, Allegro*—the last two being in binary form. Handel, even in his early sonatas admits the occasional dance into what are still in broad outline church sonatas on the Corelli model. In his Op. 5 (1739) this process is carried very much further, for almost half the movements are dances. But the opening slow–quick pair still holds out against the inroads of the 'galant'.

The terms 'sonata', 'sinfonia' and even 'concerto' were still to some extent interchangeable at the end of the 17th century. If anything, *sinfonia* was of less precise application than the others and often merely connoted 'instrumental music', especially in the sense of an introductory piece. Instrumental introductions and interludes in operas were thus often called *sinfonie*, though if we regard *sinfonia* as only the Italian for 'overture' we shall discount hundreds of works that were never operatic overtures despite their title '*sinfonia*'. They are, in fact, sonatas in the sense we have discussed with perhaps the implication of performance by a rather larger consort of instruments.

As it happens, the 'overture' to Monteverdi's *Orfeo* (1607) is called 'Toccata', but elsewhere in the opera there are *sinfonie*. Many of the overtures to the early operas were merely sectional canzonas for large instrumental ensembles, as for example in Steffano Landi's *Sant'Alessio* (1632).[1] Frequently the canzona-overture starts with a slow homophonic introduction which leads into a contrapuntal movement. We find this scheme in some of the operas of the Venetian composers Cavalli and Cesti. The *sinfonia* to Cavalli's *Giasone* (1649) is in two sections; a slow introduction in duple-time, the theme of which is modified to form the subject of the quicker triple-time fugal portion which follows. The same sort of scheme is found in Cesti's *Pomo d'oro* (1667)[2] and in the so-called 'French' overture established by Lully, which

---

[1] *HAM* 208.   [2] *GMB* 202.

in its form and five-part writing derives from the Venetian *sinfonia*. Towards the end of the century this French overture spread beyond France to England (see Purcell's overture to 'Dido and Aeneas'), to Germany, and even back to Venice. Typically, the first section is slow and rather grand, usually with plenty of dotted rhythms, stuttering up-beats, and a thick five-part texture making use of suspensions. It may end on a half-close, from which it returns to the beginning, or (second time round), continues on to the quick section. Normally this is in triple time and in fugal style. The subject may be derived from the slow introduction, but in any case a return to the style of the opening is usually made at the end. The whole of the second section is then repeated. Lully's overtures to *Alceste* (1674) [1] and *Armide* (1686) [2] are good examples of the form. Later it became the fashion to add further movements, usually dances. Handel, following the German taste for French overtures even to Italian operas, frequently does this, as in the overture to *Rinaldo* (1711) [3] which continues after the fugue with a short linking Adagio and an Allegro in gigue style. In effect this makes the overture hardly different as regards form from one of his trio sonatas, or from a harpsichord suite such as no. 7 in G minor, or (as we shall see) from one of his *concerti grossi*.

Two processes may be observed here working towards the same end. The suite frequently adopted the French overture as its opening movement, as in the Handel just referred to, and Bach's D major partita for harpsichord, among other examples. At the same time, the French overture grew a tail, sometimes a very long one as we find in Handel's overture to *Rodrigo* (1707) which ends with a string of eight dances. The result was that the suite and French overture drew near to each other and finally became indistinguishable, so that Bach could call his orchestral suites 'overtures', taking the name of the whole from the first movement.

Towards the middle of the 18th century the French overture— as an overture—declined in favour of the three-movement *sinfonia* type of overture developed in Italy about 1700. It is significant that Reinhard Keiser's opera *Croesus* was provided with one in the French style for its first performance in 1711, and one in the

[1] *HAM* 224.   [2] *MM* 36.   [3] *GMB* 278.

talian style for a revival in 1730. And just as Lully may be credited with the establishment, if not the invention, of the French overture, so we may say that Alessandro Scarlatti (1660–1725) established but did not invent the Italian variety. It is not surprising that his early overtures are types of *sinfonia* usually starting with the slow–quick pair characteristic of the sonata. But in his overture to *Dal male il bene* (1696) the opening slow section was dropped, and from then on the resulting quick–slow–quick sequence of the 'Italian Overture' became increasingly frequent. This order was already quite common in non-operatic *sinfonie*, and even among Italian overtures we can find examples prior to 1696—in the overture to *Il Barcheggio* (1681) by Alessandro Stradella (1642–1682) for example. Two examples by Scarlatti show something of the development it underwent at his hands over a number of years. The *sinfonia* to *La caduta de decem viri* (1697) [1] shows many stylistic resemblances to the sonata (and the concerto) of the period; the bustling, solid Allegro is of a kind that might well have followed a slow introductory movement, and is imitative without being fugal. The slow movement in triple time is in the dominant key, and like the corresponding movement in the church sonata (that is, the third movement) it makes great play with suspensions. [2] The form is a neat and symmetrical binary and the last movement, a type of gigue, is also in binary form. The overture to *La Griselda* (1721) [3] comes almost at the end of his life. The first movement especially is much more 'modern' in style, making little pretence at counterpoint. It is really an extended fanfare, and does not even return to the tonic (D major) but breaks off in F sharp minor from where a slow 15-bar Adagio leads back into a D major Presto—another binary gigue. The linking of movements in this way was to become a feature of the Italian operatic overture.

Most early 18th-century Italian composers recognized the *sinfonia* as a quick–slow–quick three-movement work, whether or not it was to serve as an overture. Giuseppe Torelli (1658–1709), Tommaso Albinoni (1671–1750) and Antonio Vivaldi (d. 1741) all wrote *sinfonie* which probably never saw the inside of an opera

[1] TM 44.　　　[2] Compare MM 39.　　　[3] HAM 259.

house; indeed they may be described as concertos without solo-ists. (Handel and Bach, too, wrote such *sinfonie*, but Bach also called his three-part inventions '*sinfonie*'!)

A concerto without soloist may seem a contradiction in terms to us today, though Bartók's 'Concerto for Orchestra' is one, at least, without a soloist in the usual sense. In fact, it is difficult to say exactly what was understood by the word 'concerto' before 1700. We find forms of the words 'symphony' and 'concerto' applied to certain vocal and instrumental works of the late 16th and early 17th century, in Giovanni Gabrieli's *Concerti* (1587) and *Sacrae Symphoniae* (1597, 1615), for example. But it is hard to argue that it means much more than 'ensemble music' (with a tendency to be heterogeneous rather than homogeneous in tex-ture) before Torelli's *Concerti musicali* (1698). As with so much baroque terminology it designated a style rather than a form; one which was to become associated with the Bologna school of com-posers in particular—Vitali, Corelli and Torelli. Corelli migrated to Rome before 1680, and it was there in 1682 (if not before) that his *concerti grossi* were heard, although they were not published until about the year of his death, 1713. Certain *sinfonie* of Stra-della are supposed to have anticipated Corelli's technique of con-trast between a small group of soloists (the *concertino*, i.e. the little consort) and the rest of the orchestra (the *concerto grosso*, i.e. the large consort). Really it represents the application of the idea of contrast of unequal tonal bodies to the sonata. Corelli's *concerti grossi* derive from the sonata as it was before the four movement pattern of the *sonata da chiesa* established itself firmly. They often extend to five or more movements, though underneath, the four-movement scheme may sometimes be discerned. Of the dozen published in Op. 6, the first eight are '*da chiesa*', the last four '*da camera*'; a functional distinction as well as a formal one. The eighth of this set is the well-known 'Christmas Concerto' in G minor, written to be performed on Christmas eve. The introduc-tion comprises two sections (*Vivace-Grave*) and the ensuing Allegro is in symmetrical-binary form. There follows a ternary movement in E♭ major (*Adagio-Allegro-Adagio*), then—back to the tonic—an asymmetrical-binary Vivace, a rounded-binary

Allegro in the style of a gavotte, and a final 'Pastorale' in G major, which is optional. This is only one of several different sequences found in Corelli's concertos. Handel's Op. 6 are almost equally varied, though most of them retain the opening slow–quick pair of the sonata. Succeeding movements often introduce dances, thus paralleling the later developments of the trio sonata in merging church and chamber features. Even Bach's first Brandenburg Concerto ends with a minuet with three trios (the second a 'Polacca'), though in all six concertos he dispenses with the opening slow movement, favouring the three-movement form of the *sinfonia* or solo concerto.

The solo concerto probably developed from the concerto grosso through a tendency for the first violin to take a more prominent part in the *concertino*. This can be seen happening in the third movement of Scarlatti's Concerto Grosso no. 3 (bb. 27–37) [1] but it is also possible to regard the process as one in which the first violin became the most prominent member of the full consort, gradually achieving solo status. This seems to have been Torelli's line of development. In his *Concerti musicali*, we find examples of the three-movement orchestral concerto with only a few solo episodes marked. Albinoni goes a good deal further in his *Sinfonie e concerti* (1700), and the form is more or less established in Torelli's posthumous *Concerti grossi* (1709).[2] Here we have the concerto style typified: a pounding, relentless movement in which tutti and solo sections alternate. The idea of full orchestral ritornellos alternating with reduced solo episodes had been anticipated in the operatic aria almost from the beginning of opera (see p. 99), but the achievement of the Bologna School was in uniting this static alternating principle with a dynamic, forward moving, scheme of modulations. (It may not be too sweeping to claim that, after more than a century's gestation, the classical tonal system became an accomplished fact in the sonatas, *sinfonie*, and concertos of the Bolognese.) The firm harmonic groundwork on which concerto form is based can be seen in the return of the opening tutti, or ritornello in a sequence of related keys, each return separated by modulatory episodes. A good example of this ritornello form is

[1] *HAM* 260.   [2] *HAM* 246.

the last movement of Torelli's Concerto in C minor (Op. 8 no. 8).[1] Here the opening tutti (bb. 1–17) moves from the tonic to the dominant, returns in the relative major in a shortened form (bb. 26–34), and again, finally, in the tonic (b. 47 to the end). The first episode (bb. 17–26) modulates from G minor to E flat major, the second episode (bb. 34–47) from F minor back to C minor. The accompaniment of these episodes is reduced to the continuo.

First movements in ritornello form are usually longer than this. There is often a good deal more interplay between solo and tutti, neither being excluded from the other's principal sections. But it is the ritornellos which are important from the formal point of view. They mark the main divisions of the movement, and almost invariably appear in a fixed order of keys—tonic, dominant and/or relative major, subdominant then tonic again. This does not mean there is always a ritornello in each key, or that each ritornello will be complete; it may be only partial, or omitted altogether. Vivaldi's A minor Concerto for two violins (Op. 3 no. 6)[2] provides an example of the sort of variation from the basic scheme that is common while still preserving the main outline. The opening tutti (bb. 1–25) and the closing tutti (bb. 68–93) are in the tonic, and there are tuttis in the relative major (bb. 37–48) and subdominant (bb. 52–55). What one notices here is a freer handling of the solo-tutti relationship, and a more pronounced thematic element. With Bach this is even more evident than with Vivaldi. In the 'Italian Concerto' we find all the essential concerto elements despite the fact that it is written for harpsichord alone— though the requisite two manuals permit the necessary dynamic contrast between tutti and solo sections. In the first movement the opening and closing 30-bar tuttis balance each other, and there are ritornellos starting at bar 52 in the dominant and bar 103 in the subdominant. The three episodes, starting respectively at bb. 30, 90 and 129, are each based on different motives, though the last incorporates material from the second episode as well as the ritornello. The final Presto is also in ritornello form, but the slow movement consists of a long cantilena-like melody which unwinds itself over a throbbing ostinato figure in the bass. This was

[1] HAM 246.   [2] HAM 270.

Vivaldi's practice in many of his concertos, including the one we have been considering.

The typical baroque instrumental forms are the fugue, binary and ritornello form. In general, the most important characteristics of each are as follows: 'binary'—a prominent cadence towards the middle in the dominant or (if the tonic is minor) relative major, usually complete with double bar and repeats; 'ritornello' —a fairly clear return of the opening material in the dominant (or relative major), and probably in one or even two other keys, before the final return in the tonic, as well as some differentiation between thematic and episodic material; 'fugue'—an imitative exposition, thereafter a contrapuntal texture alternating entries of the theme and modulatory episodes. But more important than their differences are their similarities, and the following diagram demonstrates the fact that each has the same basic tonality-structure, and that the differences are for the most part those of style.

Key scheme	rounded binary	ritornello	fugue
I	*A* 'opening'	*A* tutti	*A* exposition
↓	↓ modulations	↓ solo	↓ episode
↓	cadence :‖:		
V	*A* 'opening'	*A* tutti	*A* middle entry
↓		↓ solo	↓ episode
other keys	↓ modulations	*A* tutti	*A* middle entry
↓		↓ solo	↓ episode
I	*A* 'opening'	*A* tutti	*A* final entry and section
I	cadence :‖:		↓

It is not suggested that binary form is in some way the prototype of them all. This is not so: the fugue, for one, owes nothing to the binary idea. The truth is that tonality emerged as the basic component of musical form at the end of the 17th century, and in recognizing this, we recognize the principle on which classical sonata form was to be based.

We must also recognize that in addition to the cohesive role of tonality, unity in late baroque music, instrumental and vocal, fugal and homophonic, is dependent to a considerable extent on a consistent patterning of figuration within each movement. This sort of *moto perpetuo* effect becomes increasingly obvious from 1650 onwards, and can be explained in terms of the contemporary doctrine of 'affections and figures' which taught that it was through 'figures'—in other words, stereotyped melodic-rhythmic patterns—that music expressed its particular character, feeling or 'affection', and that a single basic affection should govern each piece of music as a whole. The natural result was consistency of figuration throughout, and this imparted an overall unity. Not even dance music was immune, for just as characteristic 'affects' resulted from particular 'figures', so characteristic dances resulted from particular rhythms. Towards the middle of the 18th century taste changed in favour of a variety of 'affections' within the same piece, and this is reflected in the variegated texture that is typical of the galant and classical style—as we shall see. It is this new element of conflict within the same movement that was to turn binary into sonata form.

Over and above the internal unity within each movement, there is also what we may call the cyclic unity between movements to consider. Here again tonality is all important, even though thematic relationships are not uncommon in the early suite and sonata. The suite, for all the variety it offers from movement to movement, is one because of the tonal unity to which it conforms. The sonata, *sinfonia* and concerto observe this cyclic unity too, by starting and finishing in the same key; and the very fact that one of the shorter intervening movements is often not in the tonic key, but is nevertheless related to it, actually enhances the tonal stability of the main allegro movements, which are the foundation of the whole.

III : 2 Instrumental forms of the classical period

Cyclic tonality carries beyond the baroque period as a unifying principle in the classical symphony, sonata and concerto. With them, departure from and return to the tonic is fundamental, both on the level of the work as a whole, and in the individual movements of which they are comprised. In particular, the idea which sonata form expresses is one conceived basically in tonal terms. There is this much continuity between the early and late 18th century. In other respects, however, the music of the two periods contrasts markedly though the transition is fairly gradual from one to the other.

The development of musical forms between the period of Bach and Handel on the one hand, and Haydn and Mozart on the other, is one of the least explored aspects of musical history, though it is now receiving more attention. Nevertheless there remains a comparatively little known generation of composers separating the giants of the Baroque from the masters of the classical period, and it is to their music that we must turn in order to trace the emergence of classical sonata form.

The new style is sometimes described as *galant* (a close English word would be 'elegant') or *rococo* (delicately ornamented). As never before, the social function of music was aristocratic and secular. It was cultivated as one of the artificialities of court, and thus the enthusiasms of the Baroque gave way to the affectations of the Rococo. Basically it is a homophonic style, tuneful and harmonically simple. It is lighter in character than baroque music, and is in many respects a reaction against its elaborateness. That quality of melody which Handel is reputed to have found wanting in the work of worthy Dr. Greene—good 'air'—became increasingly important. Soon it was almost the only thing that mattered; grace and 'good taste' were qualities sought above everything—and the earnest contrapuntal style became discounted. To the aristocrat it was too learned and laboured; to the intellectual it seemed a relic of the past, tainted with religion, and with its rules and strictures deriving from authority and tradition rather than reason and nature, an enemy of the Enlightenment.

The distinction between *da chiesa* and *da camera* styles was short-lived, and was to become more and more blurred as the 18th century got under way. Soon, practically the sole remnant of the church style was the slow introduction and quick fugue of the sonata and concerto grosso. Torelli, Albinoni and Vivaldi had dispensed with it in the solo concerto—a sensible move since (quite apart from the question of taste) the fugue did not really lend itself to soloistic treatment. The same composers had largely forsworn it in their *sinfonie*, as had Scarlatti in the Italian overture. Similarly in the solo violin sonata, asserting its independence from the trio sonata early in the century, Pietro Locatelli (1695–1764) and Giuseppe Tartini (1692–1770) progressively abandoned the fugal Allegro, and the substitution of a binary Allegro in its place is one of the marks of the end of the baroque era (see Tartini's *Sonata pastorale*[1]).

Yet the fluid terminology of the Baroque still persisted well into the 18th century. 'Symphony', 'sonata', 'concerto', 'overture', 'quartet', etc., were all titles whose meaning and application overlapped, as can be seen in the haphazard nomenclature of works by Giovanni Battista Sammartini (1698–1775) and Johann Stamitz (1717–1757), two of the most influential instrumental composers of the time. Even so, the essential features of what the later 18th century understood by these terms became clearer about 1750. In the case of the symphony, its three-movement baroque predecessor of the same name (*sinfonia*), whether designed as an overture or as concert music, provided the starting point. Hand in hand

[1] *GMB* 295.

with the simplifying tendencies of the *Galant*, went the adoption of binary form in each of the movements, and the frequent substitution of a minuet for the final Allegro or Presto—a common practice in Italian *sinfonie* of the 1730's and '40's. In style the symphony had a certain pretentiousness and though it might be written in as few as three parts, a string band with or without wind was required to do the music full justice.

Viennese composers such as Georg Monn (1717–1750) and Georg Wagenseil (1715–1777) seem to have been among the first to include both a minuet (as third movement) and a Presto (as finale) in their symphonies, though by no means invariably. Monn's D major symphony, dated 1740, is in four movements, the third of which is a minuet and trio, but the same composer is more liable to write a 'symphony' in the old concerto grosso form, complete with slow introduction to fugal Allegro. Stamitz, the famous director of the Mannheim orchestra, wrote symphonies in three as well as four movements; so, prior to about 1765, did Joseph Haydn (1732–1809). Roughly half of his first thirty symphonies are in three movements. From then on he was wholly devoted to the four-movement plan (with minuet and trio placed third), and it was no doubt Haydn's immense prestige which helped to establish its prevalence in Germany. Yet more than a dozen of the early symphonies of Wolfgang Amadeus Mozart (1756–1791) are of the three-movement type favoured by Italian composers like Sammartini, as well as by such un-Italian composers as Carl Philipp Emanuel Bach (1714–1788); so too are a few of his later ones including the 'Prague' Symphony (no. 38) written in 1786.

Meanwhile the operatic overture had become a one movement form, though exactly when the Italian overture began to go out of fashion is difficult to say. It is quite true that one-movement overtures are to be found here and there throughout the history of opera, but *buffa* operas were among the first to make do with a single movement as a regular practice. Anything more ostentatious would have disturbed the balance and spoilt the fun. The *Orfeo* (1762) and *Alceste* (1767) of Christoph Willibald Gluck (1714–1787) are possibly among the earliest serious operas to dispense with the three-movement form of overture, and both Haydn and Mozart wrote their last Italian overtures in the early 1770's. It was part of Gluck's teaching that the overture should prepare the listeners for the mood of the drama to follow, and in many respects his overture to *Iphigénie en Aulide* (1774) set the pattern for the serious operatic overture for a number of years, both aesthetically and in the general outline of slow introduction leading into a tense sonata–allegro—though in this case the form is not 'sonata form' and the tempo is not allegro! Gluck's last important opera, *Iphigénie en Tauride* (1779) did away with a formal overture altogether, and replaced it with a prelude depicting the 'calm' followed by the 'storm'.

The classical sonata finds its origins not so much in the ensemble sonata of the early 18th century, nor even in the solo violin sonatas of composers such as Locatelli and Tartini (despite their dissatisfaction with the fugal style), but in the Italian solo sonata for keyboard of the period 1730–1740. It is here that we find the earliest unmistakable examples of both the style and the form of the classical sonata, indeed, of the galant period itself, no doubt because it grew up outside the great baroque traditions of the Italian violinists, the French clavecinistes, and the German organists. Unencumbered by an established tradition, the spirit of the age had a free rein, and the sonatas of Domenico Scarlatti (1685–1757), and particularly of the next generation of composers represented by Baldassare Galuppi (1706–1785) and Giovanni Rutini (1723–1797) are evidence of this. These composers are representative of the two principal schools of Italian harpsichordists, respectively the Venetian and the Neapolitan, and it is significant that both these places were important operatic centres, particularly of *opera buffa*—another child of the times and one whose melodic idiom was an essential ingredient of the *galant* instrumental style.

As the keyboard sonata had never become an established form like the trio sonata in Italy during the 17th century, these composers used the word 'sonata' in its basic meaning, as 'something played'. Scarlatti's *Essercizi* (1738) contained thirty pieces each called 'sonata' and this itself clearly illustrates the simplest use of the word. Most of his later sonatas were probably intended to be grouped in pairs, each pair comprising two 'sonatas' in the same key, or sharing the same tonic, major or minor. In this he was either setting, or possibly even following the fashion for two-movement keyboard sonatas which predominate in the works of composers like Domenico Alberti (d. 1740) and Domenico Paradies (1707–1791), and which just outnumber three-movement sonatas in the works of Galuppi and Rutini. If Italian composers favoured two or three movements in their keyboard sonatas, German composers seem to have liked three or even four. C. P. E. Bach's 'Prussian Sonatas' (1742) and 'Würtemburg Sonatas' (1744) each have three movements arranged quick–slow–quick, and so have a large majority of Haydn's and all Mozart's authentic keyboard sonatas.

Like the solo keyboard sonata, the string quartet can trace no direct line from the Baroque. Several influences shaped its form. So far as its constitution is concerned it amounts, in effect, to the addition of the viola to the standard baroque trio-sonata grouping of two violins and cello, and the omission of the keyboard continuo instrument, made partly redundant by the presence of the viola as 'filler-in' and the more homophonic texture of the music as a whole. This process was well under way before 1750. We find it already in Alessandro Scarlatti's *Sonate a quattro; due violini, violetta e violoncello, senza cembalo* preserved in manuscript, and identical with four of the *VI Concertos*.[1] Several of Tartini's concertos are also called *sonate* or *sinfonie a quattro*, and in fact the baroque practice of playing concertos or symphonies as chamber music is probably the main one leading to the emergence of the string quartet as a distinct form. The first edition of Haydn's earliest string quartets bears this out, for it carries the title *Symphonies ou quatuors dialogués pour deux violons, alto et basse*.

These quartets of Haydn also point to another influence which must be regarded as contributory, that of the divertimento. The divertimento, and with it the cassation and serenade, were usually light-hearted pieces intended for out-of-doors performance, incorporating features from the symphony, the concerto and the

[1] *HAM* 260.

suite. Anything from two to five or more movements (and instruments) was usual, often including two or three minuets and other dances, marches, *rondeaux*, and sets of variations of a popular character. Haydn wrote his early quartets during the 1750's as divertimentos, which partly explains their five-movement form, with minuets placed before and after the central slow movement. His later quartets, and those of his contemporary Luigi Boccherini (1743–1805), are normally in the four-movement form of the symphony, although Haydn usually places the minuet second (instead of third, like Mozart) up to his Op. 50 quartets, that is, before about 1785.

The solo concerto of the latter half of the 18th century retained the three-movement form of the baroque plan. Whether the concerto grosso finds a direct descendant in the *symphonie concertante*, or whether they are merely analogous to each other is doubtful. Compared with the solo concerto, the concerto grosso was no longer a force to be reckoned with (except in England where Handel's influence was to remain strong for many years), yet to some extent it lived again in the *symphonie concertante*. This can be described as a sort of concerto grosso in the form of a symphony, in which a group of soloists is treated in the manner of a *concertino* contrasting with an orchestral *ripieno*, but in the style and idiom of the three-movement classical symphony. A vast quantity of such works survive from the period after 1750, most of which are unheard these days except for one or two by Haydn, and Mozart's beautiful one for violin, viola and orchestra (K. 364).

We have so far been considering the overall aspect of the musical forms of the early classical period. We must now look at the internal structure of their movements. Whether we take a symphony, a sonata or a string quartet, and whatever movement we care to examine, we notice that by far the greatest majority are divided down the middle by a double bar. This, of course, is the outward and visible sign of binary form. But what makes the typical *galant* binary movement different from its baroque predecessor is its lack of a homogeneous texture. A baroque movement maintains a certain uniformity and continuity of figuration throughout, whereas *galant* phraseology is short-winded; it is always stopping and starting. Compare the first eight bars of the finale of Monn's symphony in D major, dating from 1740,[1] with the opening of the Presto in Alessandro Scarlatti's *sinfonia*, *La Griselda* (1721),[2] also in D major. Despite the fact that Monn is a *galant* composer whose style has roots in the Baroque, and Scarlatti is a baroque composer whose instrumental style anticipates the *Galant* in some ways; and despite the close analogy of form and instrumentation between the two movements—the contrast is highly illuminating. Baroque continuity is evident in the Scarlatti; whereas the discontinuity of Monn's style is immediately apparent.

The most obvious difference between these two movements is their style, but there are important formal differences too. The Scarlatti Presto is in symmetrical-binary form with some correspondence between the cadences of the two divisions. The Monn is in rounded-binary form; the second half is more than twice as long as the first (20:30+ 16), and the opening theme returns, disguised for a moment, at b. 51, and with its modulatory sequel omitted in order to remain in the tonic. This, of course, is what we expect in rounded-binary form, but thematic differentiation being such a tendency in the *galant* style we often find the 'open' cadence and its approach associated with distinct thematic material, which in due course is heard in the tonic at the 'close' cadence. We have a rather primitive example here, for only the last eight bars of each division of Monn's movement correspond. A more developed stage can be seen in the last movement of the sonata Op. 1 no. 2 (*c.* 1742)[3] by Giovanni Platti (d. 1763), in which—disregarding the seven-bar coda at the end of the second half—the last twenty-three bars of each division correspond, the dominant of the first to the tonic of the second. Within these twenty-three bars at least four thematic ideas can be distinguished, though one would hesitate to pick any one as a 'second subject'. But we do not really need a second subject, for lengthy cadential correspondence such as this is really the essence of the early stages of sonata form. As the tendency towards thematic differentiation increases we shall find 'second subjects' enough. Nor at this stage do we need a 'development' section. We have here a lengthy modulatory passage (bb. 44–82) which shows the characteristics of a sonata development in embryo. Again, a more developed thematic consciousness on the part of composers will turn this sort of passage into a true development section.

The main divisions of this movement can be expressed thus:

A ‖: 1 (bb. 1–20)   tonic section, followed by
      2 (bb. 21–43)   dominant section and 'open' cadence:‖
B ‖: 1 (bb. 44–82)   modulating section based on 1 and 2
                  passing from the dominant to the relative
                  minor, then
      2 (bb. 83–124)   final tonic section, comprising return of
                  A1 (bb. 83–101) and A2 (bb. 102–124) in
                  the tonic key, the 'close' cadence expanded
                  by
   Coda (bb. 124–130)   :‖

It is ironical that, so far, we have confined our attention to movements which are actually 'finales' in order to illustrate the early development of sonata form. For, at a later date, sonata form was to become more characteristic of the *first* movement than any other; so much so that it acquired the alternative title of 'first-movement form'. Nevertheless, in terms of keys and modulations—and, as we shall see, these are really the truest terms—this particular finale is a typical example of early sonata form. Nor will it have escaped notice that it is also an example of rounded-binary form. In fact, it must be recognized that the only difference between the two lies in their style. The key-scheme is the same, the proportions are the same, but a melodic and discontinuous style has replaced the contrapuntal continuity of the Baroque. Tonality is still the main principle of formal organization, and an evaluation of sonata form in terms of key rather than themes conforms much more closely to late 18th-century thinking and practice. And what is more, it brings within a general rule many so-called exceptions that cannot be easily accommodated to the 19th-century conception of it in terms of thematic exposition, development and recapitulation. (However, these terms have their uses.)

Thus, at this stage we need not necessarily regard the 'exposition' as comprising a statement of the 'first subject' in the tonic linked by a modulating bridge passage to a 'second subject' in the dominant or relative major, but rather as the opposition of two 'key areas', the tonic and the dominant. (Indeed we could say that in resolving this tonal opposition and leaving the themes comparatively untouched, the classical 'recapitulation' tacitly admits that the sonata 'argument' is a tonal rather than a thematic one.) Leaving aside the fact that there may be several first and several second 'subjects', and that the bridge passage may not modulate, we can see that contrast of keys is more essential than contrast of themes simply by the frequent absence of just this thematic contrast, as when there is no well-defined second subject, or when the first subject does double duty, first in the tonic then in the dominant. (Haydn was particularly fond of this, even as late as the 'London' Symphony.) And if we look upon the 'development section' merely as a place in which previously heard subject matter is manipulated in various ways (even allowing the possibility of introducing entirely new ideas) we should also bear in mind that the means of manipulation is always modulatory whatever else it may be in addition. Finally, the idea of the 'recapitulation' as a repetition of the exposition with the bridge passage modified to lead into a return of the second subject in the tonic, takes no cognizance of cases in which the first subject is omitted altogether, or partly omitted (as frequently happens with Stamitz and the Mannheimers); in which the second subject is omitted, or the order of the two subjects is reversed; or in which the whole treatment is free, compressing or expanding the original subject material. Yet none of this disturbs the tonality-structure of sonata form.

It is true that such 'exceptions' become rarer towards the end of the century. Even so, Haydn's handling of sonata form differs considerably from Mozart's, particularly in its monothematic and developmental tendencies. For one thing, his development sections are longer and much more thorough-going; occasionally they may even contain a 'false reprise' of the main subject in the tonic, anticipating the recapitulation proper (see the 'Lark' Quartet, Op. 65 no. 5, first movement bar 105). His recapitulations, when they do come, are often quite free in relation to the exposition; nevertheless they are firmly grounded in the tonic key whatever tricks he may be up to with his themes. In the first movements of his symphonies, Haydn often precedes the sonata–allegro with a slow introduction. Undoubtedly this originates with the slow–quick opening of the *da chiesa* style. We have already noted this legacy in several of Monn's symphonies and quite a few of Haydn's earlier four-movement symphonies have their movements arranged in this way—slow, quick, slow (minuet and trio), quick—the latest being 'La Passione' (no. 49, written in 1768). Thereafter he either dispenses with the opening slow movement entirely, or permits it to survive as a vestige introducing the Allegro and sometimes linking the two thematically (clearly in nos. 90 and 98). In the end the slow introduction became the standard procedure and in the last twelve 'Salomon' symphonies, all but one—the 95th—start with a slow introduction. In this respect Mozart follows Haydn in only two of his mature symphonies, nos. 38 and 39. Beethoven, on the other hand, employs a slow introduction in four of his nine symphonies, and through him it became part of the stock-in-trade of the 19th-century symphonist.

Mozart's approach to sonata form is more regular than Haydn's, and it is his which is generally held up as an example. Yet even the first movements of his rather unadventurous piano sonatas can show examples of the following 'irregular' procedures: first subject in the dominant used as a 'second subject' (K. 576); 'development' sections where no development takes place (K. 283); recapitulations starting in the subdominant (K. 545), with first subject omitted (K. 282), with 'second subject' omitted (K. 576), with subjects in reverse order (K. 311), etc. Most of these and other anomalies disappear if sonata form is regarded from the tonal point of view rather than the thematic, even though themes in the nature of things are inevitable. The following scheme expresses this viewpoint, along with the general tonal and thematic characteristics of late 18th-century sonata form.

A   First division ('exposition')

 1   Tonic section ('principal' or 'first subject' group)

(a) tonic key established by main theme, or group of themes,
(b) link, bridge passage or transition leading towards the dominant, or (when the tonic is minor) relative major,

2 Dominant (or relative) section ('subsidiary' or 'second subject group')
(a) theme or themes representing the dominant key,
(b) closing theme associated with the 'open' cadence in the dominant, sometimes rounded off by short codetta leading back either to 1 (a) or on to B.

B Second division

1 Modulatory section ('development', 'free fantasia') may start with material from A in dominant key or introduce new material. Wider modulations often through circle of fifths leading back to

2 Final tonic section ('recapitulation', 'reprise'): the return of all or most of the thematic material from A. The link 1(b) may be modified in order to introduce 2(a) in the tonic. Closing theme and cadence usually correspond to 2(b), and the whole of B may be repeated. A coda may prolong the ending for greater effect.

This then is the general plan of sonata form; a scheme of keys expressed inevitably through themes. It accommodates most of the 'exceptions' such as second subjects which are really the first subject in the dominant, telescoped recapitulations which omit one of the subjects, or recapitulations in the 'wrong' order, all of which may be found in the works of Haydn, Mozart and their contemporaries.

Apart from its historical accuracy, this approach to sonata form has certain other points in its favour. For it underlines the binary nature of sonata form and counteracts the tendency to regard it as ternary form in which exposition, development and recapitulation correspond to ABA. It is true that in its later stages sonata form may be described as a three-part form, but this must not be taken as implying ternary structure. Properly, ternary is a compound form, the individual components of which are virtually self-contained and complete in themselves, whereas in sonata form, exposition, development and recapitulation depend—because of their tonal organization—on each other for their existence. This same tonal view is applicable to the first-movement form of the concerto, which, even up to the time of Beethoven, is of looser thematic construction than the corresponding movement of a sonata or a symphony.

So far as the thematic aspect of the concerto's first movement is concerned, the last half of the 18th century saw the gradual merging of the old ritornello form with sonata form. We are so used to ritornello form in baroque concertos that it comes as a surprise to find the same scheme adopted by *galant* composers—even to the extent of going through the whole rigmarole of relative and subdominant tuttis. But of course, it is the style not the form which is different, and gradually the reappearances of the ritornello became reduced to two; one in the dominant half-way through the movement, the other at the end in the tonic. Thus, for example, in Haydn's keyboard concerto in C major (composed before 1763) the opening tutti (bb. 1–17) begins and ends in C, and is followed by the 'first solo' (bb. 18–36) beginning with the main ritornello theme in C but modulating to the dominant. A shorter version of the tutti-ritornello is heard in the dominant (bb. 37–44) and then the 'second solo' (bb. 45–76) leads off with the same theme, modulating more widely, but leading via a cadence in the relative minor back to the closing ritornello in C (bb. 77–106). This is a fairly standard first-movement procedure, though sometimes solo episodes do not make use of tutti themes but introduce new ones. And where the ritornello is lengthy, more than one theme is often recognizable. In the concertos of Johann Christian Bach (1735–1782) this subsidiary theme is usually clearly evident, and its singing style often contrasts markedly with the main theme.

The similarities between this type of ritornello form and early sonata form are clear. The dominant ritornello leading straightway into a fairly wide circle of modulations which arrive back at a final ritornello in the tonic is an obvious parallel with the second division of sonata form. Similarly the first solo which begins in the tonic and modulates to the dominant is analogous to the first division of sonata form. Only the opening ritornello, beginning and ending in the tonic as it does, is foreign to sonata form, and as the sonata principle infiltrated into the concerto, composers came to regard the opening ritornello as a self-contained orchestral introduction. Mozart realized this as a boy of nine or so, for in arranging three of J. C. Bach's sonatas as concertos (K. 107) the opening tuttis (which he based on Bach's first-movement expositions) were just stuck on in front. Nothing could more clearly demonstrate the fact that from the first solo onwards, sonata and concerto were the same formally. In time, of course, this meant increasingly well-defined and contrasted second subjects (not necessarily incorporated into the opening ritornello) and gradually the abandonment of the dominant ritornello as this manner of introducing the modulatory section—the second solo —became rarer.

We should not, then, regard the first tutti as a sonata exposition; this really begins with the first solo. Hence to call the first solo of a Mozart concerto the 'second exposition', or to refer to the ritornello and first solo together as a 'double exposition', is nearly always inaccurate. Mozart twice (see below) and Beethoven once, in his third Piano Concerto do, in fact, write 'double expositions'; that is, they introduce the second subject in the dominant (or relative major) during the opening tutti. But these are exceptions, and do not alter the fact that the 'first tutti' is a survival from the baroque concerto, and is best called by that name. The first solo likewise derives from the corresponding section of the baroque concerto, but tends more and more to be treated as a sonata 'exposition'. It is here, not in the ritornello, that we get key contrast, indeed true second subjects, whereas frequently the ritornello presents merely a string of secondary material (in the tonic) following the main theme. Girdlestone has summed up Mozart's treatment of the opening ritornello admirably. He points out that in 13 of Mozart's 23 piano concertos the opening tutti gives a preview of the second subject in the tonic, and in the other ten 'sometimes the second subject is in the dominant (K. 413, 449); sometimes it is absent (K. 415, 459, 466); sometimes ... [what seems likely] ... to be the second subject does not reappear till the development (K. 365, 503) or the recapitulation (K. 450, 467, 482), whilst the true second subject appears first only in the solo. One cannot generalize further than to say that the opening tutti opens with the first subject and contains some of the ideas which are to return in the rest of the movement.'

Mozart treats the beginning of the first solo in a variety of ways, sometimes introducing a brief thematic diversion for the soloist before the main theme (K. 466, 482, 491). But from then on it is sonata form in our tonal sense, with modulatory 'second solo' and a final tonic section—sometimes called the 'third solo'—which may recall themes from the ritornello as well as the first solo. The solos are separated by tuttis, and the concluding tutti is interrupted on a cadential six-four chord, a cadenza intervening between it and the final dominant seventh to tonic resolution. In a way, the cadenza is like another development section, one which the performer was expected to extemporize, combining virtuoso display with a rather rhapsodic treatment of the thematic material. A final extended trill on the dominant seventh chord gave the orchestra its cue to resume the tutti and bring the movement swiftly to an end.

The slow movement was usually placed second in classical works, though in many of Haydn's quartets (and some of Mozart's) it came third. Nearly always it was in a different key from the other movements, most often in the subdominant though Haydn sometimes moves further afield. A gentle Andante in a limpid, cantabile style was favoured, not entirely to the exclusion of the Adagio, but in a majority of cases. In the early classic period some sort of binary-sonata form is still the general rule for such movements, though later, other forms such as the air with variations, ternary or rondo form became more frequent. Haydn's symphonies provide a good illustration of the trend. Well into the 1770's he continued to favour binary-sonata movements, but from then on he turned with greater frequency to 'air and variation' form, perhaps under the popular influence of the divertimento (which often contained sets of variations) but undoubtedly following his personal preference also. Some of the slow sets of variations from his middle period are indeed rather superficial, but by the end of his life he was devoted to the form, and wrote in it devotedly.

The 'Salomon' symphonies provide several examples of Haydn's variation technique. In the 'Surprise' Symphony (no. 94) we have a set of simple variations in which a binary theme (the halves separated by the famous fortissimo 'surprise') is varied— first (starting at b. 33), with a delicate counterpoint in the first violins against the tune in the seconds; secondly (starting at b. 49), with the theme in the tonic minor involving a short development; thirdly (starting b. 75), with the theme in the major again; and fourthly (from b. 107), with contrasts between full orchestra and strings leading into a final coda (bb. 139–156). The 'Drum Roll' Symphony (no. 103) furnishes an example of another type of variation that Haydn was fond of: the 'double variation' in which two contrasting sections undergo variation alternately. In this case, the first section, A: (bb. 1–26 in binary form) is in C minor, and the second section, B: (bb. 26–50, related thematically to A and in rounded–binary form) is in C major. The first pair of variations comprise A rather more elaborately orchestrated (bb. 50–84) and B set for solo violin accompanied by strings (bb. 84– 108). The second pair includes A with full orchestra contrasted with strings alone (bb. 108–134), and B in which the oboes hold the melody (bb. 134–159). The movement is rounded off with a coda (bb. 160–197)—an almost inevitable conclusion to a series of variations.

Even when the form of the slow movement is basically ternary, or 'double' ternary (that is, with two episodes) the element of variation is seldom absent, appearing as varied returns of the principal section (see the 'Clock' Symphony—no. 101—with its varied returns starting at b. 64 and b. 112).

Mozart was much less given to writing variations as slow movements than Haydn. Only one of the last ten great string quartets has such a movement (K. 464); all the others are in some sort of sonata form. Similarly, in the last six symphonies, that is, from the 'Haffner' (no. 35) to the 'Jupiter' (no. 41), all the slow movements are in sonata form, though the 'development' in the 'Haffner' is a mere 14-bar transition, and that of the 39th Symphony is omitted altogether—the exposition leading straight into the re-capitulation. This 'abridged sonata form' is fairly common, particularly in slow movements, where the material does not lend itself readily to development as such, and where considerations of length also discourage it. Some of the slow movements of Mozart's piano concertos are abridged in this way, the earlier ones in the main, though the late C major (K. 503) has a transition passage between exposition and recapitulation (bb. 59–73) which is merely an elaborated dominant seventh chord. In others the link between the main divisions is of greater length and import-ance, and assumes something of the character of a contrasting epi-sode (see the slow movement of K. 459, bb. 57–86) which gives a feeling of ternary form. Nevertheless, its sonata origins are made clear by the tonic reprise of subsidiary material originally an-nounced in the dominant or relative key. However, the F sharp minor slow movement of the A major concerto (K. 488) is quite unambiguously ternary, with a central episode in A major (bb. 35–52) and a final coda (from b. 84 to the end). Double ternary form is actually the most favoured slow movement form in Mozart's maturer piano concertos. In the C minor (K. 491) for example, the slow movement—in E flat major—contains two binary episodes: the first in C minor (bb. 20–35 with a link), the second in A flat major (bb. 46–58, again with a link), each placed between returns of the principal section (at b. 39 and b. 63), which is itself ternary. The movement is rounded off with a coda (b. 78 to the end).

Many early classical works in three movements end with a minuet, or at least a 3/8 or 3/4 *tempo di minuetto*. Sometimes even, the minuet is the slowest movement of the three, and is placed second. About half of Haydn's piano sonatas either end with minuets or have them placed second, and in four-movement works it is not uncommon for minuet and trio to occupy second place—as we can see in a majority of Haydn's quartets, especially those composed before the early 1780's, also in several of Moz-art's. The usual position in the four-movement symphony was third.

The minuet had been a common constituent of the baroque suite, as one of the *galanterien*, and indeed it epitomized the *galant* period. Sometimes it was coupled with an *alternativo* (second minuet or 'trio') after which the first minuet was repeated again: the first and third of Bach's French Suites provide examples. The minuet occurs still more frequently in the divertimento, invariably with a trio and sometimes with more than one. The term 'trio' came into use because it often happened that these alternative movements were written in three parts, or scored for three instruments, in contrast to the fuller texture of the main dance (see the last movement of Bach's first Brandenburg Concerto which has three trios, the first and third in three parts). This practice of lightening the texture, if not always of resorting to three instruments, or three-part harmony, continued beyond the end of the century, as did the baroque tendency to contrast wood-wind in the trio with full orchestra in the minuet.

Though the overall arrangement of 'minuet and trio' is thus a ternary one, the minuets were binary in themselves—symmetrical, asymmetrical and rounded examples can all be found. In the later period the third variety is the most favoured; the first division modulating to the dominant and after the repeat continuing with modulations from the dominant back to the tonic, where the first division's opening and cadential material rounds off the movement (see the minuet and trio from Boccherini's string quartet Op. 27 no. 3[1]). However, the final tonic section which rounds off the second division is sometimes so similar in length and content to the first division that on the face of it the movement may be said to be in ternary form, especially when (as happens in the minuets of Haydn's 'Military' and 'London' Symphonies, nos. 100 and 104) the first division does not modulate to the dominant, ending instead in the tonic.

It is interesting to observe an amusing feature of quite a number of classical minuets—the use of all sorts of canonic devices, even 'cancrizans'. Haydn's Piano Sonata in D (no. 26) has a *'menuetto al rovescio'* indicating that the minuet is to be played backwards at the repeat after the trio, and Mozart's Serenade in C minor

[1] *HAM* 307.

(K. 388) has a '*menuetto in canone*' with trio '*al rovescio*' (see also the minuets of Haydn's symphonies nos. 44 and 47).

We find as much variety of form in the finales as the slow movements; indeed, we find the same forms used, though, of course, the style is more lighthearted and the speed much quicker. In the early classic period, finales in binary-sonata form were almost invariable, usually in a quick or moderate triple-time often approximating to the style of a gigue or minuet. The same tendencies and general development of sonata form that were described in dealing with first movements can be traced in these finales, if anything, more clearly. But once again the popular influence of the divertimento began to oust the ubiquitous sonata form by advancing the attractions of the air with variations, and more important still, the rondo finale.

At its simplest the classical rondo is a movement in which the opening theme or section returns several times in the tonic key, each return separated by episodes which contrast more or less with the main theme. Its baroque antecedents were the *rondeau* movements of French clavecin and ballet music (the latter especially having a wide influence towards the middle of the 18th century), and ritornello form which we have considered in relation to the baroque concerto.

If the name itself did not suggest it, one would guess that it was the *rondeau* that developed into the 'rondo', rather than ritornello form, for the fact that *rondeau* and rondo are typically at home in the suite or divertimento leads to this conclusion. Together with the air and variations, the rondo was the popular instrumental form of the second half of the 18th century. They both flourished as independent pieces; their tunes were catchy; the mood was gay, and they were intended to please. When they came to be introduced into the more pretentious symphony or sonata it was usually as a finale, customarily the most spritely movement. Little by little (though never entirely) the sonata-form finale was superceded, and it has been computed that in the latter years of his life, Mozart wrote twice as many finales in rondo form as sonata, variation and minuet finales combined.

The growing importance of the rondo as the concluding movement of a symphony can be traced in Haydn's symphonies. It is comparatively rare before 1770 or so, but increasingly frequent thereafter, although his treatment of the form is not stereotyped. Several varieties of rondo are distinguishable yet whatever happens the basic rondo principle of three or more returns of the main theme in the tonic key separated by episodes is adhered to. This alternation of theme and episode is the essence of 'simple rondo'. Usually the episodes provide contrast of key and commonly introduce new material. However, they may also develop the main theme; for example, the finale of Mozart's 'easy' C major Piano Sonata (K. 545) contains an A minor developmental episode based on the principal theme (bb. 28–52). Sometimes a relationship with sonata form is suggested by the presence of a clearly defined first episode in the dominant which reappears later as the third episode in the tonic. This arrangement, and variations of it, is known as 'sonata-rondo', since it combines certain sonata-form features (the return of a dominant section in the tonic towards the end) with obvious rondo characteristics, as well as the lighter, more melodic rondo style. A typical example may be represented as follows:

Rondo aspect	*A* *B* *A*	*C*	*A* *B* *A* *Coda*
Key scheme	*I* *V* *I*	*VI* or other key	*I* *I* *I*
Sonata aspect	exposition	'development' or episode	recapitulation—coda

and illustrated clearly by the finale of Mozart's 'Haffner' Symphony (K. 385). Naturally enough the movement opens with the main theme in the tonic key (D major) and this leads to a subsidiary theme in the dominant (b. 38) clearly distinguishable and contrasted with the main theme. But instead of ending the exposition with a double bar and repeat (as in sonata form) a return is made to the main theme, again in D major (b. 80). The central episode which follows (starting b. 110) is mainly concerned with the subsidiary theme in B minor, and from there the music returns to the tonic key, where, first the main theme is recapitulated (b. 139), then the subsidiary theme (b. 182). A coda which includes a final return of the main theme (b. 232) brings the movement to a close.

The finest classical rondos are probably to be found in the finales of Haydn's symphonies and Mozart's piano concertos. Haydn was always prone to develop his main theme, and in fact the finale of the 'Military' Symphony (no. 100) is virtually a rondo with only one theme, developed in the episodes, and especially in the lengthy central episode. Mozart concentrates on the element of contrast between thematic section and episode: in the Piano Concerto in E flat major (K. 271), a cantabile *Menuetto* forms the central episode in a movement otherwise Presto; and ₵; in K. 482 (also in E flat) a 3/4 *Andantino cantabile* interrupts a 6/8 Allegro. Both composers write textbook rondos or sonata-rondos almost by accident. We can call them rondos because the main theme recurs in the tonic again and again; sonata-rondos because, in addition, we may recognize a subsidiary theme first in the dominant, later in the tonic—but for the rest it is pure *joie de vivre*.

In general then, a minuet, a set of variations or a rondo, usually provides the finale, or a sonata-form movement in the lighter style. But when the composer wrote for himself or for his fellow musicians, the *kapellmeister* in him was sometimes constrained to try his hand at the contrapuntal style, which, though it bored some, awed others. There was indeed a tradition of fugal finales which had never quite died out, and Haydn's Symphony no. 40 (1763) is a case in point. Elsewhere, over and over again he was to introduce fugal elements into his finales—of the symphonies (see the 'Clock' no. 101, starting at b. 189) as well as the string quartets. In fact, the finales of three of the six quartets in Op. 20 (1772) are fugues, a form in which he was particularly interested at this stage as a means of dividing the musical interest more equitably between the instruments of the quartet, instead of continually favouring the first violin. The lesson learned, Haydn never forgot it, but instead of continuing to write fugues as such, he used the style as an ideal means of thematic development within other forms. Thus in the middle of the finale of the Quartet in E flat major (Op. 71 no. 3, 1792) we find a fugal exposition of the main subject combined with a new counter-subject in semiquavers (bb. 30–38), entries of the subject in F minor (b. 39) and C minor (b. 44), a mock stretto (bb. 46–50) followed by an episode leading to a tonic statement of the subject in the viola over a dominant pedal (bb. 63–65), and more besides. The movement is in fact in ternary form with a fugue comprising most of the episode (bb. 30–87).

But perhaps the most famous 'fugal finale'—though it is not strictly a fugue—is the last movement of Mozart's 'Jupiter' Symphony. Though it lacks the interlocking continuity of texture usually associated with true polyphony, nevertheless within a sonata-form framework and a sonata-allegro style there is a fantastic amount of fugal display—not merely the five-part fugal exposition interpolated into an otherwise normal sonata-form exposition (bb. 36–53), but strettos and canons of all sorts (including *cancrizans*), and a breathtaking coda (bb. 356 to the end) in which all five subjects of the exposition are deployed in the combinations and permutations of five-part invertible counterpoint. Perhaps, after all, it is a fugue; one—and arguably the only one in the late 18th century—which is true in style to its period and composer. In spite of its impressive devices it does not look back to the Baroque or beyond, nor suggest any composer but Mozart. And in one way it points to the future; to a more even distribution of weight in the symphony. Emotionally, the typical 18th-century symphony peters out after the first movement; the same with the sonata. The 'Jupiter' is perhaps the first symphony in which the most important movement is the last, or is, at least, a match for the first; the first in which the romantic desire to perorate and consummate in a finale is prefigured.

III : 3 Opera and Oratorio

It is not easy to give a short definition of opera that will include every opera ever written, unless it is Dr. Johnson's 'an exotick and irrational Entertainment'. Nevertheless, we may say that in general an opera is a dramatic entertainment, in which there is a considerable amount of singing by some (at least) of the principal characters taking part. By this definition Adam de la Hale's 13th-century pastoral *Robin et Marion* might be considered one; similarly the liturgical dramas and their descendants, the mystery plays of the later Middle Ages. Indeed, the first 'oratorio', the *Rappresentazione di anima e di corpo* (1600)[1] by Emilio de' Cavalieri (d. 1602), belongs to this tradition.

In Italy, the *intermedio*, the madrigal-comedy, and the *pastorale* were the immediate precursors of true opera. The *intermedio* was a short allegorical representation performed between the acts of a play. Count Giovanni Bardi (1534–c. 1612), of whom we shall hear more, devised several for insertion between the acts of Bargagli's *La Pellegrina* (1589), with music by Marenzio, Cavalieri and others, and words by Ottavio Rinuccini (1563–1621). It included elaborate choruses, madrigals and solos, as well as instrumental pieces for a large orchestra.

In the madrigal-comedy, the dialogue was set in madrigal style. The most famous, *Amfiparnasso* (1594)[2] by Orazio Vecchi (1550–1605), was probably not intended for a stage performance, but others, including perhaps the amusing *Zapaione musicale* (1604)[3] by Adriano Banchieri (1568–1634), were sung off-stage, while on-stage the action was mimed.

---

[1] See *HAM* 183, *TM* 37, *GMB* 169. [2] *GMB* 164. [3] *HAM* 186.

The *pastorale* was a play dealing with the amatory adventures of nymphs and shepherds and the like, with songs, choruses and dances interspersed within the action. One of the earliest was Politian's *Orfeo*—performed about 1480 in Mantua. More than a century later, this time at Florence in 1590, Cavalieri composed music for a performance of Tasso's *Aminta*, which, together with Guarini's *Pastor Fido* marks the literary peak of this form.

But the immediate origin of opera lay in the attempts of Bardi's *camerata* to recreate a style of music which, it was imagined, had been used in the Greek dramas. This group of literati and musicians had been led to the conclusion that in singing their tragedies, the Greeks 'used a kind of music surpassing that of ordinary speech but falling so far below the melody of song as to take an intermediate form'. Efforts at composing examples of this 'speech-song' were made by several members of the *camerata* and exemplified in the earliest operas, all performed in Florence: settings of Rinuccini's *Dafne* (1597) by Jacopo Peri (1561–1633) and Jacopo Corsi (d. 1604) the music of which is now incomplete, and *Euridice* (1600) by Peri and Giulio Caccini (d. 1618). These were combined efforts, but Caccini completed, published and later had performed his own version of *Euridice*. Within a few years, three further operas were performed at Mantua, Monteverdi's famous *Orfeo* (1607), his *Arianna* (1608) of which only the *lamento* survives[1] and another *Dafne*, this time by Marco da Gagliano (d. 1642), also performed in 1608. (The first German opera was yet another *Dafne*, this time by Heinrich Schütz, performed in 1627.)

The dialogue of these operas was set in 'speech-song', or as they called it *stile rappresentativo*—the theatrical style. We would now call it recitative, but it is slower, more sustained and more expressive than the 18th-century variety with which we are more familiar. Some idea of its style and expressive capabilities can be gained from '*Tu se' morta*'[2] from *Orfeo*, sung by Orpheus after he has received the news of Euridice's death.[3] Note especially the expressive dissonances and affective leaps in the declamation. But these operas were not in recitative throughout. They also included choruses, dances and instrumental pieces or *sinfonie* (see excerpts

[1] *GMB* 177.   [2] *MM* 31.   [3] See also *GMB* 176, *HAM* 187.

from Peri's *Euridice*[1] and da Gagliano's *Dafne*[2]) as well as songs and duets of a more melodic type in which we may recognize the prototype of the later operatic aria.

Popular elements began to creep into the Roman and Venetian operas which followed. Comic scenes were introduced into otherwise serious operas like Stefano Landi's *Morte d'Orfeo* (1619) and even into sacred operas like *Sant'Alessio* (1632), also by Landi (see the duet '*Poca voglia di far bene*.'[3] Comic opera proper emerged with *Chi soffre, speri* (1639), music by Virgilio Mazzocchi (1597–1646) and Marco Marazzoli (d. 1662). Musically there were important innovations. Contrast between recitative and aria became more marked, the former becoming more conversational in tone, the latter more tuneful, and sometimes inordinately florid to allow the singer to show off. Strophic airs composed over a ground bass were quite common. In these and other Roman operas there is a considerable amount of chorus work—much in excess of Florentine opera—and the instrumental music is also notable. The *sinfonia avanti l'opera* (the 'instrumental music before the opera'—in other words what we would call the overture) is normally a sectional canzona, alternating slow homophonic sections with quicker contrapuntal ones.

The first public opera house was opened in 1637 in Venice, and by the end of the century there were 17 theatres there which between them had put on almost 400 operas. Popular and spectacular elements intruded more and more, yet musically they were by no means negligible. Monteverdi's last opera *L'incoronazione di Poppea* (1642) belongs to this period, and he was worthily followed by his pupil Francesco Cavalli (1602–1676). In the operas of Cavalli, and his rival Pietro Antonio Cesti (1623–1669), we may notice a further development along the lines already indicated in the works of the Roman school. Recitative is more *secco* (i.e. drier in tone) and generally clearly differentiated from the arias. The arias themselves are often composed of suavely beautiful melodies (*bel canto*) usually in three time and modelled on some dance rhythm. They are usually strophic, that is, each verse is sung to the same music, the repetitions separated by short

[1] *GMB* 171.   [2] *GMB* 175.   [3] *HAM* 209.

instrumental ritornellos, or else by a further brief recitative; see *'Ecco la lettra'* from Cavalli's *Serse* (1654).[1] Sometimes a second verse is set differently with a return to the beginning (*da capo*) indicated or written out, as in Monteverdi's *'Pur ti miro'* from *L'incoronazione di Poppea*.[2] In examples such as this we can see the origins of the *da capo* aria.

The death-scene of Erisbe from Cavalli's *Ormindo* (1644)[3] is a good example of a scene from a Venetian opera. The opening recitative is rhythmically rather stiff, though it achieves pathos through the harmonic richness of its five-part string accompaniment. Then a short *secco* recitative introduces Ormindo's *'Piangete, Amori'*, a triple time *bel canto* aria, built over a seven-bar ground bass which repeats eight times in all. The scene closes with another moving passage in recitative.

The use of the chorus declined somewhat in Venetian opera, except in prestige operas like Cesti's *Pomo d'oro* (1667) written to celebrate the marriage of the Emperor Leopold I to Margherita of Spain (see *Di bellezza e di valore*[4]). On the other hand, the role of the orchestra increased in importance, not so much in accompanying arias—this was almost invariably left to the continuo—but in the instrumental introductions to the arias (the *ritornelli*), in providing music for interpolated ballets, and in performing increasingly impressive *sinfonie* or *sonate*.

Towards the end of the century Naples rivalled Venice and Rome as the most important centre of opera in Italy, and it was there that Alessandro Scarlatti (1660–1725) worked off and on from 1684. After him the Neapolitan style became international, with the Germans, Handel and Johann Adolf Hasse (1699–1783), and Niccolo Jommelli (1714–1774) its principal exponents. It is customary to deride the rigid formalism of Neapolitan operas after Scarlatti, but we should remember that it was partly the result of a well-intentioned new look at the typical opera libretto which sought to reject many dramatically absurd elements. In the end two distinct types of opera resulted, *opera seria* where the subject matter was heroic, mythological or historical, and *opera*

[1] *HAM* 206, and also *GMB* 203.   [2] *GMB* 178.   [3] *GMB* 200.
[4] *HAM* 221.

buffa, a lighter, 'real-life' entertainment, of which *La serva padrona* (1733) by Giovanni Battista Pergolesi (1710–1736) is an early and excellent example. These *buffa* operas were performed as comic interludes (*intermezzi*) between the three acts of an *opera seria*, and are thus themselves in two acts and without overtures.

But the good intentions of such reforming librettists as Apostolo Zeno (1668–1750) and Pietro Metastasio (1698–1782) were not always shared by their lesser brethren, nor by composers, and certainly not by impresarios and singers. For one reason or another the musical elements became increasingly differentiated and stylized, resulting finally in two kinds of recitative, and several conventional aria types. Normally the action was furthered in *recitativo secco*, conversational, rapidly declaimed and sparingly accompanied on the harpsichord; see the recitative-scene from Scarlatti's *La Griselda* (1721).[1] Occasionally when the dramatic situation merited it, the orchestra would accompany the singer in *recitativo accompagnato* (or *stromentato*), a type which, though it was free in form, approached the aria in its expressive and musical qualities, as another name for it, *arioso*, implies. But *secco* recitative was the connecting medium. The typical scene began with dialogue set in this way leading up to an aria which gave emotional expression to the character's feelings. Within each act, the scenes were arranged as nearly as possible in the natural dramatic order, but bearing in mind such desirable considerations as a pleasing musical variety in the sequence of aria types, and (most important!) the need to give the singers arias in quantity and quality suitable to their relative status as virtuosi. Mostly the arias were of the *da capo* variety: that is, after a second section contrasting with the first in key and (often) movement, '*da capo*' or '*dal segno*' indicated to the singer that a return to the beginning or to a sign was to be made, and the first section sung again; see '*Cara sposa*' from Handel's *Rinaldo* (1711).[2] Each section by itself was usually in a kind of ritornello or binary form.

Tonal unity within the opera, or even within the act, was liable to be accidental rather than intentional, and the succession of

[1] *GMB* 259.   [2] *MM* 44.

arias is only rarely governed by considerations of tonal relationship. It is left to the recitative to bridge the tonal as well as the
dramatic gap from one aria to the next. Above all, Neapolitan
opera was singers' opera. Repeated sections were ornamented and
the main cadences profusely so, hence the term *cadenza* for a
cadential display. Too often opera was regarded merely as a
number of arias strung together—'number opera'. There was
even a category of opera which consisted of a patchwork of arias
drawn from various sources or composed by different composers.
This particular confection was known as a *pasticcio* (literally a
'pie'), though it has been suggested that 'hash' would be a better
word.

A number of approaches to opera as we know it were made in
France and England between 1550 and 1650. In France, the *ballet
de cour* and in England the masque, served up a mixture of dancing,
solo and choral singing, speeches and elaborate décor and stage
machinery, in which the plot (if any) was the least important
consideration. A similar form was the Spanish *zarzuela*. These
entertainments reached their peak in the first half of the 17th
century, and in England, masque songs in the declamatory style
were just about as near to recitative as English composers could
get.

The *ballet de cour* had a more fruitful existence in the end, thanks
to Jean-Baptiste Lully (1632–1687). Though Italian by birth, Lully
thoroughly adapted himself to the French tradition, and with a
long series of semi-operatic *comédies* and *ballets* behind him, many
in collaboration with Molière, he was ready to become the master
of French opera, or *tragédie lyrique* as he called it. He had provided
ballets for the Paris performances of Cavalli's *Serse* in 1660 and
Ercole amante two years later, and it was operas such as these
which provided the incentive for the establishment of the *Académie
Royale de Musique* in 1669. When Lully took over in 1672, it was
natural that these two influences, the ballet and Venetian opera,
should make themselves felt. The traditional French influence is
most noticeable in the dances with which Lully's operas were well
supplied, and in the airs and choruses based on dance forms. But

a musical continuity is achieved through the use of recitative of a type that was Lully's special creation. Its style is admirably suited to the inflexions and rhythms of the French language and owes something to the rhetorical delivery of the most celebrated actors of the *Comédie Française*. Unlike the *secco* recitative of the Italians it cannot be accommodated into regular 4/4 bars. Instead the barring is irregular, and the rhythm much more varied; see '*Enfin il est en ma puissance*' from *Armide* (1686).[1] In fact, it is much closer to the *stile rappresentativo* of the Florentines, and like it, seems often to be on the point of becoming songful. Looking to the future it may be observed that Wagner's *sprechgesang* (speech-song) is not vastly different.

If French recitative sometimes seems about to become elevated into melody, the airs frequently demonstrate the reverse trend, with the more serious ones taking on a frankly declamatory nature. Were it not for the *rondeau* form of Merope's lament 'O Mort! venez finir mon destin déplorable' in *Persée* (1682)[2] one would find it hard to say whether it was recitative or air. In general Italian-style *bel canto* and *coloratura* are absent. Instead we find simple airs and choruses usually based on dance rhythms: those in three time resembling the minuet, sarabande or chaconne in style and form, those in four time the gavotte or bourrée.

With Lully, the musical unit is the act. In part this derives from his observance of the dramatic unities, but even so, compared with Italian operas the numbers flow into each other much more easily, simply because recitatives and airs are not widely differentiated in style. Not even the scenes are self-contained, and in the whole of Act III of *Alceste* (1674) the only break in the physical continuity of the music is the semi-independent funeral scene, scene five. The end of each scene leads into the next, and this continuity of movement is underlined by an overall harmonic scheme based on keys falling a fifth until the process is arrested towards the end by what amounts to a vast perfect cadence. The tonal plan of this act is as follows: A minor (scene 1), D minor (scenes 2 and 3), G minor (scene 4), C minor and major (scene 5), G major (scenes 6 and 7), C major (scene 8). In fact, what we have

[1] *GMB* 234.　　　[2] *GMB* 232.

here is the strongest harmonic sequence possible in tonal music; one which baroque composers usually followed in their modulations, and which classical composers adopted in their development sections, based on roots falling a fifth.

German opera was open to both French and Italian influences. Vienna, and the courts of Dresden and Munich had supported Italian opera in the second half of the 17th century, but in 1678 a public opera house was opened in Hamburg, and with it German language opera began to flourish. Italian influences are most apparent around 1700, but traces of a less sophisticated tradition deriving from the earlier native form, the *singspiel*, are evident at times, especially in the earlier years. The *singspiel* had mixed spoken dialogue with musical passages in an entertainment which was often moralistic in purpose, as for example *Seelewig* (1644) with music by Sigmund Theophil Staden (1607–1655).[1] In the Hamburg operas, strophic and bipartite airs based on *lied* and dance forms were common—see the binary aria '*Schöne Wiesen*' from *Erindo* (1693) by Johann Sigmund Kusser (1660–1727)[2] and composers, particularly Reinhard Keiser (1674–1739) at his best, were a good deal less casual when it came to aspects that in Italy were considered of secondary importance, such as skilfully written and expressive accompaniments to the arias. The recitative was often in arioso style, measured and musically expressive, while choruses, dances and instrumental music showed a French influence. With Handel, German elements were almost completely submerged in Italian: he is the true successor to Scarlatti, and his operas are the finest examples of the cosmopolitan style.

When he arrived on the English scene at the end of 1710 pasticcios were the only taste of Italian opera that Londoners had had. *Camilla* had been written by Antonio Maria Buononcini (1675–1726) for Naples in 1696, but the London version of 1706 contained heavy borrowings from the operas of other composers and was sung in English. Fifty years before, the first English opera had been given with some success apparently, and although

[1] *GMB* 195.   [2] *GMB* 250.

the music for the 'Siege of Rhodes' (1656) is lost we know that it
was largely, if not entirely, in recitative. But there were to be few
English operas with continuous music in the second half of the
17th century, apart from 'Dido and Aeneas' (1689) by Henry
Purcell (1659–1695). Most were 'semi-operas' such as Purcell's
'King Arthur' (1691), and 'Fairy Queen' (1692), among others,
with a preponderance of spoken dialogue and lengthy musical
interpolations (usually at the end of each act) comprising recitatives, airs, choruses and dances. In particular, his masterly use of
vocal and instrumental chaconnes and ground basses are an
important feature of his dramatic music: Dido's lament 'When I
am laid in earth' need only be mentioned.

Handel's operas had varying degrees of success up to 1728,
when, in 'The Beggar's Opera', the English at last found their
operatic métier. It was a double satire against the Whig govern-
ment and Italian opera. The overture, by Johann Christoph
Pepusch (1667–1752), was in the French style, and the songs were
mostly ballad tunes.[1] As the dialogue was spoken there was no
recitative, and it is hardly surprising that the absence of recitative
combined with catchy tunes and a low-life story made it a popular success. In the next ten years about fifty 'ballad operas' were
put on. It was the manifestation in England of a general reaction
against the stiffness of heroic opera which found expression in
opera buffa in Italy, in opéra comique in France, in the singspiel in
Germany, and the tonadilla in Spain. A considerable amount of
interaction can be traced between these forms, particularly of
opera buffa on the tonadilla, and of ballad opera and opéra comique
on the singspiel.

Two ballad operas by Charles Coffey, 'The Devil to Pay' (1731)
and 'The Merry Cobbler' (1735) in German versions played an
important part in revitalizing the tradition of the singspiel. This
popular form was cultivated in Leipzig by Johann Georg Stand-
fuss (d. 1756) and Johann Adam Hiller (1728–1804),[2] but it soon
spread all over Germany and was eventually to culminate in
Mozart's 'Magic Flute' (1791). Ballad opera had its effect in
France too, though the existence of a popular satirical opera in

[1] See GMB 281, HAM 264.   [2] GMB 309.

Paris from about 1716, arising as it did as a reaction against the monopolist 'Royal Academy of Music' may have shown John Gay the way with 'The Beggar's Opera'. Operatic controversy was the staple diet of musical polemics in 18th-century France, and in 1752 a performance of Pergolesi's *La Serva Padrona* sparked off the '*querelle des bouffons*' between those who supported the French classical opera (of which Rameau was the chief exponent) and those who preferred the naturalism (however artificial) of Italian *opera buffa*. The musician-philosopher Jean-Jacques Rousseau (1712–1778) favoured the latter, and in his opera *Le Devin du Village* (1752) adopted a popular style, though retaining the use of recitative for dialogue. Later examples of this type of *opéra comique*, or *comédie mêlée d'ariettes* ('play interspersed with little songs') dispensed with recitative. It may not be without significance that 'The Beggar's Opera' was given in Paris in 1750, and the ubiquitous 'Devil to Pay' appeared in a musical arrangement by François Philidor (1726–1795) in 1756.

Ballad opera, *opéra comique* and *singspiel* gave rise directly or indirectly to numerous 19th-century hybrid forms that have little or nothing in common apart from their spoken dialogue. To mention Beethoven's *Fidelio* (1805) and Gounod's *Faust* (1859) in the same breath is to prove it. The productions of the 'Opéra Comique' in Paris (which were not necessarily comic), included *Carmen* (1875) by Georges Bizet (1838–1875) as well as operettas by Jacques Offenbach (1819–1880). The latter's *opéras-bouffes*, such as 'Orpheus in the Underworld' (1858), had a noticeable influence on the operettas of Johann Strauss (1825–1899), whose *Die Fledermaus* was produced in 1874, and on Gilbert and Sullivan. The tradition is alive today in the 'musical', as well as in the more serious efforts by George Gershwin (1898–1937) in 'Porgy and Bess' (1935) and Kurt Weill (1900–1950), whose 'Threepenny Opera' (1928) is actually a 20th-century version of 'The Beggar's Opera'.

Opera buffa stands apart from the other types of comic opera in that it exploits the conversational possibilities of recitative to the utmost. Musically, too, it tends to be more sophisticated, though popular elements—folk-song and dialect—are quite common. Following the rejection of comedy in the Metastasian reform, the comic *intermezzo* performed between the acts, or at the conclusion of an *opera seria*, developed into an entertainment in its own right under the influence of the librettist Carlo Goldoni (1707–1793). (There had, of course, been full-scale comic operas for almost a century.) Pergolesi's *La Serva Padrona* (1733) has already been mentioned several times, and marks the beginning of a development which stretches through Rossini's 'Barber of Seville' (1816) to Donizetti's *Don Pasquale* (1843) and even to Verdi's *Falstaff* (1893), but which reached its zenith towards the end of the 18th century in the *buffa* operas of Niccola Piccinni (1728–1800), Giovanni Paisiello (1740–1816), Domenico Cimarosa (1749–1801) and above all Mozart.

It is important in the evolution of opera for two reasons; in particular in rejecting the full scale *da capo* aria in favour of simpler forms, and in developing the use of ensembles, especially the concerted ensemble-finale. We also begin to find through-composed songs which are really in embryo sonata form. Though they lack the double bars they are recognizably manifestations of the same idea—tonic section modulating to dominant section, followed by a short transition returning to a free recapitulation and final cadence in the tonic (see Gallupi's '*Da me non speri*'[1]). Taking into account the ritornello, the similarity of form between this type of aria and the free sonata form of the concerto is apparent. It is not surprising that Mozart excelled in both.

Naturally we find many forms of aria in Mozart's *buffa* operas. The shorter and more lyrical are usually in ternary form with a coda (see '*Il mio tesoro*' from *Don Giovanni*, II, 2), but in more dramatic situations an approach to sonata form is often observable ('*Ah! chi mi dice mai*' in *Don Giovanni*, I, 3). Even where there are no verbal repetitions that naturally call for some sort of recapitulation, we may still observe the tonal plan of sonata form underlying the texture. Thematic cohesion is left to the orchestral accompaniment, and in the *terzetto*, '*Susanna, or via sortite*' from Act II of 'The Marriage of Figaro' the form—abridged sonata

[1] *HAM* 285.

form—is clearly revealed by the correspondence in the accompaniment and by the sonata key-scheme.

Exposition		Recapitulation	
bb. 1–18	(tonic section)	bb. 71–83	(tonic)
bb. 18–36	(bridge passage)	bb. 83–100	
bb. 36–61	(dominant section)	bb. 100–121	(tonic)

Transition	Coda
bb. 61–71	bb. 121–136

We find the tonal aspect of sonata form even more developed in his concerted finales. On one or two occasions he writes a 'vaudeville-finale' in which the characters sing a verse each in alternation with the chorus; the finale to Act III of the *singspiel* *Die Entführung aus dem Serail* (1782) is a case in point. (Rossini's 'Barber of Seville' also ends with one.) This simple form of finale had been used in French *opéra comique*, but more characteristic of *opera buffa* is the concerted or ensemble-finale which is rather more elaborate. Since this type of finale actually furthered the action, recapitulations are dramatically inappropriate even though the 'rondo finales' of Piccinni do in fact reintroduce previously heard material in their course. But this harks back to the vaudeville. The Mozartean ensemble-finale derives from Galuppi's 'chain-finales' in which the action is split up into short movements more or less independent in themselves, though played continuously. Mozart's symphonic approach welds everything together, not by thematic means, but through a scheme of key changes which makes each section complementary to the one before, to the one after, and to the finale as a whole. In these terms we may examine the finale to Act II of 'The Marriage of Figaro', 940 bars in length. The 'exposition' consists of the first three sections establishing the tonic and dominant keys, E flat and B flat major respectively. The 'development' spans the next four sections, the sequence of whose keys follows the circle of fifths—G, C, F and B flat major—which, with one further drop of the root a fifth, leads into the 'recapitulation': the last two sections in E flat major, and the final *prestissimo*. The way in which all this parallels the dramatic development of the action can only be described as miraculous.

'Exposition'	(tonic)	E flat major	4/4	Allegro
	(dominant)	B flat major	3/8	Molto andante
		B flat major	4/4	Allegro
'Development'		G major	3/8	Allegro
(roots falling a fifth)		C major	2/4	Andante
		F major	4/4	Allegro molto
		B flat major	6/8	Andante
'Recapitulation'	(tonic)	E flat major	4/4	Allegro assai
		E flat major	4/4	Piu allegro
'Coda'		E flat major	4/4	Prestissimo

The ensemble-finale was a highly important stage in the development towards musical and dramatic continuity in opera: a process of change which led from 18th-century 'number opera' with its self-contained arias, to the symphonic weave of Wagnerian music-drama. Continuity is partly a matter of musical cohesion, and we have seen that in cases where this is greatest— we have given examples from Lully and Mozart—it is due to some degree of influence exerted by a predominant tonality, or of modulations through an orbit of related keys which itself centres on a particular tonic, rather like the modulations in a development section in sonata form. So it is that, for all their wanderings, 'The Marriage of Figaro' (1786), *Don Giovanni* (1787) and even 'The Magic Flute' (1791) are not complete until they return to the key from which they set out in the overture.

Throughout the 17th and 18th centuries religious music was strongly influenced by opera. The forms of recitative and aria were ubiquitous, though choral writing still owed something to the polyphonic style of the 16th century, either directly through the 'Palestrina style' or indirectly through the instrumental fugue. Oratorio, Passion, cantata, motet and verse anthem all reflect the prevailing operatic styles, and by the late 17th century even the Mass had succumbed, though not to the point of setting any of the text in recitative.

We have already mentioned what is generally regarded as the

first oratorio, Cavalieri's *Rappresentazione di anima e di corpo* (1600). It is really a kind of opera-oratorio, or sacred opera, as one might expect from a composer who was one of the leading musicians in the Florentine *camerata*. Despite its musical innovations, which included songs, choruses, instrumental *sinfonie* and dances, as well as the new recitative,[1] it is really a species of *sacra rappresentazione* or late mediaeval morality play with music. (The word 'oratorio' comes from the *oratorio*—'oratory' or hall—in which similar religious entertainments were held as part of the evangelical activity of St. Philip Neri and his Oratorians.) The opera '*Sant' Alessio*', which has also been mentioned, belongs to the same category. As far as the style and form of the music are concerned there is no reason to pretend that such works are not oratorios too, for to do so would put out of court a majority of 'sacred dramas' many actually conceived in terms of the operatic stage, including several of Handel's.

Handel's ultimate concept of the oratorio was a much wider one however. Undoubtedly the operatic element was never entirely absent, but he was also open to other influences—the Latin oratorios of Giacomo Carissimi (1605–1674) and the English choral tradition, to mention two of the most important. Carissimi's oratorios were severely anti-operatic, and may be regarded as a development of the biblical dialogues of such composers as Giovanni Francesco Anerio (d. 1630) and Giovanni Francesco Capello.[2] In sticking closely to the biblical text in such works as *Jonas*,[3] *Jephte*[4] and *Judicium Salomonis*[5]; in using an *historicus* or narrator to connect up the dialogue; in eschewing the aria in favour of a continuous but flexible recitative and important chorus work—Carissimi's oratorios contrast in almost every way with the operatic trends of the mid-century. The fact that during the reign of Pope Innocent X (1644–1655) opera was out of favour in Rome may have led him to write in this manner. Carissimi's oratorios did not have much influence in Italy, where no doubt his musical style was considered too aloof and austere in comparison with *oratorio volgare*—that is, operatic oratorio in

---

[1] Examples in *HAM* 183, *GMB* 169 and *TM* 37. [2] *GMB* 180.
[3] *HAM* 207. [4] *GMB* 198. [5] *MM* 32.

Italian. But his French pupil Marc-Antoine Charpentier (1634–1704) wrote numerous oratorios after the manner of his master (see excerpts from *Le Reniement de St-Pierre*[1]) and in Germany, Christoph Bernhard (1627–1692) and Johann Caspar Kerll (1627–1693) spread his influence generally. The latter's *Pia et fortis mulier* (1677) is an example of a Jesuit 'school-play' with music; a type of oratorio which the Jesuits sponsored for didactic purposes.

Handel certainly knew Carissimi's music, but it is in their attitude to the chorus rather than in their handling of it that these composers resemble each other. A still more direct influence is the late 17th-century English choral style as Handel found it exemplified in the ceremonial odes of Purcell and others. Handel himself first essayed this style in his 'Birthday Ode to Queen Anne' (1713) and in his 'Utrecht Te Deum' of the same year. Twenty years later when he turned from the precarious business of writing operas to the fresh fields and pastures new of oratorio, he seized on the chorus as one of its main properties, at the same time cutting down the arias, particularly those in *da capo* form. The two oratorios of 1733 provide significant pointers. In 'Deborah' there are as many airs as choruses (19 of each but only 8 *da capo* arias); in 'Athalia' arias slightly outnumber the choruses (18 to 15, but here only 5 are *da capo*). And in the only two oratorios in which he set biblical texts, the process is carried to the extreme, for in 'Israel in Egypt' (1739) the chorus is everything, and it also plays a very important part in 'Messiah' (1742).

Here too, we may note another increasing tendency—the use of accompanied recitative instead of *recitativo secco*. Some of the most expressive pieces in 'Messiah' are in arioso style, for example 'Comfort ye' and 'Thy rebuke hath broken His heart'. Among the few *da capo* arias are 'He was despised and rejected' with its vividly contrasting middle section in the relative minor. Most are in some sort of ritornello form with the principal theme reappearing in related keys before returning to the tonic—'Rejoice greatly' is one. The choruses are mostly in Handel's free style which mixes homophony and polyphony in a way which can only be described as Handelian. They range from the strictly

[1] *HAM 226, TM 42.*

fugal 'And with his stripes' through many of much looser contrapuntal structure to those which are more or less sectionalized. The
last chorus but one, 'Worthy is the Lamb', for example, is in
two principal sections: the first, homophonic (Largo-Andante)
proceeding from the tonic, D major, to the dominant, then
(Largo-Andante) from the dominant back to the tonic; the second,
contrapuntal (Larghetto) starting with a free fugal exposition and
continuing with numerous strettos on the two halves of the subject.
Finally, an adagio cadence (only a half-close) leads into the fugal
'Amen' which ends the work.

It is ironical that one of Handel's least typical oratorios should
have virtually defined oratorio for subsequent generations. The
English Handel tradition directly influenced Haydn in 'The Creation' (1797) and in the early 19th century Germany became oratorio's second home, and Mendelssohn its principal exponent
with 'Elijah' (1846). Elgar's 'Dream of Gerontius' (1900) and
William Walton's 'Belshazzar's Feast' (1931) are more recent
examples, and Honegger's 'King David' (1921) and Stravinsky's
Oedipus Rex (1927)—both of which require a spoken narration,
the latter mimed action as well—should be mentioned. Michael
Tippett's 'A Child of our Time' (1942) uses negro spirituals
rather as Bach uses Lutheran chorales in his cantatas and Passions.

The development which culminated in Bach's Passions is
another aspect of the oratorio. The four Gospel accounts of the
events leading up to Christ's death had been performed semi-
dramatically in the Holy Week Masses as early as the 15th century.
The chant was apportioned between three deacons; a tenor
'evangelist' (historicus or chronista) who chanted the Gospel narrative, a bass (Christus) to whom the words of Christ were assigned,
and a high tenor (turba or synagoga) who took the part of the
crowd and sang all the other parts. Later, the turba sections were
set polyphonically—the earliest setting is by a late 15th century
English composer John Davy—usually with the original chant in
the tenor. This was the most common way of setting the Passion
in the 16th century, though there are numerous examples set in
polyphonic style throughout, not merely the turba sections. This

type has been called the 'motet-passion' (being in the style of a lengthy motet) to distinguish it from the more realistic characterization of the 'dramatic-passion' just described.

The first setting of the Passion in German was by Luther's friend Johannes Walther (1490–1570) in 1530. It is of the 'dramatic' type, with simple homophonic sections for the *turba*, and this treatment is found as late as Schütz's 'St. Matthew Passion' (1666) though the narration is in a kind of unaccompanied recitative not very different in style from plainsong, and the *turba* is set in madrigal style.[1]

The motet and dramatic Passions drew their texts from the Gospels, but about the middle of the 17th century the practice of interpolating reflective and devotional material, and even of supplanting the Gospel narrative with a new poetic text, grew up. The 'St. John Passion' (1643) of Thomas Selle (1599–1663) and Schütz's 'Seven Last Words of Christ on the Cross' (1645)[2] are early examples, while Brockes' poem 'The Passion of Jesus' (1712) was to be set as a Passion-oratorio by Keiser (1712), Handel (1716), Telemann (1716), Mattheson (1718) and others, including parts of it in Bach's 'St. John Passion' (1723).

Bach's two great passions are the culmination of both traditions. The Gospel story is set in *secco* recitative; the evangelist a tenor, Christ a bass, the other parts allotted as appropriate (usually bass), and the crowd—Disciples and Jews—the chorus. This is the dramatic-passion within the Passion-oratorio, comprising the poetic text set in accompanied recitative and *da capo* arias, with Bach's selection of chorales (and chorale settings) arranged so as to form a devotional commentary on the Gospel. Thus, the two Passions, distinct in style, are one in theme.

In the 'St. Matthew Passion' (1729) the 'dramatic' elements are the highly rhetorical *secco* recitative of the evangelist and Gospel characters, which contrasts with the gentler declamation of Christ, accompanied by strings, not continuo alone. (Selle had already contrasted the accompaniment of Christ's words with those of the evangelist.) The choruses are brief and highly dramatic, often involving antiphonal effects between the double

[1] *GMB* 192.   [2] *GMB* 191.

choir. The 'oratorio' elements are the reflective and deeply moving ariosos[1] which preface the lengthy but no less expressive *da
capo* arias usually sharing the same solo voice and *obbligato* instruments; the chorale preludes which open and close the first part,
and the final chorus; and the amazingly varied chorale harmoni-
zations.

Bach's *da capo* arias differ in several ways from Handel's. For
example, Bach's middle sections rarely provide the same degree
of contrast in mood and movement, only of key and (sometimes)
texture through the thinning out of the accompaniment. More so
than with Handel the instrumental influences of the concerto and
sonata intrude, and in an aria like '*Gebt mir meinen Jesum wieder*'
(no. 51 in the 'St. Matthew Passion') the style and form of the
concerto is unmistakable. In fact, beneath the explicit *da capo*
structure of many, the ritornello principle is clearly evident.
'*Können Tränen meiner Wangen*' (no. 61) for example, starts with
a ritornello in G minor (bb. 1–13), then comes the first solo introducing new material and modulating to the relative major
(bb. 13–24). A ritornello in that key follows (bb. 25–32), then the
second solo which modulates back to the tonic via C minor (bb.
33–51). A tonic ritornello closes this section (bb. 52–64) which
is the *A* division of a ternary aria, but obviously itself in ritornello
form. Then comes the shorter *B* division, followed by the return
to the beginning. Thus, beneath the overall ternary structure
lies a wealth of formal symmetries.

		A			B		A
1–13,	13–24,	25–32,	33–51,	52–64:	64–77,	78–91:	*Da capo*
r^1	s^1	r^2	s^2	r^1	$a:b$		
G min	⟶	B ♭ maj	⟶	G min			

At other times, the return *dal segno* merely supplies the final
ritornello, as in '*Erbarme dich, mein Gott*' (no. 47) which has the
character of a slow concerto movement in siciliano rhythm. The
opening ritornello in B minor (bb. 1–8) introduces the first solo
which uses the theme of the ritornello and modulates to the

[1] MM 49.

dominant (bb. 8–22). There is then a ritornello in the dominant key (bb. 22–26) followed by a second solo modulating at greater length back to the tonic (bb. 26–46). The opening ritornello is then repeated *dal segno*, thus rounding off the movement.

Bach's so-called 'church cantatas' may be defined as oratorios on a small scale; a definition which Bach recognized when he gave the title '*oratorium*' to the six cantatas that go to make up the 'Christmas Oratorio' and the single cantatas known as the 'Easter' and 'Ascension' oratorios. The word cantata means literally 'sung', that is to say, a piece to be 'sung' as against a piece to be 'played'—*sonata*—and it had been so used since the early 17th century in Italy. It derived from the solo monodies and continuo songs of composers such as Caccini and Alessandro Grandi (d. 1063), and within the general category of 'cantata' we find single airs (strophic, binary, *da capo* and rondo), strophic variations (vocal ground basses), and later, extended composite forms consisting of a succession of recitatives and arias. The names particularly associated with the form in the mid-17th century were Luigi Rossi (1598–1653)[1] and more especially Carissimi, among whose solo cantatas the composite type predominates. It was subsequently developed by Stradella, Scarlatti[2] and Agostino Steffani (1654–1728) as an adjunct to their operatic works, and by Handel too.

The Lutheran 'church cantata' is analogous to this form, though not directly derived from it. It developed from the early baroque motet in *concertato* style, that is, a motet in which a variety of soloists and instruments might be employed, and which shows some heterogeneity of texture (see Schütz's *O Herr, hilf*[3]). In Germany, this 'motet' or 'concerto' (as it was usually called) developed operatic traits, as did the analogous English form, the verse-anthem. Naturally Lutheran chorales were often incorporated into the musical structure (see Schein's *Erschienen ist der herrliche Tag*[4]), to the extent that in the chorale-cantata each movement presents a different treatment of the same chorale tune. The parallel with the chorale-partita is clear, and a late example of the

---

[1] *HAM* 203.   [2] *HAM* 258, *GMB* 260.
[3] *MM* 33, also *GMB* 212.   [4] *TM* 38.

form is Bach's motet *Jesu meine Freude*. Franz Tunder's *Wachet auf*[1] is a short chorale-cantata in which, following the *sinfonia*, the first section (4/4) treats the chorale simply, the second (3/4) more freely. His *Abendmusik* (evening-music) at the Marienkirche, Lübeck was continued by his successor Buxtehude, who expanded the dimensions of the cantata, setting literary as well as biblical and chorale texts. In 1700 the Lutheran Church officially countenanced the cantata, and found a place for it in the liturgy.

Bach probably wrote a cantata for every Sunday of a five-year cycle, though not quite 200 survive. Most of them end with a four-part chorale harmonization, and in roughly a quarter there are no other choruses beyond this, merely a sequence of recitatives and arias. Those with chorus usually start with a chorale-prelude for chorus and orchestra, less often with a brilliant ritornello movement, and end with a simple chorale. In some cantatas chorale treatment is not confined only to the beginning and the end, but may occur in several movements (*Wachet auf* no. 140, for example), or even in each, as in *Christ lag in Todesbanden* (no. 4[2]), though this is the only example in which a chorale is treated so thoroughly.

Bach's other great choral work, the B minor Mass, is an example of the encroachment of the operatic style on liturgical music. Not that there is any irreverence in the effect, far from it, for even composers like Alessandro Scarlatti restrained themselves—and even wrote fugues—when it came to composing large scale ceremonial Masses. (They could also write the most seductive 'Palestrina' counterpoint, particularly the later Neapolitans.) Soloistic and instrumental elements had been introduced into settings of the Mass quite early on in the 17th century, as may be seen from Monteverdi's remark that certain *concertato* movements could be substituted for the corresponding section of his Mass (1641) written otherwise in the old-fashioned style, and in the Mass for 52 vocal and instrumental parts with continuo written by Orazio Benevoli (1605–1672) for Salzburg Cathedral in 1628. The old and the new styles were practised side by side (and together) throughout

[1] HAM 214.　　　[2] MM 46 and 48.

the 17th century, and even in 18th-century Masses the antique style was never quite forgotten; the second *Kyrie*, the *Gratias*, *Credo*, and *Confiteor* of the B minor Mass are cases in point.

The tendency towards sectional differentiation within each movement of the Mass in the latter part of the 17th century parallels that of the *canzona*. The text fell naturally into certain short sections, and in the end each was treated as a more or less self-contained movement. The canzona's 'quilt' form, even the canzona's style, is evident in the Gloria from the *Missa Sancti Henrici* (1701) by Heinrich Biber (1644–1704) where the movements are differentiated as follows:

I
: *Et in terra pax*, C major, ₵ (two sopranos, 6-part strings and continuo)
: *Gratias agimus*, full 5-part choir and orchestra (2 *clarini*, 3 trumpets, 3 trombones, tympani, strings and continuo).

II *Domine Deus*, A minor, 3/2 (bass solo, two violins and continuo)

III *Qui tollis*, A minor, ₵ *Alla breve*, (fugue in antique style on chromatic subject).

IV
: *Qui sedes*, C major, 3/2 (full)
: *Quoniam* (soloists)
: *Amen*, (full, based on *Qui sedes* material)

When we come to Bach's B minor Mass, each movement is much more clearly defined in itself and contrasted with its neighbours. The movements keep within an orbit of related keys though, and this is a unifying factor. For example, the eight movements of the Gloria are in D major (chorus), A major (aria), D major (chorus), G major (duet), B minor (chorus), B minor (aria), D major (aria), and D major (chorus). Choruses comprise five-eighths of the work as a whole, and compared with the 'St. Matthew Passion' the arias are shorter and avoid *da capo* form. And, of course, there are no recitatives. Most of the choruses are fugal, or else in ritornello form (or both), but an exception is the *Crucifixus*, composed over a chromatically descending four-bar chaconne bass.

The B minor Mass was probably never performed in its entirety during Bach's lifetime, for the Lutheran Mass at this stage retained only the Kyrie and Gloria of the Latin Mass. Contemporary Masses by Italian composers were likewise divided into numbers—the so-called 'cantata-mass' which contained many solo movements—but in South Germany a more instrumental tradition survived (we have just seen an early example by Biber) passing through Johann Joseph Fux (1660–1741) and Florian Gassman (1729–1774) to the Viennese School of the late 18th and early 19th centuries. The Masses of Haydn and Mozart still show certain operatic traits, but increasingly they take on symphonic characteristics. Instead of the individual soloist, it is the ensemble, the chorus and, above all, the orchestra which are important. Attempts at large-scale formal integration through the recapitulation of opening sections are sometimes noticeable, not only in the Kyrie–Christe–Kyrie which naturally invites ternary treatment, but also in the longer movements. In the Credo of Haydn's *Missa Cellensis* (1782) the opening returns at the *Et resurrexit*, and the same idea is found in the Gloria and Credo of Mozart's 'Coronation Mass' (1779), where also the final *Dona nobis pacem* repeats the music of the opening Kyrie (as Bach's had repeated the *Gratias*).

On the whole, composers did not try to disguise the sectionalization which was almost inevitable. Compared with the early 18th century they reduced the number of sections, making each longer instead. The fact that the text of the Gloria and the Credo falls logically into three or four main sections enabled these movements to be treated either as a symphony (observing the characteristic symphonic sequence of movements with the appropriate keys), or as a single though episodic movement. The former approach is well illustrated in Schubert's Mass in A flat major (1822) where the Gloria is in three distinct movements:

I   Gloria, E major 3/4 *Allegro maestoso e vivace* (ternary form)
II Gratias agimus, A major 2/4 *Andantino* (ternary form)
III Domine Deus, C sharp minor, ₵ *Allegro moderato* (introduction) leading to
    Cum Sancto Spiritu, E major (fugue).

On the other hand, the Gloria of Schubert's E flat major Mass (1829) is a single movement in B flat with the opening recapitulated at the words *Quoniam tu solus sanctus* (leading into another *Cum Sancto Spiritu* fugue), and a middle section *Domine Deus* in G minor. The Gloria of Bruckner's Mass in F minor (1872) is similar, but recapitulates the opening material in reverse order (i.e. *bogenform*):

A   *Gloria* and
B   *Gratias agimus*, C major, ₵ *Allegro*
C   *Qui tollis*, D minor, 3/4 *Adagio*
B   *Quoniam* and
A   *Cum Sancto Spiritu* culminating in a
Coda   *In gloria Dei Patris. Amen.* a multiple fugue ending with a
         recollection of *A*.

It should be said that the Church had never really approved of these elaborate Mass settings. The use of orchestral instruments in church has always been frowned upon, and had been censured repeatedly during the 18th and 19th centuries. As part of the musical reaction which characterizes the 20th century, there has been a tendency to revert to a more austere style. But for one reason or another few composers have been drawn to the Mass in its liturgical form, or achieved much when they have. Vaughan Williams' Mass in G minor (1923) is an example which allows mediaeval modality to flavour it; Stravinsky's Mass (1948) is also spiced with mediaevalisms, though of a more abrasive kind.

So far as the larger forms of church music in the late 18th and early 19th centuries are concerned, the analogy with instrumental music is clear. It is through balance of tonalities that unity is achieved (even though we have noted examples of thematic recapitulations which supplement rather than oust tonality in its role). This is true whether the analogy is with the single symphonic movement in sonata form, or the symphony as a whole in three or more movements. We have seen that the same can be said for the concerted-finale of *opera buffa*, and together they demonstrate convincingly that in vocal music, when sheer length and the developing sense of the words makes the problem of unification most acute, it is the gravitational pull of the tonic which holds the music together.

III : 4 Beethoven: expansion and integration

Beethoven took the forms that Haydn and Mozart left him, and transformed them; not changing them so much as exploiting them within a new order of musical subjectivism. It was a process of intensification in which the drama and dynamism inherent in sonata form, indeed in the whole concept of the sonata, was to be realized. He was able to amplify the latent possibilities of contrast and expansion, both in terms of thematicism and tonality, yet at the same time achieve unprecedented emotional and musical unity. So far as form is concerned, then, we shall discover expansionist tendencies counteracted by others fundamentally integral which help to relate the parts to the whole.

Expansion is not only a question of simple addition. It is true that Beethoven goes one beyond the usual four movements in the 'Pastoral' Symphony (no. 6), and still further in his late string quartets; the B flat major (Op. 130) having six, the C sharp minor (Op. 131) having seven. (But Haydn's Symphony no. 7, 'Le midi', has five movements, and his 60th symphony has six!) Even so, Beethoven's symphonies, sonatas and quartets are longer than those of his predecessors because of expansion in other directions, within the individual movements. This is not merely the result of longer themes, or more of them. It is doubtful if Beethoven's themes are longer on the average than Mozart's, but even if they are this factor alone would not be enough to affect the overall length of a sonata-form movement significantly. Nor were Beethoven's themes any more likely to come in groups than Mozart's: multiple second subjects are about as common in one as in the other, and multiple first subjects perhaps more common with Mozart. Beethoven's greater length is the result of something more; what, for want of a better term, we shall call expansion in depth.

The elements here are mixed, but their root lies in an increased thematic consciousness which results in themes strikingly individual in themselves and thus all the more highly differentiated from their neighbours. This in itself leads to a longer exposition, other things being equal, since the exposition of two or three contrasted themes needs a wider framework than a simple modulation from the tonic to the dominant. All the more so when the key for the second subject is further removed from the tonic than the dominant or relative major, as it is increasingly with Beethoven, especially in the direction of keys based on the mediant. This, of course, is a wider application of the tonic-relative major relationship already established in minor keys; nevertheless it does provide a precedent for the 'third relationships' which become increasingly frequent in the 19th century. Among the first movements of Beethoven's piano sonatas, Op. 28, Op. 31 no. 1, and Op. 53 have second subjects in, or starting in, keys a third above their respective tonics, while Op. 10 no. 3 and Op. 106 have them in keys a third below. When the subject matter is so emphatically characterized and the element of contrast—thematic and tonal—so pronounced, it follows that not only will the exposition be on a larger scale, but the development needs to be commensurate if climax rather than anticlimax is to be achieved. Again, this tendency is accentuated by the increased range of modulations which Beethoven utilized in the development section. And since the length of the recapitulation is largely determined by the proportions already established, this in its turn cannot be brief. Furthermore, we may notice a significant change in the traditional role of the recapitulation as primarily a reaffirmation of the tonic; one which begins to imply a thematic rather than tonal outlook. For Beethoven sometimes works on the principle of recapitulating second subjects a fifth lower (or a fourth higher) rather than in the tonic key. Usually, of course, this amounts to the same thing, since the dominant is most frequently the original key of the second subject and a recapitulation a fifth lower will bring it back in the tonic key. But from the point of view of traditional practice it is the right thing done for the wrong reason, and in the case of non-dominant second subjects leads to non-tonic recapitulations —in the 'Egmont' Overture, for example. In such cases, the re-capitulation does not fully re-establish the tonic key, and in fact, introduces an element of non-finality (compared with a thorough-going 'classical' tonic recapitulation) which a later switch to the tonic cannot quite dispel. It is one of the functions of the coda to reinforce this finality.

Beethoven's use of the coda is on the face of it the most obvious aspect of his expansionist tendencies. Sometimes it makes a long movement even longer. The coda of the already vast first move-ment of the 'Eroica' Symphony increases its length by roughly a quarter (from 551 bars to 691 bars), that of the fifth Symphony by almost a third (from 374 bars to 502 bars), and that of the 'Lebewohl' Piano Sonata, Op. 81a (from 142 to 239 bars) by two-thirds—not counting repeated expositions. In the past the coda had been used principally as a means of rounding off a piece more effectively, so as to avoid an abrupt finish. With Beethoven it is this and some-thing more. It is more even than the 'terminal development'—to use Vincent D'Indy's phrase—into which the flood of Beet-hoven's invention overflowed. It is perhaps to be regarded as a substitute for the repeated second division of sonata form now obsolescent. The reason for the omission of the second repeat may have had something to do with the increasingly uneasy juxtaposi-tions of tonality between the final cadence and the return to the start of development, or the inordinate length that would often result if the repeat was made. But it is more likely that the dramatic concept of the sonata, which saw the recapitulation as a resolution of conflicts undergone in the development could not tolerate going through the whole experience again; it would be as unmeaningful as repeating the last act of a play. Beethoven marks the repeat of the second division occasionally, even as late as the first movement of the Op. 78 and Op. 79 piano sonatas (the latter with quite a long coda to follow), and in the finale of his last String Quartet, Op. 135, with the remark 'Si repete la seconda parte al suo piacere'. But in its absence the Beethovenian coda does take over its functions, incorporating elements of thematic development and recapitulation dramatically appropriate to what has gone before. In its developmental aspect the coda is rarely the rival of the development section proper; it is shorter and the modulatory range is more limited. But in its recapitulatory aspect it sometimes outdoes the 'first recapitulation'—not in length but, as has been suggested, in its affirmation of the tonic key.

All this is well illustrated in the 'Waldstein' Sonata (Op. 53) in C major by comparing the coda with the development and recapitulation. By itself, the development section is 70 bars long and can be divided into three sections; the first 26 bars (bb. 86–111) being concerned with the main theme in keys generally related to F minor, the next 30 bars (bb. 112–141) relating to the second subject of the second group centred first around B flat minor and moving gradually to the dominant of C, the last 14 bars (bb. 142–155) preparing for the return of the principal theme in the tonic at the beginning of the recapitulation (b. 156). The recapitulation itself is 82 bars long and contains all the subjects in the original order, but the return of the second subject is in A major initially, a fourth higher than in the exposition. Now comes the coda, 54 bars long; a kind of summary in lieu of a repetition of the previous 159 bars. Its first 33 bars constitute a further development of the main theme, starting in D flat major but soon moving back to keys closely related to C. Following a brief cadenza-like passage the last 19 bars recapitulate first the principal second subject now in the tonic, then the first subject mounting rapidly to a fortissimo finish.

Here then we have a coda which is something more than a 'terminal development'. It is both development and recapitulation, and viewed as the formal analogue of the repeated second division of sonata form, we can see how it gives new life to a formality which was becoming increasingly meaningless.

The intensification and expansion that Beethoven brought to sonata form, he brought to other movements of the symphony and sonata as well. The Beethoven 'Adagio' is an emotional rather than a formal phenomenon; so too is the *grazioso* or *allegretto* rondo or sonata-rondo finale that we find in some of the piano sonatas. Most remarkable is the transformation undergone by the minuet and trio. It is not quite true to say that Beethoven completely replaced it by the 'scherzo', for as late as 1812 he composed a genuine minuet and trio for the third movement of his eighth Symphony, and there are numerous examples of minuets written up to that time—in the String Quartet in C (Op. 59 no. 3) for example. Yet even before 1800, in two of the three sonatas dedicated to Haydn (Op. 2) he had taken Haydn's hint and given the third movement the title 'Scherzo'. For Haydn had all but anticipated him. He had labelled the minuets of his Op. 33 quartets (1781) 'Scherzo' or 'Scherzando', though perhaps only the sixth approaches the scherzando quality of the presto 'minuets' in the late string quartets. The word 'scherzo' means 'joke' or 'game' and was certainly not new in Haydn's time; Monteverdi's *Scherzi Musicali* (1607) are a collection of light vocal pieces, and there is a 'Scherzo' in Bach's A minor keyboard partita. Haydn had already used the term in two piano sonatas side by side with true minuets, as Beethoven did in the Quartet Op. 18 no. 4 and the Piano Sonata Op. 31 no. 3. But in general it is true to say that the minuet did actually become the scherzo in Beethoven's works, although it is not called 'Scherzo' as often as is sometimes thought. (For example, the only symphonies to contain named scherzos are the second and third, and among the quartets later than Op. 18 the nearest we get is the '*Scherzando vivace*' in Op. 127.) But whatever they are called, they may be recognized by their *da capo* form (inherited from the minuet and trio), and increasingly by their relentless, almost hectic motion. They are found either as second or third movements, and are usually in a very quick triple-time with one beat to the bar. However, 2/4 is sometimes encountered (in the piano sonatas Op. 31 no. 3 and Op. 110, for example). There is often contrast of key between scherzo and trio (though they are in the same key in all the symphonies except nos. 5, 7 and 9). *Minore* for *maggiore* or vice versa is common, otherwise related keys or the key a third below the tonic are favoured. (As an example of the latter scheme see the seventh Symphony where scherzo and trio are respectively in F and D major.)

Apart from exceptions such as the scherzo in rondo form which ends the Piano Sonata in G (Op. 14 no. 2), the sonata-form scherzo of the first 'Rasoumovsky' Quartet (Op. 59 no. 1), and others mentioned above, Beethoven's treatment of the form falls basically into two categories. The first includes simple ternary form, with or without coda, and with or without the repeat written out with modifications. Internally, scherzo and trio are usually in binary form, but by the ninth Symphony the scherzo has become a fully fledged sonata-form movement complete with second subject group returning in the tonic in the second division (though this is still marked to be repeated). It was, after all, only a matter of time before the binary minuet had to be thus emancipated; the signs were there almost from the beginning. The second category has been called 'grand scherzo' and involves a double *da capo*; that is, two returns of the scherzo with the trio played twice, both times in the same key and basically the same in other respects. This arrangement may be described as extended or double ternary form (*ABABA*), and it is characteristic of Beethoven at his most longwinded. Examples are to be found in the fourth and seventh Symphonies, the 'Archduke' Trio (Op. 97) and the quartets Op. 74, 95 (but with the trio in different keys) and 131.

Beethoven introduced another type of movement altogether in place of the scherzo on a few occasions. The 'scherzo' of the piano sonata in A major (Op. 101) is actually a quick march with canonic trio of highly contrasted character. Similarly in the A minor quartet (Op. 132) there is a short *Allegro marcia* in rounded-binary form. Actually, marches were fairly common in the early classical sonata, probably on account of the influence of the divertimento. They usually serve as light movements such as the '*Rondo alla Turca*' finale to Mozart's Piano Sonata in A major (K. 331), but in the third movement of Beethoven's Piano Sonata in A flat major (Op. 26) and the second movement of the '*Eroica*' Symphony we have examples of the *marcia funebre*—the funeral march.

So far we have concerned ourselves largely with the expansion of form that we find in Beethoven's work; not yet with the unifying devices that were necessary if increasing size was not to lead to flabbiness, and flabbiness to disintegration. The ordinary listener can hardly fail to sense the cohesiveness, the oneness, of a

work like the *'Eroica'* Symphony, or be unaware of the distinct
and separate character that marks each of Beethoven's symphonies,
even those composed simultaneously like the fourth and fifth,
the seventh and the eighth. This character we may recognize as a
manifestation of the 'idea' which lies behind the music and which
motivates it. This 'idea', or motivating force, may be 'abstract'
or it may be capable of visual or verbal definition (in which
case we have 'Programme Music'), but whatever its nature, it will
clearly tend to exert a unifying influence on the musical material.

One school of analysts accounts for this internal unity of a work
by demonstrating that each theme derives from a basic thematic
idea. Whether in most classical music before Beethoven this is not
to mistake the melodic clichés of a composer and the period, or
the inevitable influence of tonic and dominant triads in melodic
formation—in other words, accidents—for significant thematic
relationships, is an arguable point. It is true that in pre-tonal
music we do find a thematic principle at work, in the cyclic Mass,
for example, and in the variation canzona, but by the 18th century
tonality has become the main unifying agent, and thus thematic
resemblances are virtually beside the point.

But we have already noticed an undermining of structural
tonality with Beethoven, not only in occasional non-tonic recapitulations of second subjects, but also in the general widening
of the tonal orbit and consequent weakening in the gravitational
pull of the tonic. We cannot doubt that Beethoven looked to
thematicism as an additional means of unification. As we shall see,
thematic cross references from movement to movement are frequently to be observed, though we must allow the subconscious
mind of the composer to be the cause of many of these. For in
contemplating a work as a whole, it is very likely that some common denominator will run through it, whether the composer
wills it or not. Thus the rhythm, at least, of the four-note motive
that begins the fifth Symphony, and to some extent the actual
notes, relates the first movement to the scherzo, which, being
linked physically with the finale and recurring again within it,
extends the relationship and binds the whole together. Something of the same sort is found in the last movement of Haydn's

46th Symphony which is interrupted towards the end by a return of the minuet, and in the finale of the same composer's 'Horn Signal' Symphony (no. 31) where the opening of the first movement is also brought back at the end. Obviously the finale is the natural place for retrospective quotations, and the best known example with Beethoven is, of course, in the ninth Symphony, where references to the three previous movements are made before the 'Ode to Joy' finally gets under way. But the same idea is to be found in the much earlier *Sonata quasi una fantasia* (Op. 27 no. 1) where the last movement is interrupted with a recollection of the Adagio before breaking into a brief concluding presto section. Both these cases point to a growing tendency to regard the finale not only as a movement in its own right, but as a summary—a sort of coda—of the whole work. We shall find this again and again with composers after Beethoven.

At the same time Beethoven moved towards actual physical continuity of music from movement to movement. We have already mentioned the intermeshing of the last two movements of the fifth Symphony; the last two movements of the 'Emperor' Piano Concerto and the last three movements of the 'Pastoral' Symphony are also continuous. The same process may be observed in the late piano sonatas and string quartets. The seven movements of the C sharp minor Quartet (Op. 131) flow into each other despite a highly sectionalized structure and frequent changes of mood, tempo and key.

As an example of these cohesive features—movement continuity and thematic change and interchange—the A flat major Piano Sonata (Op. 110) will repay closer examination. Basically, the work is in four movements; the first a Moderato in sonata form, the second a scherzo and trio, the third an *Arioso Dolente*, and the fourth a fugue. But in fact, the only real break occurs between the first and second movements, for the scherzo and arioso are linked by a transitional 'recitative'—an appropriate introduction to the arioso to follow, and an idea which Beethoven had already used in his Piano Sonata Op. 31 no. 2 and was to use again in the finale of the ninth Symphony. (Instrumental recitatives are found before Beethoven; in the second movement of Haydn's *Le Midi*

Symphony, for example, in the first of C. P. E. Bach's 'Prussian Sonatas', and as far back as 1700 in Kuhnau's 'Biblical Sonatas'). Further, the arioso and fugue are dovetailed together through the alternation of sections thus—arioso$_1$, fugue$_1$, arioso$_2$, fugue$_2$. In addition to this physical continuity, there is a wealth of thematic interconnection throughout the sonata. For example, the melody of the arioso is obviously related to that of the scherzo (Ex. 12 (ii–iii)), and the harmonic scheme of its accompaniment is the same as the opening of the first movement (Ex. 12 (i–ii)), though in the tonic minor. Possibly Beethoven was unaware of these relationships in composing the sonata, nevertheless they are the outward sign of an inward unity unconsciously realized. The three-part fugue which emerges from the arioso is clearly derived from the subject of the first movement (Ex. 12 (v–vi)). After following a fairly placid course—though examples of stretto between treble and bass (bb. 66–70) and bass and alto (bb. 76–80) occur, also diminution (treble bb. 82–83)—the arioso reappears in G minor. Then the fugue returns, this time in G major with the subject inverted mirrorwise (Ex. 12 (vii)); a shape in which it resembles a retrograde version of the original fugue subject, hence of the main theme of the first movement. It also recalls the figuration pattern of the trio (Ex. 12 (iv)), though Beethoven was probably only aware of it as an inversion of the subject, whatever else it may be. In the course of the fugue it undergoes inversion again, augmentation and stretto by double diminution before returning to A flat major in its original form and abandoning part-writing for a brilliant pianistic ending.

Ex.12

(i)   I Moderato cantabile molto espressivo

The above brief analysis has pointed to some of the conscious and unconscious factors which help to integrate such a work so that it may be likened, not too fancifully, to a growing and developing organism. Growth and development were the potentials of sonata form which Beethoven realized. In doing so he necessarily brought to it a remarkable flexibility of treatment, preserving in the main the traditional outline and balance of tonality, yet achieving an unprecedented freedom within. Most striking perhaps is the elimination of links in the conventional mechanical sense. An idea once stated is freely developed in a logical continuation which brings forth other ideas. The development section proper continues the process already begun; one in which tendencies latent in the thematic material assert themselves more unconstrainedly until they reach their final affirmation in the recapitulation.

Some of these aspects may be illustrated in the first movement of the String Quartet in A minor (Op. 132). The eight bar introduction (*Assai sostenuto*) presents a mysterious four-note theme forwards, backwards, upside-down and inside-out before breaking into the Allegro. (This four-note theme can be found throughout the last quartets in various guises; with its upward glide of a sixth expanded into a leap of a diminished seventh in the *Grosse Fuge*, Op. 133, for example.) The main allegro theme is in A minor, announced by the cello (b. 11) and developed immediately with modulations to F major, only to be interrupted briefly by the appearance of another, less important fugato subject in D minor given to the first violin (b. 40). F major is definitely established for the next subject (second violin b. 48) and the exposition closes with shaded recollections of the opening chords of the introduction interspersed with a jagged cadential figure (bb. 67–74). The four-note theme in canon between cello and viola starts the development (b. 75) and appears in combination with the main theme during the first stage (bb. 75–151), passing through G minor, C minor and major on the way to E minor. After a reference to the fugato subject in A minor (b. 151) the second subject in C major is given to the cello (b. 159). The return to the recapitulation follows the transition from exposition to development quite closely.

The four-note theme returns in the tonic with drastic economy—eight bars telescoped into two (bb. 193–194)—and, in fact, the whole recapitulation is highly condensed, with all the themes in the tonic minor or major contained within 38 bars as against the exposition's 74. The coda (bb. 232–264) takes up the main theme once more, bringing the movement to a suitably forceful ending.

The broad principles of sonata form are clearly recognizable in this movement. The most obvious departure from tradition lies in the abandonment of the repeat of the exposition, but this is an increasingly frequent occurrence in late Beethoven (only Op. 106 and Op. 111 among the piano sonatas, and Op. 130 among the string quartets have repeated expositions in their first movements). This is more important for what it implies than in itself, for it recognizes that exposition and development are no longer really separate. Naturally themes have to be announced somewhere near the beginning of a movement, and tonalities have to be established before they can be expanded; but otherwise, the development may be said to explore more searchingly what has already been begun in the exposition. To call the cumulation of this process a recapitulation is perhaps to use the wrong word. For the recapitulation represents a state of equilibrium in which the musical and emotional forces at work during the course of the movement are resolved. It was this concept of sonata form, already incipient with Haydn, that Beethoven passed to his successors, most of whom—with one exception—missed the point. And the one exception chose to write operas.

Something of the same transformation that Beethoven wrought in sonata form he brought also to the 'air and variations'. As in certain other respects, he seems to have inherited some of Haydn's talent and predilection for this type of composition. Among slow movement variations from the early and middle periods may be mentioned those in the G major Piano Sonata (Op. 14 no. 2), the A major quartet (Op. 18 no. 5), the opening Andante of the A flat major Piano Sonata (Op. 26), not forgetting the 'Appassionata' Sonata (Op. 57) and the fifth Symphony, most of which are of the ornamental type which display increasing elaboration of the theme and accompaniment from one variation to another.

Two important independent sets of variations for piano are the '15 Variations with Fugue, on a theme from *Prometheus*' (Op. 35) —known as the '*Eroica*' Variations because some of the material was used again in the finale of the '*Eroica*' Symphony—and the '32 Variations on an original theme' in C minor, composed four years later in 1806. In these, the sheer number of variations demands a more resourceful treatment than would have been appropriate in a shorter set designed for inclusion within a sonata or symphony, and it is interesting to observe how important structurally the bass becomes when something more than progressive elaboration is needed. The '*Eroica*' set starts with the bass alone, and continues with four introductory variations on it before bringing in the theme proper as a melodic counterpoint. Thereafter theme and bass are equally important factors in the variation process, with the final fugue on the 'bass' itself leading to a restatement of the theme just before the coda. The '32 Variations' are even more dependent on the bass, which in this case is actually a type of chaconne ground. Here Beethoven glances back at the baroque period, rather as Brahms was to do in the finale of his fourth Symphony.

But the point of departure for the more respectable sets of variations by 19th-century composers, such as Schumann's *Études Symphoniques*, Mendelssohn's *Variations Sérieuses* and Brahms's sets, was Beethoven's '33 Variations on a Waltz by Diabelli' (Op. 120)—the ultimate of resourceful variety within strict variation form. But the need for variety and contrast in sets of variations of such length inevitably inhibits the shaping of an overall design. However, by placing a suitably weighty movement such as a fugue at the end, a kind of culminating apotheosis is achieved, which seems to function retrospectively as a cohesive agent. In this role, the virtues of the fugue as a conclusion to a set of variations have not been lost on subsequent composers.

Nevertheless in the 'Diabelli' Variations, Beethoven shows us that there are other ways of making variations than by progressive elaboration of a theme. Melodic accentuation, harmonic rhythm, phrase structure, chord progressions, modulation and formal balance are all material to be worked on. The 'Diabelli' Variations display these elements of variation in the abstract: that is, as static developments, without the sense of progression which runs through the development process of a sonata or fugue. On a smaller time scale an inner consistency was possible, and Beethoven used variation form as an ideal type of slow movement in his later quartets and sonatas. In it, he expresses contemplatively what, in the fugue, he expresses dynamically. Both forms are concerned with the pursuit of a single idea, and it is true that, with Beethoven, a variation theme and a fugue theme are both to be commended not for what they say, but for what they leave unsaid. Yet he requires no more than half-a-dozen variations to achieve an eloquence all the more intense for being firmly directed.

Usually some sort of expansion or cumulative effect is involved in the overall scheme. This may be apparent in the increasingly involved decorative treatment of the melody, as in the slow movement of the ninth Symphony, or in the progressive complexity of accompanimental figuration as in the last movement of the Piano Sonata, Op. 111—indeed, these were traditional procedures. However, the movement away from the simplicity of the theme might follow an uneven course, taking the form perhaps of a double arc in which a minor climax is achieved after the first two or three variations, followed by a reaction (analogous to the traditional *minore* variation) and build-up towards a major climax just before the end. The last variation, or, more likely, the coda, eases the tension with a return to a simpler statement of the theme, or some aspect of it. The finale of the Op. 109 Piano Sonata in E major provides an example; the first arc ending in the minor climax of the third variation, the second culminating in the major climax in the course of the sixth variation, followed by a return to the theme in the coda.

Beethoven discovered that fugue was, if anything, even more suited to the thematic developmental process of composition than sonata form. That it is naturally so is shown by the fact that fugato is so often utilized within sonata-form developments, especially in the string quartets of Haydn and Mozart. Yet despite this, the formal fugue had its disadvantages, particularly the lack of contrast in its continually unfolding texture; for although the fugue might have two or three subjects, fundamentally they were complementary to each other. Beethoven was conscious of this at an early stage, and compromised by writing his fugues in sonata form (as Mozart had done in the 'Magic Flute' Overture). Hence the scherzo in the C minor String Quartet (Op. 18 no. 4) starts like a regular fugue, but as it proceeds it is clear that it is organized according to the sonata-form plan, with a repeated exposition, a development section and recapitulation with keys properly adjusted. The Andante of the first Symphony is a similar sort of movement, but here only the first theme is treated fugally. There is a magnificent F minor fugato in the second episode of the slow movement of the 'Eroica' Symphony (bb. 114–143), and a very different kind of fugue in the trio of the third movement of the fifth Symphony—in Berlioz's phrase 'like the gambols of an elephant'. Still within the framework of sonata form Beethoven writes a fugue as the finale to the third 'Rasoumovsky' Quartet (Op. 59 no. 3), complete with inversions of the subject, but an unmistakable sonata type of development, in which the theme is broken down into fragments and developed exhaustively. Another extended fugal episode is found in the second movement of the Quartet in F minor (Op. 95, bb. 34–112), a work which takes us to the threshold of his last period.

We have only to observe that Beethoven's intention was to finish the Op. 130 Quartet in B flat major with the *Grosse Fuge* (now Op. 133), and to compare the other great fugue in B flat— the finale of the 'Hammerklavier' Sonata (Op. 106)—to realize that Beethoven regarded the fugal-finale as something rather special. (These are by no means the only fugues to be found in the works of his last period.) To begin with, its associations were serious and high-minded, and this certainly recommended the fugue to the mature Beethoven above rondo, or even sonata form. Further, familiarity with the fugues of Bach, had shown him what might be done. And as his harmonic language approached the richness of Bach's, he became increasingly aware of how its expressiveness might be realized through the fugue; through the opportunity for thematic and harmonic development it afforded; through the continuity and drive naturally inherent in fugal texture which seemed to guarantee cohesion.

But Beethoven's attitude was not Bach's. He neatly epitomizes his approach in the heading to the finale of the '*Hammerklavier*'; '*Fuga a tre voci, con alcune licenze*'—Fugue in three voices with certain licences!

It is not proposed to analyse it in detail here; merely to point out first, the manner of thematic development; secondly, the elements of contrast; and thirdly, the integration of these and the cohesion of the whole.

Thematic development is effected by (i) the use of fugal devices such as augmentation (bb. 84–100), stretto by augmentation and inversion (bb. 101–106), retrograde motion (bb. 142–164), mirrorwise inversion (bb. 198–224), close stretto of inverted and uninverted forms (bb. 284–298)—devices, incidentally, which Bach uses much more sparingly in his fugues than Beethoven who (intoxicated by his master Albrechtsberger's text-book) cannot resist them, and (ii) episodes which seize on motives in the subjects and countersubjects and toss them from one voice to another modulating the while. All this involves a certain amount of contrast too, but more striking contrasts are presented by (i) the introduction of a second subject in B minor (bb. 143–164), a third subject in D major (bb. 240–268), as well as independent episodes in G flat major (bb. 75–83) and A flat major (bb. 120–143). These second and third subjects are integrated within the thematic scheme by combination, the second with the main theme backwards (b. 143), the third with the main theme in its original form at the re-establishment of the tonic key (bb. 269–278).

Overall there is the tonal plan setting out from B flat major and ranging as flat as G flat major, and as sharp as B minor before triumphantly reaffirming the tonic in the last 121 bars. Yet tonally and thematically everything relates to what has gone before and what is to come. Indeed, it is impossible to gauge the effect of either the tonal or thematic processes independently. They complement each other's logic, and together contribute to the forward and upward sweep of the whole fugue.

To Beethoven then, the fugue became the form, which—in allegro tempos at least—offered the greatest opportunities of continuous development within a highly integrated texture; more even than sonata form which lacked the ultimate in tautness of construction and emotional fervour. Hence the fugue's position as a finale, where, in allowing the fullest realization of Beethoven's thematic approach to structure, it found its logical place as the culmination of the whole.

IV

Thematicism and the development of the 'cyclic principle'

IV : 1 'Programme music': lyric and dramatic aspects of form

Romanticism implies an approach to art which explores the world of fantasy and feeling. Romantic composers regarded music as a means of realizing and intensifying these experiences, and of communicating them to their fellow-men. To the generation of composers born around 1810, it seemed as if Gluck, Weber and Beethoven had shown how this could be done, though in fact there was already a tradition dating from the middle of the 18th century—and supported by a highly developed system of musical aesthetics (*affektenlehre*)—which recognized that music was about feelings. The lyrical strain of Romanticism which we tend to think blossomed suddenly with Schubert, derives (in part at least) from the *empfindsamer stil* of C. P. E. Bach and the Berlin school, and can be traced in the songs of Johann Friedrich Reichardt (1752–1814) and Carl Friedrich Zelter (1758–1832), and in the piano music of Wilhelm Friedemann Bach (1710–1784). Indeed, this 'sentimental style' together with its emotional complement, the turbulent *sturm und drang* ('storm and stress') can be seen as directly contributing to, if not actually inaugurating the romantic movement in music. This, of course, is only part of the whole complex movement in literature and the arts at this time towards emotionalism.

These two extremes anticipate what we may call the lyric Romanticism of Franz Schubert (1797–1828), Robert Schumann (1810–1856) and Frédéric Chopin (1810–1849) on the one hand, and the dramatic Romanticism of Hector Berlioz (1803–1869), Franz Liszt (1811–1886) and Richard Wagner (1813–1883) on the other—not that these labels can be applied too rigidly. In general, the lyric style was expressed through static forms; that is, forms without development processes, like ternary and rondo forms, such as we find in most 19th-century 'character pieces' for piano solo. The dramatic style favoured developmental forms which press on towards a final resolution of the argument. This, of course, is the essence of sonata form in the Beethovenian sense; and understood in that sense it was ideally suited to what Liszt and Wagner set out to do in their music.

It is in the realm of lyric expression that these early romantic composers excel. We think of Schubert primarily as a song writer, at his best in the short, strophic *lied*, in which the melody (though not necessarily the accompaniment) is substantially the same for each verse. The style has the appearance of simplicity, often with a folksong flavour and with folksong-like repetitions of the melody at the beginning which are frequently echoed at the end. However, we should remember that not all Schubert's strophic settings are as obvious as those of Zelter, or his own *Heidenröslein* or *An Sylvia*. Very often the treatment is freer; melody, harmony, key and accompaniment may each change, particularly towards the end of the song (obvious examples are *Die Forelle* and *Du bist die Ruh*). Then there are his through-composed songs in which, frequently owing to a longer text and more complex verse structure, wholesale repetition from verse to verse is absent.

More often in his earlier years than later he seems to have been drawn to the form of the *scena*—perhaps through the example of Reichardt—wherein recitative, arioso and melodic elements were mingled in a kind of rhapsody following the sense of the words. Goethe's *Prometheus* was set by both Reichardt and Schubert in this style. Similarly, in his youthful predilection for the narrative ballad he was perhaps following Johann Zumsteeg (1760–1802); yet it led to the composition of two early masterpieces, the *Erl-könig* and *Gretchen am Spinnrade*, both through-composed but welded into a dramatic unity by means of the insistent and descriptive figuration of the accompaniment, and the recurrence of certain vocal phrases throughout the songs. The accompaniments of these two songs are typical of the way in which Schubert was able to establish the mood of a song immediately and maintain it, thus imparting a subjective unity over and above the objective unity resulting from his wonderfully resourceful manipulation of piano figuration.

Schubert wrote two song-cycles: that is, sequences of songs arranged in order so that, as Richard Capell says 'a drama is revealed to us in a series of lyrical movements'. This is a far remove from opera, for it is through soliloquy rather than dialogue that the narration unfolds. Furthermore, there is no physical link between the songs, only an emotional continuity. In neither the *Schöne Müllerin* nor the *Winterreise* cycles can we discern conscious thematic connections between songs. But Beethoven in his *An die ferne Geliebte* recalls the opening melody of the first song towards the end; so does Schumann in what might be called the piano epilogue to his *Frauenliebe und leben*. Likewise his *Dichterliebe* cycle is summed-up (though no themes are quoted) in a lengthy piano coda to the last song. Schumann and Hugo Wolf (1860–1903) after him, showed a more literary approach to word setting than Schubert, writing a smaller proportion of strophic settings and lacking his melodic freshness—and naïvety. Their declamation is more dramatic, while Wolf's accompaniments in particular, provide the sort of musical continuity and commentary that we find on a much larger scale in the orchestral 'accompaniments' of the Wagnerian music-drama. Yet if we apply the term 'art-song' to the songs of Schumann and Wolf primarily, it implies no criticism of Schubert, or for that matter Brahms, both of whom in favouring strophic form and folk-like qualities of melody—musical rather than literary characteristics—seem to prefer nature to art.

The lyric impulse of romantic composers found another outlet in the 'character piece' for piano. This term includes all the many independent movements for piano whose titles indicate the character or style of the music rather than its form. Some have abstract titles such as 'Bagatelle', 'Moment Musical', 'Impromptu', 'Intermezzo', 'Étude', 'Prelude' (not necessarily an introductory piece, but often one in its own right), etc., others are mood pictures such as 'Nocturne', 'Romance', 'Barcarolle', 'Berceuse', etc.; others are more overtly descriptive, though they may be collected together under a general title such as *Lieder ohne Wörte* ('Songs without words'), *Albumblätter* ('Album Leaves'), etc.; still others are dances such as the 'Waltz', 'Ländler', 'Mazurka', 'Polonaise', 'Écossaise', etc. The piano music of Beethoven, Schubert, Schumann, Chopin, Mendelssohn and Brahms will furnish examples of all these and more. As has already been hinted, the majority are in some sort of ternary form, with contrasting episode. Modifications may include a brief introductory section, perhaps not more than a bar or two, a second episode which may or may not be related to the first, varied returns of the principal section, and a coda which may recall episodical material in bringing the piece to an end.

More wide-ranging in mood and extended in scale are the 'ballades', 'capriccios', 'fantasias', 'rhapsodies', and 'scherzos' of Chopin and Brahms. Chopin's scherzos are no longer jocular though still basically ternary in form. The ballads are even freer and, though repetition is involved, in no case is it a simple matter of *ABA*. Structurally the simplest, the F major Ballade (Op. 38) actually ends in a different key (A minor) from the beginning, alternating an F major *Andantino* opening section with a *Presto con fuoco*, first in A minor then in D minor, but concluding with an *Agitato* section in A minor, and a coda which alludes to the opening *Andantino* without confirming its key. The rhapsodies of Brahms, on the other hand, are much more firmly knit than the works we have been considering; the one in G minor (Op. 79 no. 2) actually being in strict sonata form.

But it was to symphonic music—not necessarily the symphony —that the Romantics looked for the fulfilment of their most grandiose concepts. Liszt and Wagner were to realize sonata form in 19th-century terms, and the developmental continuity which we have found in Beethoven (the principle of 'developing variation' as Schoenberg called it) was to find its logical outcome in the process of thematic transformation in the works of Liszt, and the use of leitmotives in Wagner's operas. In contrast to the introverted romanticism of Mendelssohn and Schumann, a much more dynamic concept of musical expression is illustrated in the orchestral music of Berlioz and Liszt, in which an attempt is made to convey a different type of experience, not of subjective feeling but of objective description. Whether, when we use the term 'Programme Music' we mean only the latter, or whether programmaticism involves both the lyric and the dramatic (or whether all music is not programmatic) need not concern us, fortunately, for the truth is that established musical forms were not incompatible with either approach. We have already seen how ternary form provides a suitable vehicle for lyrical expression, and we shall discover how the late 18th-century overture form, with its slow introduction leading to sonata-allegro, was adaptable to a programme dealing with narrative, or dramatic conflict.

The overture (at least, after Gluck) was, in fact, a kind of programme music in the sense that one of its functions was to set the mood of the opera to follow. Perhaps the first to do this in a way which was significant for the future was Gluck's *Iphigénie en Aulide* (1774), and we can see the same thing in Mozart's overture to *Don Giovanni* (1787), and in Beethoven's *Coriolan* (1807) and *Egmont* (1810) overtures (neither, incidentally, overtures to operas, but to plays). Still more overtly programmatic are the second and third *Leonore* (1805–1806) overtures, in which themes from the opera are incorporated and the dramatic climax of the opera foreshadowed in musical terms. Beethoven himself referred to *Leonore* No. 1 as a 'characteristic overture'; 'characteristic' implying descriptiveness as in the 'character piece'. Weber too, in his overture to *Der Freischütz* (1821) uses motives drawn from the opera, treating them within the orthodox framework of sonata form with a slow introduction, and with undeniably atmospheric effect.

It is with Felix Mendelssohn (1809–1847) and Berlioz that the overture as an independent concert piece—the concert overture—came into its own. In most cases these overtures were not intended to precede a stage performance but are merely illustrative orchestral pieces. Nevertheless they tend to follow the same form as the operatic overture: slow introduction followed by sonata-allegro.

In Mendelssohn's 'Midsummer Night's Dream' Overture (1826) there is strictly speaking no slow introduction, only four held woodwind chords which set the fairy atmosphere of the piece with incredible effectiveness. The movement is in orthodox sonata form (as usual in the overture without repeated exposition), as is the very different but equally evocative 'Hebrides' Overture (1830). The form of 'A Calm Sea and a Prosperous Voyage' (1832) was to have broken with tradition and comprised 'two pictures standing side by side', following Goethe's pair of poems of the same title as the overture; but in its final form the first picture (representing the 'calm sea'), serves as a slow introduction to the main allegro section, the 'prosperous voyage'—again in sonata form. We find a similar arrangement in Berlioz's 'Waverley Overture' (1828) where the same scheme represents respectively the first and second lines of the epigraph from Scott's 'Waverley' —'Dreams of Love and Ladies' charms/Give place to Honour and to Arms'.

From the dates it will be seen that Mendelssohn and Berlioz were active in the field of the concert overture about the same time. Berlioz also made the sonata-allegro the basis of his overture form. In 'King Lear' (1831) there is a slow introduction leading into an *Allegro disperato* in sonata form, though in the later overtures, 'Roman Carnival' (1844) for example, the slow 'introduction' is itself introduced by a brief anticipation of the main Allegro.

So it appears that neither the allegedly conservative Mendelssohn, nor the allegedly revolutionary Berlioz sacrificed sonata form for the sake of descriptiveness in their concert overtures. There was no need. The slow introduction and sonata-allegro gave ample scope for the varied treatment of a wide range of musical material which could give metaphoric expression to non-musical ideas.

Both these composers carried some of their ideas over into their symphonies, though here important differences emerge. The visit to Scotland in 1829 that had inspired Mendelssohn to write the 'Hebrides' Overture also suggested to him the idea, and some of the themes, of his 'Scotch' Symphony (no. 3). This was not completed until 1842, and it was actually the 'Italian' Symphony (no. 4 in A major) which he produced for a first performance in London in 1833. The programmatic element is less pronounced in these symphonies than in his overtures and there is nothing quite so atmospheric in the 'Scotch' Symphony as in the 'Hebrides' Overture. Even so, we realize just how appropriate music and title are to each other when we compare the 'Scotch' and the 'Italian' symphonies. It is not just a question of A minor and A major—though this may have something to do with it (however, the A minor symphony ends in A major, and the A major symphony ends in A minor!). Still less does their respective character depend on the incorporation of national musical idioms characteristic of those countries, though these are evident to a limited extent (in the *saltarello* last movement of the 'Italian' Symphony, for example). In some more subtle way Mendelssohn evokes the mist and romance of Scotland, and the sunlight and high spirits of Italy, no less certainly for being more generalized than in his overtures.

But whereas Mendelssohn was content to convey only a general impression of his subject, Berlioz attempted a much more detailed description, and it is with his name that the 'programme symphony' is usually associated. Actually, this is a nice irony, for the programme symphony was already a fact before he was born. and Berlioz, rather than write his symphonies to a programme was more inclined to write programmes to his symphonies. The fashion for programme symphonies had grown up among the lesser symphonists of the late 18th century, stimulated no doubt by an audience eager for such novelties. We can find antecedents to Beethoven's 'Pastoral' Symphony in the works of Justin Heinrich Knecht (1752-1817) and the Abbé Vogler (1749-1814), and in general 'Pastoral', 'Hunt', 'Storm', and 'Battle' symphonies proliferated. Mention should also be made of the twelve 'Ovid' symphonies (1785) by Karl Ditters von Dittersdorf (1739-1799), each of which is based on a text from the 'Metamorphoses'. In France a certain amount of theorizing had gone on regarding the descriptive capabilities of music. Bernard, Comte de la Cépède (1756-1825) maintained that the composer should consider the movements of a symphony 'as three grand acts of a theatrical piece' and gave details of how the drama was to be worked out in terms of scenes, characters and so on. More famous and significant is Berlioz's own teacher Jean François Lesueur (1760–1837) who held similar views, and no doubt impressed his pupil with them.

But it is difficult not to view Berlioz's attitude with a certain scepticism. His 'Fantastic' Symphony (1830) is supposed to follow a highly detailed programme which the composer thought the audience should be acquainted with if the music was to make its fullest effect; the titles at least of the five movements were to be made known to the audience. These represent five episodes in a dream sequence of 'a young musician of extraordinary sensibility and abundant imagination', who

'. . . in the depths of despair because of hopeless love, has poisoned himself with opium. The drug is too feeble to kill him, but plunges him into a heavy sleep accompanied by weird visions. His sensations, emotions and memories as they pass through his affected mind are transformed into musical images and ideas. The beloved one herself becomes to him a melody, a recurrent theme (*idée fixe*) which haunts him continually.'

The movements are titled 'Dreams and Passions', 'A Ball', 'Scene in the Fields', 'March to the Scaffold' and 'Dream of a Witches' Sabbath', and in each of them, the Beloved—represented by the *idée fixe*—makes her appearance transformed in various guises. Despite all this, it should be observed that a great deal of the music had already been written before the programme was formulated. Thus the symphony is, to some extent, a patchwork, more or less appropriate to the scenes it purports to describe, but artificially related internally through the device of a programme and the use of the *idée fixe*. Thus, the *idée fixe* is largely a stop-gap means of forcing thematic relationships between movements otherwise diverse in character and origins.

However, in a sense, we are not so much interested in what Berlioz the opportunist did, as in what he seemed to do. To all appearances the 'Fantastic' Symphony is a programme symphony; so too is 'Harold in Italy' (1834). Here again we know that some of the music was originally intended for a cantata on the death of Mary, Queen of Scots; some of it had belonged to the 'Rob Roy' Overture; yet despite its Scottish associations they were not so strong as to prevent it from being used in a work with the title 'Harold in Italy'. (We have seen Mendelssohn depict these national characteristics much less equivocally in his symphonies!) The four movements of the 'Harold' Symphony are intended to portray 'Harold in the Mountains—Scenes of Melancholy, Happiness and Joy', 'March of the Pilgrims singing the Evening Prayer', 'Serenade of an Abruzzi Mountaineer to his Mistress', 'Orgy of Brigands'. These titles are probably as good as any to describe the movements, but what we really have, in effect, are four character pieces arranged in order of mood and speed approximating to that of the normal four-movement symphony. In the classical sense, neither this nor the 'Fantastic' Symphony is a true symphony, for the classical symphony is greater than the sum of its parts; to some extent the individual movements subordinate their identities in a higher interest. But here, the movements are of such unrestrained and irrepressible character that it needs a programme and the eleventh-hour use of the *idée fixe* to impose an artificial unity on the music. Mendelssohn had a finer appreciation of what the symphony was in the classical sense for all his romantic inclinations. Had he been Berlioz he might have used the 'Hebrides' Overture as one of the movements in his 'Scotch' Symphony (or perhaps even in his 'Italian' symphony!), but, not being Berlioz, he knew that a symphony composed of four concert overtures is no symphony. At best it would have been the sum of its parts, no more.

When it comes to the form of the separate movements Berlioz is almost as orthodox and as traditional as Mendelssohn. Typically, Berlioz's handling of sonata form is based on the slow introduction leading into a sonata-allegro scheme which we have already noticed in his overtures, and which can be traced back to Haydn's symphonies, and further. It has already been shown how this offered scope for descriptiveness, and this (together with the blessing bestowed upon it by the 'trinity'—Gluck, Weber and

Beethoven) no doubt recommended it to Berlioz. And just as Mendelssohn divided the title of his overture 'A Calm Sea and a Prosperous Voyage' between the slow introduction and Allegro, so did Berlioz with the first movement of both his symphonies; 'Dreams (*Largo*) and Passions (*Allegro agitato e appassionato assai*)' in the 'Fantastic', and 'Scenes of Melancholy (*Adagio*), Happiness and Joy (*Allegro*)' in 'Harold in Italy'.

The opening Adagio of the 'Harold' Symphony (bb. 1–94) does indeed evoke a mood of brooding melancholy. The 'Harold' theme is first heard in G minor (wood-wind bb. 14–21) and later in G major (b. 38) where it is given to the solo viola—the part was originally written for Paganini though he declined to play it. One of Berlioz's most effectively orchestrated passages makes a transition to the main theme of the Allegro in G major (b. 95), derived from bars 3 and 4 of the 'Harold' theme (Ex. 13 (i–ii)). The second subject is in the dominant (b. 174) and like the first is related to the *idée fixe* (Ex. 13 (iii) in the tonic to show the similarity more clearly). In true classical style, and as in the 'Fantastic' Symphony, the exposition is marked to be repeated, and the development section (starting at the second-time bar) deals with the main theme in various keys. The subjects return in the reverse order in the recapitulation, the second in the tonic, at bar 260 and the first, also in the tonic, thirty bars later. There follows a long coda beginning with a fugato on the 'Harold' theme (bb. 324–352), working up from the lower strings in combination with the first subject in the wood-wind, then in the wood-wind in combination with the first subject in the strings (bb. 352–372). Berlioz makes the most of this by repeating forty-odd bars again with only minor differences of orchestration. A quicker tempo is taken up (b. 439) together with the second subject and a crescendo builds up to a rousing finish.

Ex. 13

(i)   (Idée fixe - 'Harold')

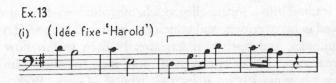

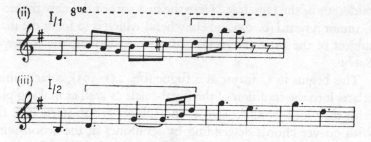

So much for scenes of happiness and joy; though of Harold in the mountains we are little wiser. Emotions such as happiness and joy are probably more easily expressed in music than in any other way. But what does Berlioz do when the programme is less generalized—in the last movement of the 'Fantastic' Symphony, for example? Here again, a modification of the same overture form provides opportunities for purely descriptive writing as well as for more abstract musical construction. In this case we have three introductory sections before the commencement of the main sonata-allegro. The first, *Larghetto* (bb. 1–20) sets the atmosphere in which the artist 'sees himself at a Witches' Sabbath surrounded by a fearful crowd of spectres, sorcerers, and monsters of every kind, united for his burial. Unearthly sounds, groans, shrieks of laughter, distant cries to which others seem to respond.' All this is brilliantly depicted in the music. The next section, *Allegro–Allegro assai–Allegro* (bb. 21–101) is less subtle, but clearly illustrates the next stage of the programme, as well as anticipating the two principal tonalities on which the exposition of the main Allegro is based; C major (already heralded by horn calls and drum rolls in the previous section) and E flat major: 'The melody of his beloved is heard, but it has lost its character of nobility and reserve. Instead it is now an ignoble dance tune, trivial and grotesque [b. 21]. It is She who comes to the Sabbath! A shout of joy greets her arrival [bb. 29–39]. She joins in the diabolical orgy [bb. 40–101].' The shrill notes of the E flat clarinet, and the jig-rhythm of the *idée fixe* bizarrely ornamented add to the descriptiveness of this section. Next comes a setting of the *Dies Irae* chant marked *lontano* and accompanied by bells—'The funeral knell, burlesque of the Dies Irae.' Here the first part of the new theme in C minor is heard (b. 106 and elsewhere) which is to form the main subject of the principal section of this movement, the *Ronde du Sabbat*.

This begins in C major as a fugue (bb. 241–305), a fact which relates it to the tradition of the fugal-finale as well as making play with the word 'ronde'. The second subject group starts in E flat with quaver chords descending by semitones in the wood-wind (bb. 306–309 and elsewhere)—a reminiscence from the first intro-ductory section (bb. 4 and 15)—and after various treatments of this idea the *Dies Irae* is reintroduced, still in E flat (bb. 348–362). The development consists of another fugato for strings based on a chromatic version of the first subject (starting b. 364) and this works up to a crescendo leading back to the recapitulation (b. 403) of the first subject and *Dies Irae* combined in the tonic key. The coda (bb. 479–524) develops the *Dies Irae* further and ends (need-less to say) fortissimo.

Once again, Berlioz, the 'musical anarchist', has written a movement which is basically quite conventional from the formal point of view. In general, it is true that thematic development is not confined to the development section only but is liable to occur anywhere, in the recapitulation which is usually free, and in the coda. He is clearly conscious of the need for thematic integration, and we notice this in his fondness for incorporating introductory and episodic material into subsequent developments, and in his predilection for the contrapuntal combination of themes originally stated separately. It may already have been suspected that Berlioz had a natural contrapuntal bent, and it is true that his fugal writing is not only 'correct' (unlike his harmony and modulation!) but has a vitality which is rare in the 19th century. He might have turned the tables and taught Cherubini a thing or two in this respect.

The concert overture and the programme symphony came together in the Lisztian symphonic poem. The term itself—'symphonic poem'—was a happy choice. It implied that the composer was setting out to do with musical sounds what the poet did with words; to communicate narrative, description, atmosphere, feeling. Form and scale were, as it were, by-products of the composer's method, which might vary from the static presentation of a comparatively simple impression to the dynamic working out of multiple ideas. In doing so, Liszt made use of the technique of thematic change and interchange in the interest of both formal cohesion and programmatic symbolism. To some extent this latter aspect derived from Berlioz's concept of the *idée fixe* but it was also, in part, a fruit of the Wagner–Liszt 'dialogue' that was in progress during the 1850's; a decade in which both composers came to their full maturity, and in which Liszt as a champion of Wagner and a composer in his own right was relishing the opportunities for operatic and orchestral performance which his post at Weimar afforded. Some sort of cross-fertilization occurred between the two. Having (possibly) suggested to Wagner the structural potentialities of thematic transformation, Liszt in return was to seize on the dramatic possibilities of the *leitmotiv* in his series of twelve symphonic poems produced between 1848 and 1858. These in their turn were to be so influential that from then on thematic transformation became a technique of melodic invention and development that few of his successors could afford to disregard. The fifty years which separate the first of Liszt's twelve symphonic poems from the last of Richard Strauss's eight 'tone-poems' (his own term, but identical in meaning to Liszt's) mark the period of its development and ascendancy. Bedřich Smetana (1824–1884) composed his first two as early as 1858, and his cycle of six symphonic poems titled *Má Vlast* (1874–1879) gave a great impetus to composers such as Borodin and, at a later date Sibelius, who saw the form as a means of realizing nationalistic sympathies in music, as Liszt had himself in *Hungaria* (1856). Indeed, nearly every composer of the time tried his hand, with the significant exception of Brahms.

But to return to Liszt. Like Berlioz, he was not above serving up yesterday's dinner with a different sauce. *Les Préludes* (1856), for example, started out as an overture to a choral work called the 'Four elements', and had nothing to do with Lamartine's *Méditations Póetiques'*. The fact that this work began life as an overture, and that several other symphonic poems were originally written as such, points to the derivation of the form. Whether the concert overture could have achieved the greater flexibility in programmatic treatment that is characteristic of the symphonic poem without the fertilizing influence of the programme symphony is doubtful; certainly the urge to express sequential rather than static ideas, scenes, etc., was stimulated by Berlioz's experiments with the symphony, and, of course, Beethoven's great example.

It was the ever adaptable overture form—sonata-allegro plus coda, with or without introductory or interpolated sections—that was to provide the framework for many symphonic poems. *Les Préludes*, which is perhaps the best known of Liszt's, is a clear example, starting with a slow introduction (bb. 1–34) leading into a C major movement complete with second subject group in E major (bb. 54–108), development section (bb. 109–315) with interpolated pastoral episode (starting b. 200) leading back to a tonic recapitulation of all the subject matter in reverse order—*bogen*-like (b. 316 to the end). Actually, Liszt's last-minute programme fits quite well, especially from the start of the development section onwards:

'What cruelly wounded soul, issuing from one of these tempests, does not endeavour to solace its memories in the calm serenity of rural life? Nevertheless, man does not resign himself for long to the enjoyment of that beneficent stillness . . . and when "the trumpet sounds the alarm" he takes up his post . . . that he may recover in combat the full consciousness of himself and his powers.'

—yet it is a completely integrated sonata movement making frequent and obvious use of the device of metamorphosis. The opening unison germ theme (Ex. 14 (i)) gives rise to a countersubject of the main theme (Ex. 14 (ii)), and the first subject of the second group (Ex. 14 (iii)) as well as other subsidiary forms. Even the *Allegretto pastorale* (starting b. 200) ties in with what has gone before. Its 6/8 horn-call theme is announced over the same I–VI–IV harmonies that we heard originally as the accompaniment to the main *maestoso* subject, and later this pastoral theme is combined with the second of the two second subjects (Ex. 14 (v)).

But not all Liszt's symphonic poems are so much of a piece as this. He frequently divides the poem or story into two or three episodes, and this results in a free symphonic structure in which contrasted sections, linked and thematically related, are

somewhat analogous to the movements of the normal symphony. Thus *Tasso* (1849) is in three 'scenes' representing the
poet in Venice, Ferrara and Rome respectively, but each based
on a Tasso *leitmotiv* of falling triplets which we hear at the
outset.

On the other hand, the three movements of the 'Faust' Symphony (1854)—which, significantly, he dedicated to Berlioz—are
more self-contained, though certain themes are common to all
movements. Here we have three 'character pieces', 'Faust',
'Gretchen' and 'Mefistofeles', corresponding closely to the normal
character and sequence of the movements of a symphony.

Yet for all the internal relationships, Liszt's construction is, and
sounds, episodic. His periods are four-square and padded out with
sequences, and too often his favourite *'grandioso'* effects are little
more than empty posturing. Nevertheless he had a tremendous
influence on the younger generation of composers, as can be seen
particularly in the music of Camille Saint-Saëns (1835–1921)
César Franck (1822–1890) and Peter Tchaikowsky (1840–1893).
Saint-Saëns' *Phaëton* (1873) and *La Jeunesse d'Hercule* (1877) are
cast in the Lisztian mould—though not *Danse Macabre* (1874),
which is really a simple character piece—while Franck's *Le
Chasseur Maudit* (1882) is in the same tradition. Tchaikowsky,
like Liszt himself, took inspiration from Shakespeare and Dante.
The fantasy-overture, *Romeo and Juliet* (1869) and *Hamlet* (1888)
are in overture form with slow introduction from which material
is later incorporated into the main body of the sonata movement.
The orchestral fantasy *The Tempest* (1873), is, by comparison,
episodic and as he said himself 'diffuse', partly because he tried
to depict selected incidents from the play in chronological
order, instead of conveying an overall impression as in the two
fantasy-overtures. *Francesca da Rimini* (1876) is in ternary form
with a slow introduction.   The *Allegro vivo* (A) sections represent the chastisements of the second circle of Hell, while the
Andante cantabile (B) section is Francesca herself, and her unhappy
story.

The development of the symphonic poem culminated in
Richard Strauss (1864–1949) and it was through his tone-poems

that he made his early and lasting reputation. Using the full apparatus of thematic metamorphosis he developed the descriptive aspect almost to its limit (though the ultimate in this respect is perhaps to be found in a work such as Honegger's 'Pacific 231'). Strauss, however, was keenly aware of the need to find a satisfactory musical form which could carry the programme. Hence, the adventures of *Don Quixote* (1897) are cast in free variation form, and 'Till Eulenspiegel's Merry Pranks' (1895) in rondo. In fact the 'mock sermon' and 'philosophical disputation' are episodes in both a narrative and a musical sense. The first is in B flat major (starting p. 27 Eulenburg Miniature Score), the second in A minor (starting p. 45), and they are placed within an F major movement dominated by two ubiquitous motives representing Till. The principal thematic section preceding the 'mock sermon' episode is recapitulated after the 'philosophical disputation' and this leads into a rumbustious coda which further develops the two main themes together with the 'sermon' theme, now irrepressible. The excitement works up to the moment of Till's execution, after which a short epilogue recalls the 'once upon a time' opening of the work. The construction of the work may be expressed schematically as:

Prologue: A_1 B A_2 C A_1 Coda: Epilogue.

Strauss's other tone poems may be regarded as basically sonataform structures. The procedure is fairly orthodox in *Don Juan* (1888)—if we allow for the interpolation of two episodes into the development section—but a work like *Also sprach Zarathustra* (1896) forces us to revise our ideas of sonata form to some extent. Its programme deals with the opposition of man's nature and spirit in the course of his evolution, and seen overall it may be described as an emergence from darkness to light, with major tonalities triumphing in the end over minor. This is presented in musical terms not only though leitmotives, but by continual conflict between the key of C and the key of B, a conflict which is all-pervading and never finally reconciled. The work is vast and thematically complex, but the two principal motives are both announced within the first 34 bars (Ex. 15 (i–ii)). This perhaps is all the exposition there is. Thereafter, these themes are developed along with new leitmotives which are continually being added, at least as far as the '*Grablied*' section (starting p. 47, Eulenberg Miniature Score). This and the following fugue, '*Von der Wissenschaft*' (p. 61) are exclusively concerned with developing subjects through transformation and combination—see how the fugue subject incorporates both in its first two bars (Ex. 15 (iii)). At the climax (p. 94) C major asserts itself, and the first theme gives rise to the '*Tanzlied*' (p. 126)—a gigantic waltz the impetus of which mounts and carries through the whole recapitulation. But in the end C major slowly fades, the tempo slackens, and the second theme now serene and in B major has the last word, or almost. For the last three notes, *ppp* and pizzicato on cellos and basses alone, are bottom C.

Ex.15

(i)

(ii)

(iii)

Here we have a view of sonata form in which it is no longer possible to distinguish clearly three divisions each characterized by a particular or predominant function. The opening section is primarily concerned with presenting the musical material as germinal motives, but it is extremely short and almost immediately (that is, following the luscious '*Von den Hinterweltlern*' episode) the full potential of the material is realized, culminating in a sort of 'plateau of attainment'—the recapitulation. Exposition and development are not so much successive as simultaneous, the developmental function taking over as the movement sweeps 'onwards and upwards' gathering all the material—episodes included—into the vortex. In such a way the conflict inherent in sonata form is played out.

IV : 2 'Abstract music': the quest for unity and continuity

We must now return to the beginning of the 19th century and follow a parallel course to that we have just taken. Perhaps parallel is the wrong word, for parallel lines are supposed not to touch, whereas 'programme music' and 'absolute music' can hardly be separated. We have seen how serviceable sonata form was as a vehicle for programmatic expression; we shall see how the *idée fixe* and the device of thematic metamorphosis developed throughout the 19th century as a means of securing an overall unity and integrity in works nominally abstract in intent.

When it came to the more extended forms of the symphony and the sonata, the proximity of Beethoven to the early romantic composers was almost as much an impediment as it was an inspiration. They were impeded by the impossibility of realizing themselves fully in terms dictated by one of such vastly different temperament, yet inspired to make the attempt nevertheless. It has already been suggested that they were more at home in lyric forms than in the fundamentally dramatic arena of the Beethoven 'sonata'. Certainly Schubert, Schumann and Chopin all wrote music in sonata form, but in varying degrees it was against their nature and better judgement. Thus when Schubert recapitulates his first subject in the subdominant and his second subject in the tonic, as he often does (in the 5th Symphony, for example), he is in no sense resolving the conflict of tonalities posed in the exposition, but merely repeating them at a pitch which will enable him to finish in the tonic. His lovely key-juxtapositions are the very negation of the purposeful modulation so characteristic of the development section of the classical sonata. Similarly, Schumann betrays how ill at ease he is with sonata form in numerous details, particularly in his piano sonatas, and occasionally in his quartets and symphonies. This is not to say that neither composer ever arrived at a true appreciation of the nature of sonata form. Yet the fact that they often missed the point is in itself an indication that the sonata idiom was not their natural language.

Nevertheless, Beethoven was both the law and the prophets, and all that lesser mortals could do was to obey. In particular, they followed the trend in Beethoven's music towards the integration of formal elements within a work, reasoning that the stronger the internal links, the more forceful the emotional impact of the whole. The desire to achieve the single, overwhelming artistic experience lay close to the heart of romantic musicians, and though they did not all agree that music should or could do this by itself, they recognized that the impact of music would be weakened unless there was maximum formal cohesion.

This was not just a question of doing away with the gaps between movements; rather of organizing material so that not only should there be variety of mood, but continuity of thought and unity of purpose as well. The principal means of attaining that unity which romantic composers so ardently desired was through the 'cyclic' device of transfer and transformation of musical ideas throughout a work, and of continuity from one movement to another. In both respects the influence of Beethoven is clear, but Schubert's 'Wanderer Fantasia' (1822) also provides us with an early example of physical continuity between its four 'movements', as well as the metamorphosis of a theme from movement to movement. Nothing that was to follow immediately was quite so remarkable in these respects. Certainly we get linkage, as for example between the first two movements of Mendelssohn's Violin Concerto (1844), and cyclic elements are not lacking. The same composer's early A major String Quartet Op. 13 (1827) makes use of thematic transfer and transformation between movements, while the first Piano Concerto, Op. 25 (1831) and 'Scotch' Symphony are each continuous and cyclic. Berlioz carries the idea a stage further, and both the 'Fantastic

Symphony' and 'Harold in Italy' have an *idée fixe* which is an obvious cyclic device. Schumann, too, came under the spell in the early 1840's. His fourth Symphony (1841)—played without a break—is cyclic, so are the Piano Concerto (1845), the last two movements of which are also linked, and the Piano Quintet (1842).

These last two works provide a good example of the two basic cyclic procedures that we find in the 19th century, thematic recall and thematic transformation, both of which, incidentally, are characteristic of the symphony's distant but direct ancestor— the canzona. In practice, these often overlap, since transformation is, after all, a type of recall; but at its simplest, thematic recall implies the return in a more or less recognizable form of an important theme from earlier in a work (often the opening theme of the first movement) in one or more subsequent movements, especially in the finale. This is what we have in the coda of the finale of the Quintet, where, the principal theme of the first movement is reintroduced and combined in a double fugue with the theme of the last movement (Ex. 16). Thematic transformation, on the other hand, implies a less obvious, more organic relationship between the themes of the various movements such as we find in the Quintet also, but more simply illustrated in the first and last movements of the Piano Concerto (Ex. 17 (i–ii)).

Ex.16

Ex.17

(i)

(ii)

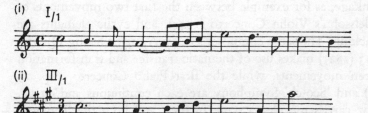

For all their experiments in running movements together and relating them thematically, these composers adhered to the traditional concept of the symphony, sonata or concerto so far as the number, order and character of movements were concerned. Admittedly the 'Fantastic Symphony' and Schumann's 'Rhenish' Symphony take a hint from Beethoven's 'Pastoral' and add another movement making five in all; so too did Schubert in the 'Trout' Quintet, Op. 114, (1819) and in the 'Octet', Op. 166 (1824) he went one further. And Mendelssohn followed Beethoven in writing a choral finale to his Second Symphony, the *Lobgesang* (1840). But generally composers were content to accept the conventional order and nature of the movements; first, a sonata-allegro often with a slow introduction; then, a slow movement followed by a scherzo (or these two reversed) and lastly, the finale.

The slow introduction to the first movement frequently contains a germinal theme destined to be used in the ensuing Allegro, and probably elsewhere in the work. Thus in Mendelssohn's 'Scotch' Symphony, the theme of the opening *Andante con moto* becomes the main theme in the Allegro, and is used again in the coda of the finale. The Allegro itself usually follows the thematic scheme of sonata form, with sometimes a remoter key than the dominant or relative minor for the second subject, such as a key a third above the tonic. In Schumann's C Major Symphony (no. 2, 1846), for example, the second subject is in E flat major (b.24 of the *Allegro ma non troppo*). The exposition is normally marked to be repeated, and in general the freedom with which Beethoven handled sonata form is seldom approached in the works of these composers. The development section is inclined to take itself seriously and rather self-consciously manipulate the thematic material of the exposition working up to a climax at which point the recapitulation starts fortissimo. The recapitulation may be freer than in classical sonata form, and as with Beethoven it is not infrequent for the key of the second subject to return a fifth lower than in the exposition, and not necessarily in the tonic. The coda reinforces the triumphal aspect of the recapitulation.

Significant changes occurred in the form of the first movement of the concerto, the most important being the abandonment of the opening orchestral tutti, notably in the concertos of Mendelssohn and Schumann. We may regard this as the final, long-delayed step in the changeover from ritornello form to sonata form in the concerto. Beethoven had hinted at a fusion of orchestral and soloistic functions, without ever dispensing with the opening tutti, by allowing the solo piano to invade the preserves of the orchestra at the start of the fourth and fifth piano concertos, so also did Mozart in his E flat Piano Concerto (K. 271). Whether or not it was Beethoven's example which prompted Mendelssohn to do away with the orchestral preamble is difficult to determine, for it was a period of transition both with regard to the form and the idea of the concerto, and composers like Louis Spohr (1784–1859) and Ignaz Moscheles (1794–1870)—to mention only two—were experimenting with unconventional designs. No doubt Mendelssohn was familiar with Spohr's Violin Concerto in the continuous form of a vocal *scena* (1816), and he himself was a notable exponent of Weber's *Konzertstück* in F minor (1821) in four sections but played without a break. Indeed, it was from the works of these composers, and Beethoven, of course, that he got the idea of linking the movements in his Piano Concerto in G minor. The same originality of outlook led to the transference of the cadenza in the first movement of his Violin Concerto from what would have been the normal place in the final tutti, to just before the recapitulation. Being to some extent developmental and climactic, the placing of the cadenza just before the start of the recapitulation was a typically logical move (which Tchaikowsky and Sibelius followed in their violin concertos), though there were probably other reasons for it as well. By tradition the cadenza contributed to the blaze of glory which brought the first movement to a rousing conclusion. But possibly Mendelssohn meant to play down this aspect for the very reason that the first two movements were to be linked, and that too great a sense of climax would detract from the continuity he was seeking. This may also have been why he wrote no cadenzas at all in his earlier piano concertos, though it must be recognized that bravura display would have been distasteful to him in works written for himself as soloist. Schumann's Piano Concerto and Cello Concerto (1850) dispense with the orchestral tutti: the latter also lacks a first-movement cadenza, renounced in favour of an orchestral link to the slow movement.

The two middle movements of these early romantic works often have programmatic associations, and there is a marked tendency to treat the slow movement and scherzo as static character-pieces. In particular, composers seem to have been drawn to the march as a suitable contrast to the first movement, probably on the twin precedents of Beethoven's third and seventh symphonies. The slow movement of Chopin's 'Funeral March' Sonata (B flat minor) and Mendelssohn's 'Italian' Symphony parallel these two works respectively, and other examples include the 'Pilgrim's March' from 'Harold in Italy' and the slow movement *In modo d'una marcia* of Schumann's Piano Quintet. In this latter example we have a rondo-sonata movement, with the principal section strongly slanted towards F minor despite a key signature of three flats, and with the first episode appearing first in C major and finally in F major. The middle section is an *Agitato* in F minor.

The march is just one example of the romantic inclination to make the slow movement a character-piece, usually in some kind of ternary form. The same tendency is observable in the scherzos, and one is not surprised to find that the scherzo from Mendelssohn's 'Octet' (Op. 20) was originally associated with a text from Goethe's 'Faust'.

In many cases the scherzo retained the minuet and trio form; sometimes, as in Mendelssohn's 'Italian' Symphony, it still has the character of a minuet, occasionally, that of a *ländler* as in Schubert's ninth, and Schumann's third Symphony. On the other hand, the scherzo of Mendelssohn's 'Scotch' Symphony is in duple time and sonata form, as is that of the Octet already mentioned. In many instances, particularly with Schumann, the quick 3/4 of the Beethoven scherzo has made the logical change to 6/8. Schumann's A major quartet (Op. 41 no. 3) has a scherzo in variation form, but the most obvious trend with Schumann is his use of the double trio. This is not the same thing as Beethoven's 'grand scherzo', for with Schumann the two trios are different. Both the first and second symphonies furnish examples, as do the Piano Quintet and the Piano Quartet. In the Quintet, the scherzo is based on a *marcato* scalic figure and is in rounded-binary form. The first trio (in G flat major) is more subdued and is canonic between 1st violin and viola; the second trio (in A flat minor) is longer and maintains a continuous semi-quaver movement. In between and at the end, the scherzo section returns, ending in a *con brio* coda.

These early romantic composers regarded the finale rather ambiguously. The symphonic finale was supposed to be the culmination of a work; the point to which the other movements had been directed. This view of the finale as a summing-up obviously derived from Beethoven's ninth Symphony, and in several instances composers adopted the principle of thematic recall which Beethoven had used. The 'Orgy of Brigands' which concludes Berlioz's 'Harold in Italy' starts with numerous '*souvenir*' passages in which all the previous movements are re-sampled before the orgy finally gets going, and we have observed Mendelssohn attempting a kind of apotheosis in the coda to the 'Scotch' Symphony. Other examples which may be mentioned include Schumann's recall of the *Feierlich* theme at the end of the 'Rhenish' Symphony, and the derivation of the thematic material of the last movement of the fourth Symphony from the first movement.

In their chamber music they were often content to allow the finale a less important place in the scheme of things, though the days of the relaxed, carefree rondo were virtually over. More often a rather manufactured liveliness is the main characteristic of what is frequently the feeblest movement of the four. Yet the sixteen-year-old Mendelssohn wrote a fugal finale to his Octet, hardly inferior in its way to the exquisite scherzo which it follows (and quotes in the coda). So too, in the coda to the finale of the Schumann Piano Quintet, where (as we have just seen) the principal themes of both the first and the last movements are combined in a double fugue.

In their dealings with the late 18th-century forms of the symphony, sonata, etc. these composers were, on the whole, ill at ease. They wrote in these forms because it was expected of them, and because their own self-respect demanded it, not because these were the means which best fitted their own creative ends. Perhaps only in their concertos did Mendelssohn and Schumann achieve viability. After all, the early 19th century was almost as much a period of transition as the early 17th century, or the middle of the 18th century, and we expect too much if we look for a perfect matching of form and content (Mendelssohn's scherzos excepted) at a time when forms were old and contents new—to put it crudely. Even so, these composers were defining new formal principles; in particular, movement continuity and cyclic unity, at the same time exploring rather tentatively, the compatibility of abstract form with programmatic content.

The tendency towards movement-continuity and thematic integration that is so characteristic of the music of Mendelssohn, Schumann and their contemporaries, finds its major focal point in the B minor Piano Sonata of Liszt. Apart from the general example of Beethoven's later works, Schubert's 'Wanderer Fantasia' was probably one of the key factors leading Liszt in this direction, for, as we have seen, this work is in four linked movements and makes use of thematic change, or metamorphosis, from one movement to another. It was a work which Liszt frequently played as a pianist and in 1851 he transcribed it as an arrangement for piano and orchestra. By this time his own piano concertos had been written (but not published) and in them he goes still further in the direction of cyclic continuity, so that in the A major Concerto (no. 2, but begun as early as 1839) it is hardly correct to speak of linked movements thematically related, but rather of a single work in several sections. Liszt himself is the historian of this development in the concerto. He wrote: 'In the old days, a concerto was in three movements: the first with three solos interspersed with the orchestra; the adagio; then the rondo. Field in his last concerto, has introduced the adagio via the second solo. Moscheles's "Concerto Fantastique" united the three parts into a single one. Weber first and Mendelssohn afterwards . . . attempted a similar design.'

It would seem as if John Field's introduction of the slow movement in place of the second solo, in other words, where there was normally development, anticipated Liszt's procedure in the B minor Piano Sonata by some years (Field had died in 1837). Not that the sonata lacks a development section; on the contrary, it is vast. Formally, the work exists on two levels; as a one-movement work in sonata form, and as a highly integrated three-movement work in the conventional quick–slow–quick pattern. The first movement, *Lento assai* leading into *Allegro energico*, introduces the main subject groups in B minor and its relative major respectively, within a continually developing thematic texture. This leads into an *Andante sostenuto*—the 'slow movement'—starting with a new theme, but also continuing the development of previous material, to be further explored in a fugue—the 'finale'—*Allegro energico* again. In this section the keys gradually come round to B minor, in which key the recapitulation of the subject material starts, with the second group following in B major—the tonic major. The coda recalls the *Andante sostenuto* and closes with a quotation from the opening *Lento assai*. It is, then, a giant sonata-form movement in which an extended development is interrupted by an andante episode. But for the *Grandioso* theme which marks the beginning of the second group, the principal subject material is all contained on the first page; the rest is metamorphosis and development.

In this and similar works Liszt established a new concept of the sonata which represented a significant step in the direction Beethoven had already foreshadowed in his mature works. Even so, just as Beethoven's immediate successors were in certain respects too timid to take his ideas further towards their logical conclusion, so too were Liszt's, and in many ways Saint-Saëns, Franck and Tchaikowsky are to Liszt rather as Mendelssohn, Schumann and Berlioz were to Beethoven. Saint-Saëns' first Violin Concerto (1859) is a one-movement work consisting of a sonata movement with a slow episode in place of the development. Its antecedents are obvious. He did the same sort of thing in his first Cello

Concerto in A minor (1873), this time separating the development from the recapitulation with an episodic *Allegretto con moto*, and also in the fourth Piano Concerto in C minor (1875) where the second movement is really a scherzando development of material contained in the first. As one would expect, there is a considerable amount of thematic metamorphosis in all these; so too, in the third Symphony (1886).

César Franck's name is inseparably linked with the cyclic method, and in the Piano Quintet (1879), the Violin Sonata (1886), the Symphony (1888) and the String Quartet (1889) he uses it to obtain an overall thematic unity without attempting movement-continuity. Tchaikowsky's symphonies too, are cyclic; not so much in the rather obvious return of the initial 'fate' motive towards the end of the finale in the fourth Symphony (1877) as in the quotations and derivations which permeate the fifth (1888) and sixth (1893) symphonies.

In the general run of late 19th-century sonata-movements it is still possible to distinguish the three main divisions, even though the dividing line between exposition and development is not always so obvious as the double bar of old (though Brahms's first three symphonies have the expositions of their first movements marked to be repeated). But the increasing trend towards chromatic harmony and vacillating modulation continued to undermine the structural function of tonality.

It is true that Liszt, Franck and Tchaikowsky usually go through the conventional motions with regard to key contrast in the exposition and return to the tonic in the recapitulation of their first subjects at least. Even so, sonata form to these composers is less a balanced modulatory process than a cumulative thematic one. Structural tonality is almost an irrelevancy, and exposing and recapitulating in accordance with tonal principles—even the business of beginning and ending in the same key—is largely a matter of convention. Any key will sound right if the shaping of the emotional and dynamic forces has made the moment right, as Mahler was to demonstrate.

However, with Johannes Brahms (1833–1897) and Anton Bruckner (1824–1896) we have a pair of composers who, for their own reasons and in their own very different ways were conservatives, eschewing the use of a programme and observing the normal arrangement of movements in their symphonies. Each uses cyclic devices and regards tonality as an important unifying principle, although the range of modulation within a movement, and of keys within a symphony is expanded. The movements themselves are separated, yet one recognizes an inner emotional unity—with Bruckner more so than with Brahms—which binds the whole together.

We need not be detained by Bruckner's or Brahms's handling of sonata form in detail. It may not have come naturally to either of them, but Brahms mastered it and used it like a craftsman and Bruckner at least found that it gave him a serviceable plan to follow. The three-fold division is usually clear, though with Brahms the texture is much more continuous and close-knit than with Bruckner, who is apt to be episodic and discursive. Their ideas of what constituted exposition, development and recapitulation were quite orthodox. Thus in the exposition, as a result of the tendency for cadence themes to secede from the second group, we often get three groups of subject material which Bruckner frequently treats as almost self-contained units, distinguishing the second by the title *Gesangsperiode* (i.e. 'melodic section') from the more motivic character of the first section. Each thematic group in a Bruckner first movement tends to start softly, building up to a climax and tailing off again. Development sections, too, start from nothing. Ponderously sequential, they get under way, modulating enharmonically and making much of thematic combinations and mirror inversions of the subject material. The recapitulation of the first group is in the tonic key, but the others merely return, not necessarily in the tonic or even in the key a fifth lower than the exposition, in which case it is left to a soaring coda to re-establish the home key and bring the movement to a close. Most of these points are illustrated in the first movement of the fourth Symphony (1874), though they apply fairly generally. Similarly, the scherzo of that Symphony may stand for the others in its bucolic high spirits and clear-cut ternary form.

Links between the movements of Bruckner's symphonies are often discernible. In this respect, perhaps the most interesting are the fifth (1877, the fugal finale of which, like much else in Bruckner, follows Beethoven's ninth by starting off with recollections from the previous movements), and the eighth (1887, where themes from all four movements are woven together in the coda of the finale). Brahms instinctively recoiled from bringing back earlier themes in triumph; the Lisztian 'return of the prodigal' was not for him. Yet a more subtle interrelationship of themes throughout a particular work is often traceable, the result sometimes of an unconscious process no doubt, as well as a natural tendency to base themes on triads. Brahms's veneration for Schumann is also a factor to be borne in mind, and we have seen that thematic metamorphosis became an obsession with Schumann in his later works. Thus the often remarked upon and unmistakable family likeness displayed among the themes of the second Symphony (1877) is but a happy example of a process which Brahms inherited from Schumann and made his own (Ex. 18 (i–x)).

It is what one might have expected from such a superb writer of variations. Melody and figuration are the principal variables in his most famous sets; the harmonic implications of their themes

Ex.18

and particularly their periodic structure are normally preserved from one variation to another. In fact, Brahms strongly favours the 'Goldberg' type of variation where form and harmonic progression provide the underlying, unchanging material, in contrast to the freer, more loosely connected variation technique of Franck's *Variations Symphoniques* (1885) or Elgar's 'Enigma Variations' (1899). The difference between strict and free variation treatment can hardly be better illustrated than by comparing Brahms's two sets of 'Studies on a theme of Paganini' (1863) with Rachmaninov's 'Rhapsody' on the same theme (1934), and we have further examples of Brahms's approach in variations on themes by Handel for piano (1861), Haydn for orchestra (1873) and the finale of the fourth Symphony. In the latter case we have his variation technique laid bare. There is no theme in the usual sense, merely eight chords harmonizing a chaconne bass taken from Bach's cantata no. 150 (which Brahms no doubt found in volume 30 of the *Gesellschaft* edition, to which he subscribed, and which came out in 1884, the year he was at work on the symphony). This ostinato is repeated thirty times in all, each time with different melodic and figuration treatment before culminating in the coda. Not only does the technique remind one of the 'Goldberg Variations'; so does the fact of there being thirty variations divided into two halves, a fresh start (so to speak) being made at Variation 16.

Clearly Brahms was a traditionalist; his insistence on the full-scale opening orchestral ritornello in his concertos is further evidence of this. If he modified the traditional form of the symphony in any way it was in his more relaxed treatment of the middle two movements. Slow movements become Andantes; scherzos become Allegrettos. For example, the second movements of his symphonies bear the following markings respectively—*Andante sostenuto, Adagio non troppo, Andante* and *Andante moderato*; while the third movements are marked *Un poco allegretto e grazioso, Allegretto grazioso (quasi andantino), Poco allegretto*, and—the only real scherzo—*Allegro giocoso*. Similarly in his chamber music, where, symptomatically he actually calls the scherzo of the G minor Piano Quartet Op. 25 (1861) 'Intermezzo'—a fitting term for movements which are more wistful than jocular. Normally he favours ternary form with one or two trios contrasting in mood, tempo and key; though in the second Symphony the episodes are presto variations on the allegretto refrain, while the scherzo of the fourth is a sonata-rondo movement.

At least one other aspect of Brahms's music is worth commenting on—the introduction of national or folk material into his chamber works, though it is not directly relevant to form as such. Brahms perhaps affected the gypsy style as an exoticism, rather as classical Viennese composers did in their rondos 'all' ongarese' or 'alla turca'. Thus we have the 'Rondo alla Zingarese' finale to

the G minor Piano Quartet, Op. 25. His admiration and friend-
ship for the Hungarian violinist Joseph Joachim may have had
something to do with it, for there are Hungarian characteristics
scattered throughout his chamber music. In the case of Smetana
and Antonin Dvořák (1841–1904), of course, we expect
nationalistic tendencies to appear. Smetana's autobiographical
String Quartet 'From my Life' (1876) has a scherzo in polka
rhythm, while Dvořák's chamber music provides copious
examples of the *dumka* and *furiant*—see particularly the quartet
in E flat, Op. 51 (1879), and, of course, the 'Dumky' Trio, Op.
90 (1891).

The polarities represented by the Bruckner–Brahms pair find a
more exaggerated expression in Gustav Mahler (1860–1911) and
Jean Sibelius (1865–1957). Brahms had revelled in the discipline
imposed by strict sonata form, and Sibelius's own constructivist
approach is revealed in his conversation with Mahler regarding
the essence of the symphony. 'I said that I admired its severity
and style and the profound logic that created an inner connection
between all the motifs.' To which Mahler replied, 'No! The
symphony must be like the world: it must embrace everything',
and in so doing he spoke as much on behalf of Bruckner's narrow,
inarticulate but deeply felt world as for his own feverish eclectic-
ism. Not that we should be too eager to associate Mahler and
Bruckner together, despite traces of Bruckner's style in some of
Mahler's Adagios. Mahler's symphonies, which span the years
1888–1909, seem, superficially at least, to stem more directly
from Berlioz and Liszt. Indeed, Berlioz and Mahler have a lot in
common: not only in the all-embracing heterogeneity of their
symphonies, but also in their penchant for marches and massed
effects, their contrapuntal facility, their originality in orchestration, and often in the vulgarity (and delicacy) of certain passages.

Mahler's purely orchestral symphonies are numbers one, five,
six, seven and nine. These are more conventional in their exterior
than the others (which have vocal and/or choral movements),
and are not overtly programmatic. Even so, they illustrate many
of the characteristics that typify instrumental movements in all
the symphonies. For example, the fifth, sixth and seventh each

begin with march-like movements (so does the second), and march episodes are to be found in nearly all the symphonies. The same three symphonies have scherzos strongly influenced by the waltz and *ländler*, and this too is typical. Marches and dances not lending themselves to sonata treatment, it is not surprising to find Mahler naturally drawn towards ternary and rondo forms, not only for such movements, but as a general tendency. In fact, with Mahler, sonata and rondo forms are barely distinguishable, for his enormous codas tend to make a sonata-movement into a rondo, by adding yet another development and recapitulation. Thus:

Sonata form			Coda	
Exp.	Dev.	Recap.	Dev.	Recap.
A^1	B^1	A^2	B^2	A^3

Rondo

Long codas, multiplicity of themes and general prolixity combine to make Mahler's symphonic movements the longest in existence, a situation which is aggravated in at least two instances by the recapitulation of long introductory sections as well (the first movement of the third Symphony and the last movement of the sixth).

The fifth Symphony (1902) illustrates many of these points. Its five movements are divided into two balancing 'Parts', as we find also in the third and eighth symphonies. The opening 'Funeral March' in C sharp minor and the 'stormy' sequel to it (in A minor) comprise Part I; the 'Scherzo', '*Adagietto*' and 'Rondo-finale'—respectively in D major, F major and D major—form Part II. Immediately noticeable is the lack of key-unity in the symphony as a whole. This is quite common in Mahler's symphonies, and is in part a manifestation of his all-embracing view of the form, rather than a premonition of approaching atonality—for Mahler was reasonably conservative in matters relating to the internal tonal structure of individual movements. This 'progressive tonality' is not quite without system, as we shall see.

Copious thematic relationships can be traced both within and between the movements of each Part. It is largely the similarity of movement, rhythm and accompaniment that relates the main theme of the 'Funeral March' (Peters 1904 ed. fig. 2) to the second theme of the following movement (5 bars after fig. 5); an overall relationship which is strengthened by the upward leap and semitonal fall of the 'wild' trio of the March (oboes and flutes fig. 7) permeating the whole of the second movement from bar 6 onwards (see flutes, oboes and clarinets). However, the second movement is something more than a development of the 'Funeral March,' as has been claimed: it is complementary to, rather than dependent on, the preceding movement. (We shall find something comparable in Sibelius's fifth Symphony.) Indeed, the second movement of the Mahler may be regarded as a sonata-allegro movement (with typically Mahlerian rondo touches) following a slow introduction.

Apart from the omnipresent motive of the falling semitone, the exposition of the second movement presents two principal subjects, the first—'stormy'—in A minor, the second, a self-contained episode in F minor (figs. 5–9) derived from the march theme in the first movement. A return to the opening theme in A minor suggests that the movement will continue as a rondo, a suggestion which is strengthened momentarily by what follows— the march theme again, now in E flat minor (fig. 12). But this is not so much the beginning of another episode as the commencement of the development section; a montage of thematic material from both movements. The recapitulation starts in A minor (fig. 18) with only a bare allusion to the first subject, but the second subject is treated at length starting in E minor (fig. 20). From there further developments and reminiscences lead to a chorale in D major (fig. 27); D major reverts to D minor (fig. 30), and after more development of the first theme the movement subsides in A minor.

Thematically and tonally, this movement links up both with what has gone before and what is to follow; with the first, as well as the second Part of the symphony. It is interesting to observe that the key of the second movement is anticipated in a lengthy A minor episode at the end of the first movement (starting at fig. 15), and not only is the key of the second Part of the symphony prefigured in the blazing D major chorale towards the end of the second movement, but the themes of the finale actually derive from this chorale which is finally and magnificently reassembled at the conclusion of the work (figs. 32–34, last movement).

Yet, taken as a whole Mahler's construction, unlike Sibelius's, is episodic rather than truly organic. Without succumbing to the programme-domination and luxurious warmth of the post-Liszt Romantics, Sibelius found himself naturally drawn towards the idea of unity through continuity and thematic metamorphosis. The second Symphony (1901) shows us the composer in control of the essential features of orthodox sonata form in the first movement, but already he gives us a hint of things to come by joining the scherzo to the finale without a break in a way which is perhaps not very different from Beethoven's in his fifth Symphony. In the third Symphony (1907) the last two movements are even more closely integrated; the finale growing out of the scherzo by a process, which, like much in Sibelius, can only inadequately be demonstrated on paper. To the ear it sounds absolutely natural and inevitable.

The first two movements of the fifth Symphony (1915) are also continuous; the opening movement serving as a kind of slow introduction to the 'scherzo' which follows. Formally there is a high degree of integration between the two movements, and in fact, taken together they form a giant rondo-like structure with returns firmly in E flat major, and developmental episodes. The way in which these two movements are integrated may be shown as follows:

A1 {
Tempo molto moderato. The movement begins with an orthodox sonata-form exposition with principal horn-call theme (Ex. 19(i)) in E flat followed by a group of secondary themes in G major, but instead of being developed they are immediately recapitulated in E flat (6 bars after E–J). Strictly, the movement so far is an example of abridged sonata form, but with regard to the whole it may be described as a double exposition.
}

B { From J a development of the chromatic second subject starts speeding up towards N and making a transition to *Allegro moderato*, although the return to E flat and the true beginning of the Scherzo occurs at the new B.

A2 { The horn-call theme is metamorphosed (Ex. 19(ii)) and provides the main subject of the scherzo exposition (B–E).

C { Yet another form of this subject (Ex. 19(iii)) is developed in the episode starting in B major.

A3 { The final return starts 9 bars after N with highly condensed references to first and second subjects, thus recapitulating both the *molto moderato* and *allegro moderato* sections, and ending with a *Più presto* coda.

Ex. 19

Here then we have two movements each of which fulfils some formal function with respect to the other, since the exposition of the scherzo is at the same time the first return of the principal subject in the tonic key. This interdependence is carried further in the seventh Symphony (1924) which is in one movement. Actually, in form it bears certain resemblances to the pair of movements we have been considering. Again, we have a sort of rondo, though in this case it is the central adagio section that functions as the first return. Germs of nearly all the themes are to be found within the first twenty bars of the work, two of the most important occur on either side of letter A (Ex. 20 (i) and (iv)). The two principal themes which emerge almost immediately (Ex. 20 (v) and (ii)) are not markedly changed in themselves throughout the symphony and thus provide easily identifiable landmarks which we may recognize in the course of our journey; but the actual substance of the music is a protoplasmic connecting tissue of derived motives in a process of continual development. We may follow the transformation of two of them during the course of the first episode or development. One (motive z) is basically scalic and obviously derives from the opening bars of the symphony, the other (motive y) at its simplest comprises three notes descending by step then rising a semitone. Near the beginning, at letter G (Ex. 20 (vi)) both these motives are still somewhat vague in form, but as the tempo increases they become more concise until, at the change to 6/4 after letter I, (Ex. 20 (vii)) a stable form is achieved which provides the thematic basis of the *Vivacissimo* development from J onwards. Following the adagio return of the two main themes in C minor—the tonic minor (L–N)—the development is resumed, but a new theme (Ex. 20 (iii)) in C major bursts out at the *Allegro molto moderato*, marking the beginning of the scherzo episode. Although the first phrase of this tune does not seem to arise directly from any previous material, its unabashed C major with a prominent D does recall the second of the two principal themes (Ex. 20 (ii)), and a few bars later (P) there are positive references to this theme. The second limb of the scherzo theme (Ex. 20 (viii)) is motive x in another guise, while the second subject in A minor (Ex. 20 (ix)) derives from y. Although the main theme of the scherzo returns in C major as a sort of false reprise at letter R the recapitulation proper starts in E flat major, with the second subject following nine bars after U in C minor, that is, still in the relative minor.

The transition to the final section of the symphony, the recapitulation of the work as a whole, starts *Vivace* and accelerates to *Presto*. But slowly rising scales on the horns over a throbbing pedal G, and a gradual rallentando lead into the C major *Adagio* which reviews the most important themes of the work in virtually their original form.

So far as the motivic construction of the work is concerned there is a great deal more that could be pointed out, and though

Ex. 20

there is room for argument about the precise mode of deriving one motive from another, enough has been shown to give an idea of Sibelius's thematic process. It may be a particular rhythmic characteristic which provides the thread linking one idea with another, or a brief melodic idiom, perhaps no more than a striking interval, a scalic progression, or the contour of a piece of apparently insignificant figuration. Because of the amorphous nature of his themes, they are all the more flexible. One never gets the impression that Sibelius is self-consciously forging new themes from old; they always seem to be lurking in the shadows. It is a process of free association, an amoeba-like plasticity which, though it may seem natural, is demonstrably art imitating nature.

When it comes to the structural function of tonality, Sibelius presents us with a stark contrast to the profuse and colourful modulations of the late 19th-century Viennese composers. In their work, modulation is so frequent and key juxtaposition so extreme that the pull of the tonic is almost cancelled out. This is far from the case with Sibelius, who goes to the other extreme and seems to banish all keys except the tonic. His music is 'mono-tonal' and neither the tonal inequilibrium that drives a classical movement to its conclusion, nor the tonal incidents which help to propel a romantic work from one bar to the next play an important role in his composition. The returns to the tonic from what might be described as a sort of tonal 'outer-space' are due more to a kind of vast gravitational pull generated through lengthy ostinatos and pedals emphasizing the tonic note, than through the interaction of different key-areas. Both the main themes in the seventh Symphony appear throughout in C, and for the most part one is unaware of any other key-centre of any significance. It is true that the recapitulation of the scherzo starts in E flat major, but this is surely an instance of Sibelius's indifference to key-duality as a structural component. For though the first subject is recapitulated in E flat, the second subject returns in precisely the same relationship to it as in the exposition, i.e. in the relative minor. In other words, as with Schubert's subdominant recapitulations, nothing is resolved between the two at all.

Sibelius's symphonies, though a side-shoot from the late 19th-century Teutonic tradition of the symphony, are a logical outcome of the development towards thematic integrity and continuity of movement that began with Beethoven. In this respect the seventh Symphony—and *Tapiola* (1925) among the Symphonic poems—marks a point beyond which progress is scarcely possible without some radical reorientation; a *ne plus ultra*, or a dead-end, depending on your point of view. (On the other hand, a less thorough-going approach has not prevented equally satisfactory essays in symphonic form: Elgar's first and Vaughan Williams's fourth Symphony—to mention only two English examples, but particularly fine ones—employ cyclic devices more conventionally, but cogently and with powerful benefit to the four-movement structure as a whole.) However, the most advanced 20th-century composers have fought shy of the symphony in either Sibelius's or Mahler's terms (though to some extent Mahler may be said to live on in the symphonies of Shostakovich), and perhaps only in Bartók's string quartets do we find a significant up-dating of what are basically 19th-century thematic devices of construction.

But the specifically 20th-century applications of the cyclic principle are Schoenberg's twelve-note method of composition, and the serial techniques to which it has given rise. The reasoning that lay behind the twelve-note system and the situation which called it into being will be considered in greater detail later, but for the moment it will be sufficient to point out that in seeking to derive all the thematic and harmonic material of a piece from a basic set of notes (which amounts in effect to a chromatic 'motto theme') Schoenberg was, to this extent, merely reapplying the idea of thematic transformation which is, as we have seen, the foundation of cyclic unity in the 19th-century sense.

IV : 3 Grand Opera and Music Drama

In many respects, opera in the 19th century shows a parallel development with instrumental music especially in the trend towards continuity and thematic integration. Before this could take place, however, a much more serious approach to the dramatic functions of music was needed than that prevailing in 18th-century Italian *opera seria*. On the other hand, French opera had never been so mesmerized by purely musical aspects, and it is to the Lullian tradition rather than the Neapolitan that one must turn to discover the beginnings of this new orientation.

The seriousness of purpose and elevated style of Jean Philippe Rameau (1683–1764) was to influence the better composers of *opera seria*, and in particular Gluck in his so-called 'reform operas'. What Gluck (prompted no doubt by his theorizing librettist Ranieri Calzabigi) wanted to reform were the conventions of Italian opera which recognized the importance of the singer, the music and then the drama in that order, instead of the reverse. Thus in the preface to *Alceste* (1767) he stated, 'I have striven to restrict music to its true office of serving poetry by means of expression and by following the situations of the story without interrupting the action or stifling it with useless superfluity of ornaments.' *Orfeo ed Euridice* (1762) was the first opera in which he put these principles into practice, and although it was originally written in Italian for Vienna, it embodies many elements of the French tradition. Both *Orfeo* and *Alceste* were later given in Paris in French versions, respectively in 1774 and 1776, and it was for Paris that he wote *Iphigénie en Aulide* (1774) and *Iphigénie en Tauride* (1779).

As with the older French operas, the chorus and the ballet remain important ingredients. However, the overture is no longer of the Lullian type, and the recitative has lost the flexibility that was such a feature of the musical declamation of Lully and Rameau. A great deal of it is more or less *secco* in style—though dignified enough—but by far its most important aspect is that it is accompanied by the orchestra throughout. Rameau, and the later 'Neapolitans' Hasse and Jommelli, had used *recitativo accompagnato* extensively, but by going the whole hog Gluck made one of his most important contributions to the development of opera. For in discarding the conventional harpsichord continuo accompaniment, the transition from recitative to air and back again, which had spoiled the dramatic and musical continuity of *opera seria*, inevitably became smoother. This continuity of orchestral timbre, coupled with the less frequent use of the perfunctory perfect cadence at the close of recitatives, was to facilitate the closer integration of recitatives, ariosos, airs and choruses into dramatic units which sometimes extend over several scenes in his later Paris operas. All this is perhaps best exemplified in *Iphigénie en Aulide*, which, of all the reform operas shows how unimportant the air had become. It was necessary that it should be so if the halting dramatic movement of *opera seria* was to be remedied.

Airs were not purged altogether, though they became fewer and shorter: the full scale *da capo* aria with its lengthy ritornello and opportunity for vocal display became a thing of the past. Instead we find simpler airs in binary and ternary form, together with a variety of forms built of alternating sections often involving chorus. Others are through-composed, freely adapting, transposing and repeating sections in their course.

Gluck is really the fountain-head of French Grand Opera, though in the hands of Luigi Cherubini (1760–1842), Gasparo Spontini (1774–1851), Gioacchino Rossini (1792–1868) and Giacomo Meyerbeer (1791–1864) it undoubtedly fell from grace subsequently. It is a wry fact that none of these lions of French opera was a Frenchman, and, since three were Italian, and all four had spent some time in Italy before they went to Paris, it is hardly surprising that Italian influences should be discernible in their music. However, not all Gluck's gains were lost, and the set-piece aria gradually gave up its independence in the interests of unity and continuity of music and drama.

To some extent the aria achieved a reprieve by being absorbed into the *scena*—which might be described as a subdivision of the action which is musically continuous and dramatically all of a piece. As such, it is the dramatic and musical unit in early 19th-century Grand Opera, and within it, the aria was still the main point of focus, though less so than it had been in the 18th century. The musical components were generally more flexibly treated, and might comprise one or two arias, a duet, a *terzetto* or chorus perhaps, as well as recitative, or the *scena* might be in recitative throughout. The stylistic dichotomy between recitative and aria is still quite pronounced with Gaetano Donizetti (1797–1848) and Vincenzo Bellini (1801–1835) and there is no mistaking the arias. On occasions they may be fairly long but the construction is usually quite simple, being often in a kind of binary *ballade*-form, strophically treated, or based on some alternation scheme with or without chorus. The more languid airs were sometimes called *cavatina, canzone, romanza*, etc., while *cabaletta* denoted a lively conclusion or sequel to an aria in lyrical style. Despite the musical self-sufficiency of the *scena*, it does not necessarily begin and end in the same key—the form is, as it were, left open. Yet underlying the sequence that goes to form the larger whole, the act, we may often perceive a plan of modulations still based on natural key-relationships, in particular those a fifth apart. Thus between the end of one *scena* and the beginning of another a tonal link is established which gives cohesion between the two, yet conveys the idea of progress forward as well.

As an example of a *scena* the famous '*Miserere*' scene from *Il Trovatore* (1853) by Giuseppe Verdi (1813–1901) may be quoted. Here we have recitative, air and chorus, yet we are conscious of the *scena* as a whole rather than its parts. It opens in F minor with an almost whispered dialogue between Ruiz and Leonora in recitative. This leads into a slow aria '*D'amor sull'ali rosee*' beginning simply in F minor and continuing with a balancing section in A flat major. But instead of a return to the tonic, the chorus interrupts with the *'Miserere'* to be followed by Leonora's query *'Quel suon, quelle preci'* and Manrico's *'Ah! che la morte ognora'*, answering A flat minor with A flat major. This tripartite sequence is then repeated to different words, with the A flat melody extending into a coda in which Leonora and the chorus also participate. Seven bars of linking recitative modulate from A flat major back to F (F major this time), and the *scena* ends with Leonora's agitated *'Tu vedrai che amore in terra'*, a *cabaletta* in binary form, the words and music of which are repeated and concluded with a rousing coda.

Verdi's operatic career spans a vast period; La Scala, Milan, presenting his first opera in 1839 and his last, and possibly finest work, *Falstaff*, in 1893. In the intervening years his style changed enormously, but throughout he conceived opera essentially in melodic terms, eschewing Wagner's symphonic approach. Even so, the instrumental aspect became increasingly important towards the end, while the regular, rather short-winded melodic phrases of his earlier style developed a wonderful flexibility and resourcefulness in his later operas. Formally, the basic components of recitative and aria are more subtly integrated, the sectionalization less apparent; see Act III of *Aida* (1871), for example. But it is not really until *Otello* (1887) that the *scena* as a musico-dramatic entity disappears altogether, swallowed up in the larger unit, the act. Even here we can still find arias: in the last act, two for Desdemona—the 'Willow Song' and *'Ave Maria'*—both in a type of *ballade*-form (*AABC*), but they are led into and away from almost imperceptibly by the recitative, and furthermore, being dramatically appropriate, they do not hold up the action unnecessarily.

Parallel with the development of musical continuity within the *scena* is the enlargement of the scope of the finale in Grand Opera. The finale, in fact, is the *scena* which concludes the act. Its early development belongs, as we have seen, to the history of *opera buffa* (see pp. 107–9), but towards the end of the 18th century it was transplanted into *opera seria*—Paisiello's *Pirro* (1787), provides an early example—whence its obvious potential as a musical and dramatic climax was to be developed in French Grand Opera. As a result there was a tendency to relegate the airs to the earlier part of the act where they would not hold up the action or disrupt the cumulative effect built up in the finale by means of swiftly alternating dialogue and a rapid succession of ensembles and choruses. This forward drive helped to shape and give continuity to the whole act by virtue of the momentum generated, and in this respect the finales of Rossini—in 'William Tell' (1829), for example—and Meyerbeer should be mentioned. Some idea of their length and variety of movement may be gained from the fact that in the 804 bars in the finale of Act 1 of Meyerbeer's last opera *L'Africaine* (1865) there are 38 double bars marking the structural subdivisions that change of time and key-signature normally indicate. But there is no break in the continuity of the music itself.

In many respects it was the French concept of Grand Opera that Richard Wagner (1813–1883) inherited, though by the year of *L'Africaine* he had well and truly disowned it. *Rienzi* (1840) is quite another story, and the mark of Spontini and Meyerbeer is heavily upon it. But he was also influenced by German Romantic Opera, and we can see some of the origins of Wagner's approach in the *singspiele* of Carl Maria von Weber (1786–1826)—*Der Freischütz* (1821)—and Heinrich Marschner (1795–1861)—*Der Vampyr* (1828) and *Hans Heiling* (1833)—both of which had an influence on Wagner's 'Flying Dutchman' (1841).

Undoubtedly *Der Freischütz* is a starting point, but in *Euryanthe* (1823) Weber went a stage further in setting the complete text of the opera to music. Thus banishing spoken dialogue from German opera (though it was the only time he did so) he made musical continuity a possibility at least, and his use of 'identifying themes' (virtually leitmotives—there are a dozen or more) showed how they could provide a cohesive element in the overall musical structure, as well as underline a dramatic point. Not that he was the first to do so, for isolated examples can be cited well back in the history of opera. We find them in Grétry's *Richard Cœur de Lion* (1784) and Méhul's *Ariodant* (1799), for instance, and as a unifying device among the orchestral episodes accompanying spoken dialogue in the 'melodramas' of Georg Benda (1722–1795). Indeed, it is not only in their use of identifying themes that these late 18th-century melodramas point to Wagner: dialogue spoken against an orchestral background (used—following Benda—by Mozart, Beethoven, and freely in Weber's *Der Freischütz*) is a premonition of Wagnerian *sprechgesang*, with its vast symphonic commentary by the orchestra, and not only that, but the proto-type of Schoenberg's *sprechstimme*.

Wagner had largely assimilated the French and German influences in *Tannhäuser* (1844), still more in *Lohengrin* (1848), though he still pandered to the German fondness for the super-natural and the French for the spectacular. Formally, however, we have something new. Instead of the 'stop-go' alternation of aria and recitative the division into 'numbers' is almost entirely obscured. Further, we find the beginnings of Wagner's continuous flow of 'unending melody' (to use his own term): an expressive, melodic recitative which with greater flexibility was to become the '*sprechgesang*'—speech-song—of his later works. It is true that there are still a few set pieces in *Lohengrin*, and some barely disguised old-fashioned recitative, but the direction he was to take in the future is clearly indicated. There is no overture, as such; he had written his last for *Tannhäuser*. Instead we have an orchestral prelude, suggestive of the spiritual background of the opera. Like the prelude to 'Tristan and Isolde' (1859) its form is really that of a gradual crescendo building up to a climax, then dying away, ending as it began. The key of the prelude, A major, is associated with the hero Lohengrin throughout the opera, and in the finale of Act III material from the prelude is recalled as Lohengrin answers the 'forbidden question' and discloses his name and origin. Similarly, leitmotives identifying certain people or ideas are used as appropriate to the story, though still rather stiffly.

Everything in *Lohengrin* points in the direction of greater unity and continuity: unity through the use of themes and keys which have a dramatic and structural significance, continuity through the 'unending melody' of the *sprechgesang* and the orchestral texture. This was to be most fully realized in the four music dramas of 'The Ring' (1853-1874). Ensembles as such are almost entirely absent from 'The Ring', and there is much less chorus work than in *Lohengrin*. The movement is generally ponderous, and the *sprechgesang* makes infrequent deviations in the direction of 'pure' melody. Viewed structurally these four music dramas may be seen as vast symphonies, each act a movement (each opera a movement even!), the whole held together by an intricate network of thematic cross-references. Wagner himself said, 'the new form of dramatic music must have the unity of a symphony movement to become a musical work of art. This unity is given by a tissue of basic motives permeating the whole composition. These motives act upon one another, linking up, separating, complementing, like motives in a symphony movement.' Not the least important aspect is the broad key-scheme which underlies the symphonic structure. Lorenz has described *Das Rheingold* (the first of the four) as a vast movement in ternary form, basically in D flat major, but with an introduction in E flat. In fact, throughout 'The Ring', the key of D flat has a structural function similar to the tonic key in a purely instrumental symphonic work.

It has been suggested that the basic principles underlying the structure of Wagner's 'unending melody' is that of the minnesinger 'bar' (*AAB*). Whether this is really so, or whether repetition followed by continuation is such a basic (and often unconscious) element of vocal form that one can always find some evidence of it, is a matter for argument—actually, these two propositions amount to the same thing. However, it cannot be denied that in 'The Mastersingers' (1867) Wagner reveals himself fully aware of the rules of bar-form, for Kothner instructs Walther in Act I scene 3: 'A bar consists of two strophes ('*stollen*') of several lines each, the same tune for both. Then comes the '*abgesang*', again several lines in length, but to a different melody.' Furthermore, he puts precept into practice in Beckmesser's '*Den Tag seh'ich erscheinen*' (*AAB, AAB, CDE*—which, though formally correct is not to be taken seriously as music). Walther's '*Am stillen Herd*', '*So rief der Lenz*' (intentionally inept) and finally the two versions of the 'prize-song' '*Morgenlich leuchtend*' show his progress in form, and composition, as well as love! Of course, the story of the 'song contest' with which the opera deals, justifies the inclusion of these more or less set-pieces which otherwise could have no place according to Wagner's theories. 'The Mastersingers', beginning and ending in C major, and *Parsifal* (1882), beginning and ending in A flat major (for all its wanderings), show the same sort of tonal unity that we have observed in connection with 'The Ring'. On the other hand, the elusive tonality (and in places near 'atonality') that is exemplified in 'Tristan and Isolde' may be cited as the point of origin of many of the harmonic developments of the 20th century.

To the legacy of Verdi and Wagner respectively, Giacomo Puccini (1858–1924) and Richard Strauss brought sensationalism and a rather more advanced harmonic vocabulary. Both used leitmotives; Strauss the Wagnerian *sprechgesang* and symphonic texture in his *Salome* (1905) and *Elektra* (1909). Sickened perhaps by the excesses of these operas, and feeling rather as Schoenberg did at the same time and in a similar position, that colossal romanticism was played out, he retired to the 18th century, at first only in the actual setting of *Der Rosenkavalier* (1911), but later in aesthetic as well. This period of reaction, reaction to Wagner in particular, was not confined to Strauss and Schoenberg alone, or to opera. It was a manifestation of a general trend towards a neo-classical outlook just before 1920, the beginnings of which can be traced back a good deal earlier. Strauss's words in 1916, 'I promise that I have now definitely cast off the whole armour of Wagner for evermore' recall Debussy's in 1893, when (starting to compose *Pelléas et Mélisande*) he wrote, 'the ghost of old Klingsor, *alias* R. Wagner, appeared at the turning of one of the bars, so I tore the whole thing up and struck off on a new line'. (Not that Debussy's reaction was as perverse as Stravinsky's who in his 'Rake's Progress' (1951) reverted to 'number opera' complete with *recitativo secco* accompanied on the harpsichord.) Debussy's declamation is consistently moulded to the words— French *sprechgesang*, if you like; the orchestral texture is continuous and uses leitmotives. But he abjures the Wagnerian bombast; the drama is carried on *sotto voce* rather than in full voice, and (as he said in effect) 'my silences are expressive, whereas Wagner's (if there are any) are dramatic'. The whole opera is intensely personal, and perhaps owes more to Moussorgsky's *Boris Godounov* (1869) than to any other single opera—apart from 'Tristan'!

The most important break through the Wagnerian sound barrier came with *Wozzeck* (1921) by Alban Berg (1885–1935). Schoenberg's 'monodrama' *Erwartung* (1909)—actually a *scena*—showed the way to some extent by relying less on leitmotives than the sheer expressionism of the music to convey meaning and feeling. Further, in *Pierrot Lunaire* (1912), though it is not an opera, Schoenberg took Wagner's *sprechgesang* a step further (or rather, a step back), by treating spoken monologue with musical accompaniment in a manner derived from the melodrama, though in a lyrical manner. This resulted in a kind of musical declamation that was spoken rather than sung, which nevertheless observed the rhythm and approximate pitch of the notation. He called it *sprechstimme* (literally 'speaking voice') and the debt to the melodrama is implied in the subtitle—*Melodramen*. This presented new possibilities in setting dialogue, possibilities which Berg exploited in his turn, and many other composers since.

But for our purpose, the main interest of *Wozzeck* is in its approach to formal problems caused on the one hand by a highly fragmented drama (27 scenes cut down to 15), and on the other by a musical idiom which at this stage had forsaken the unifying potentialities of tonality, or, as Berg himself said, 'how to achieve the same degree of cohesion and of structural unification without the hitherto accepted medium of tonality and of its creative potentialities'. (We shall consider the implications of the breakdown of the tonal system and the emergence of 'twelve-note technique' in more detail in the next chapter.) In practical terms, the problem existed on three levels; the need to integrate the acts within the opera, the scenes within the acts, and the scenes themselves. At the first level, the use of leitmotives, musical and dramatic parallels between the acts, and the device of ending each on the same 'tonic'—G major!—may be cited. At the second level, in addition to leitmotives and the actual continuity of the orchestral texture, a wealth of devices linking scene to scene might be quoted, but one only must stand for them all, namely the anticipating of the passacaglia theme of Act I scene 4 in an apparently insignificant passage for clarinet at the end of the preceding scene (bb. 486–487). At the third level, he adapts abstract forms and procedures such as fugue, sonata, rondo, etc., to each scene, so that to this extent they are musically self-sufficient.

The following summary extracted (and slightly rearranged) is from a lecture Berg himself gave on the form of his opera.[1]

'The two flanking acts ... furnish the framework for the middle Act, like the element "a" in the scheme of the tripartite "lied-form". This Act II is musically much more closely integrated, its five scenes being inseparably linked like the movements of a symphony ... The structure of the two flanking acts is much more loose ... One could call the five scenes of Act I "five musical character pieces" ... The five scenes of Act III correspond with five musical forms the cohesion of which is achieved through some or other unifying principle.'

The following tabulation sets out the formal aspects of the opera in greater detail, with annotations again drawn from Berg's lecture. There is no overture or prelude: by the fourth bar the curtain has risen.

Act I   ('Five musical character pieces.')

Scene 1   'a Suite of more or less stylized archaic dance-forms (such as Prelude, Pavane, Cadenza, Gigue, Gavotte with double refrain)'.

Scene 2   'the unifying principle ... is of an harmonic nature; these [three] chords represent the harmonic vertebra of the scene'.

Scene 3   'Military March (with its intentionally "wrong basses") and ... Lullaby'.

Scene 4   'Passacaglia, or Chaconne ... based on a dodecaphonic subject ... This is followed by 21 variation-forms.'

Scene 5   'a rondo-like Andante affettuoso'.

Act II   ('the movements of a Symphony').

Scene 1   'a Sonata-movement'.

Scene 2   'an Invention and a Fugue with three subjects'.

Scene 3   'The slow movement of this symphony-like Act II is a "Largo".'

[1] Printed in Hans Redlich's *Alban Berg* (London, 1957) pp. 261–285.

Scene 4 'The Ländler . . . is the first subject of this Scherzo . . . A song . . . would correspond with a first Trio, a Waltz, . . . with a second Scherzo, the hunting chorus . . . a second Trio . . . Now follows . . . the repeat of . . . Ländler, Lied, Waltz, . . . as much as possible variational'—in other words, $A_1B_1C_1/D/A_2B_2C_2$.

Scene 5 'Rondo Marziale.'

ACT III ('Six inventions.')

Scene 1 'a theme, subjected to variational treatment'.

Scene 2 'Low "B" . . . now becomes a unifying element and, indeed, the cohesive principle.'

Scene 3 'rhythmic pattern on which the scene is based . . . establishes cohesion and unity'.

Scene 4 'based on only one chord'.

Scene 5 'is preceded by a . . . orchestral interlude representing a thematic development-section, utilizing all the important musical characters related to Wozzeck. Its shape is tripartite and its unifying principle is—an exception to the rule of this opera—Tonality . . . D minor . . . the final scene . . . with its continuous quaver-movement . . . a "perpetuum mobile".'

We have dealt with *Wozzeck* at some length because it represents a fascinating formal exercise, and because it is perhaps the one opera written this century which successfully advances the Wagnerian concept. But as a solution of the problem it set out to solve it can only be regarded as a stop-gap. By its very uniqueness it could provide no broad pattern for the future, and Berg recognized this when he adopted Schoenberg's twelve-note system in his second (and unfinished) opera *Lulu*.

Operas using this technique have, to a greater or lesser extent, proliferated over the last thirty years, though most seem in retrospect rather ephemeral. Quite recently serial and electronic techniques have been used. For those who see opera in terms of symphonic structure, like Wagner, it may be that some form of serialism will provide a workable basis. But composers like Leoš Janáček (1854–1928) and Benjamin Britten (b. 1913) have shown that opera more than worthy of the name can flourish outside the traditions of Grand Opera and Music Drama. Janáček's declamation, grounded as it is in the rhythms and inflections of his native language and folk music—like Moussorgsky's and like Bartók's in 'Bluebeard's Castle' (1911)—is capable of tremendous effect, as operas such as *Kátya Kabanová* (1921) and 'From the House of the Dead' (1928) illustrate. Vastly different are Britten's chamber operas; a genre intended for small-scale production requiring only modest orchestral forces that he has turned to again and again, notably in 'The Rape of Lucretia' (1946), 'Albert Herring' (1947) and 'The Turn of the Screw' (1954). Although he abjures the symphonic approach he uses leitmotives. But there is no attempt to obscure the stylistic differentiation between recitative and song, duets, ensembles and choruses. His recitative is often artificial, in many ways like Purcell's, dwelling on certain words in order to bring out their meaning either for comic or pathetic effect, and (in his chamber operas) often using *recitativo secco* complete with piano 'continuo'. The 'songs' are unashamedly tuneful and depend to a great extent on ostinatos in the accompaniment for their effectiveness.

In point of fact, Britten relies a great deal on the orchestra for all his economical use of it; nowhere more than in the 'interludes' which are so important a structural feature of his operas. In 'Peter Grimes' (1945) the 'Sea Interludes' preface the acts and bridge the scenes. In 'The Rape of Lucretia' this function is allotted to a 'male chorus' and a 'female chorus' (actually soloists), but again in 'Albert Herring' and 'Billy Budd' (1951) important orchestral interludes help to give continuity. Yet it is in 'The Turn of the Screw' that we find the most original exploitation of this connecting device. In this opera the two acts are preceded by a Prologue, and divided into no fewer than 16 scenes, the intervening 'interludes' being treated as variations on the 'theme' announced between the prologue and scene 1. The theme is actually a 'note-row', alternately ascending a perfect fourth and falling back a minor third thus: A, D, B, E, C sharp, F sharp, D sharp, G sharp, F, B flat, G, C—although the treatment is far from atonal. Indeed, to a great extent the opera depends for its shape on the mounting 'white-note' tonalities of the first act— A, B, C, D, E F, G and A flat—scene by scene, which in the second act decline via the predominating black-note keys—A flat, F sharp, F, E flat, C sharp, C, B flat and A.

Here then is another highly individualistic solution to the problem of form in post-Wagnerian opera. In fact, it may be that apart from operas which are traditional in conception and more or less conservative in technique, every modern opera reflects a different approach to the problem of unity and continuity. Consequently, one can hardly speak of opera today, only operas.

IV : 4 20th-century developments

We enter the 20th century with Debussy and Schoenberg. Almost every development in music so far this century can be traced back to the works of these composers. Between them they destroyed the tonal system with its traditional key-relationships grouped round the tonic-dominant polarity, in its place substituting a new concept of tonality—in Debussy's case one favouring modal, pentatonic and whole-tone scales which lack semitones; in Schoenberg's, one based on the semitone scale of twelve notes.

True, they did not do this single-handed. The whole-tone scale had had its occasional devotees before Debussy, and Schoenberg at least could claim (and did claim) that he was merely the instrument of progress, that this was the direction in which Wagner, Strauss and Mahler had indicated music should go. Traditional key-relationships had already been profoundly weakened, and with them the fundamental logic of sonata form. Eventually Schoenberg solved the problem of form without tonality to his own satisfaction with his twelve-note system. Debussy, however, was to discover that his own particular brand of atonality—which was not really keylessness, but rather a kind of nebulous tonality—would work only on a restricted scale, where the brief, quasi-improvisatory impression of a piece of music was to some extent self-justifying with or without the suggestion of a return to the beginning at the end. To this category of works belongs the *Prélude à l'après-midi d'un faune* (1894), the *Nocturnes* (1899) for orchestra, and above all the *Préludes* (1910, 1913) for piano. When it came to writing a work on a large scale—one might say, when it came to composing rather than improvising—in *La Mer* (1905) for instance, he submitted himself to a formal discipline almost for the first time since his early cyclic String Quartet (1893). *La Mer* too, is cyclic; and even with respect to tonality a unity is observed, for to all intents and purposes the work is in D flat major. The opening movement, '*De l'aube à midi sur la mer*', starts with a slow introduction in B minor, but this soon leads to D flat, *Modéré*, *sans lenteur* (Durand miniature score, p. 5) and eventually concludes in that key. Similarly, the third movement, '*Dialogue du vent et de la mer*', starts in C sharp minor but ends in the enharmonic major, D flat.

A closer look at the finale will show us just how close-knit the music is thematically. Like the first movement it starts with an introduction in which the main themes emerge, as it were, from the deep. Both introductions actually present the same material slightly altered, but the rising semitone motive (first heard in the wood-wind at the top of p. 2) is also present in the finale in an inverted and slightly expanded form (fig. 43), and after further modification it becomes the first subject of the movement proper (fig, 46). The key is C sharp minor, and a transition starts at fig. 47 leading to the second subject on p. 99, a whole-tone version of a theme already foreshadowed in the introductions of both move-ments (fig. 1, p. 2, and fig. 44, p. 85). The exposition closes with a chordal theme *très soutenu* in E flat minor on horns, (p. 106) previously heard in the recapitulation of the first movement (fig. 14) and itself a metamorphosis of one of the main themes of the exposition, where it is also given to the horns (fig. 3). Whether what follows is development or recapitulation is open to argu-ment. Undoubtedly the climactic return of the principal theme in the tonic key occurs at fig. 60, and this is followed 14 bars later by a recapitulation of the horn theme, now in B flat minor. But between the end of the exposition (fig. 54) and this return there are two reappearances of the main subject in the tonic (figs. 55 and 56), the second louder than the first, and each followed by short developmental digressions, the latter including a return of the whole-tone subjects (cornets, p. 120) now not quite so whole-tone and tasting strongly of D flat (C sharp) minor. From the tonal point of view this suggests recapitulation rather than development, but the emotional shaping of the movement points nevertheless to the final return of the two principal themes from fig. 60 onwards as the recapitulation, following the dynamic build-up which has gone before—albeit in the tonic key. A short coda (starting fig. 61) based on the second subject treated in ostinato fashion by cornets whips up the excitement in a way that for Debussy is rather theatrical but nonetheless stunningly effective.

This renunciation of some at least of his earlier sensuousness in favour of a greater formal consciousness is carried a stage further in the three comparatively austere sonatas for various instruments he composed at the end of his life. But there had always been a classical strain in Debussy's make-up. We find it, for example, in the seemingly rather precious use of old dance styles in the *Suite Bergamasque* (1890–1905), with its *Menuet* and *Passepied*; the suite *Pour le Piano* (1896–1901) comprising *Prélude*, *Sarabande*, *Toccata*—and elsewhere among the piano music where he pays his respects to the French clavecinistes of the 17th-century. Maurice Ravel (1875–1937), too, in his *Tombeau de Couperin* (1917) followed and helped to consolidate this neo-classical trend. Behind it perhaps we can discover the influence of Erik Satie (1866–1925), whose *Trois Sarabandes* for piano had been published as early as 1887, and who, after the death of Debussy exerted (together with Stravinsky) tremendous influence on 'Les Six'—a group of young French composers whose approach to music was highly irreverent. A frequent irreverency of theirs was to pretend that the 19th century had never existed (so far as serious music was concerned) and to adhere to the letter of 18th-century classical forms. Of the original six, Darius Milhaud (b. 1892), Arthur Honegger (1892–1955), and Francis Poulenc (1899–1963) became the best known. But this 'back-to-the-18th-century movement' was not an entirely French phenomenon, even though its headquarters were in Paris during the 1920's and 1930's. In Russia, Sergei Prokofiev (1891–1953) had composed his 'Classical Symphony' (1917) in flippant imitation of 18th-century models; the first and last movements in strict sonata form

complete with second subjects in the dominant and tonic recapitulations, and a gavotte and musette in place of a minuet and trio.

Igor Stravinsky (b. 1882) also reacting from the extravagance
of such early works as 'The Rite of Spring' (1913), decided there
was virtue in emotional and material economy in his *Histoire du
Soldat* (1918), and went back to Bach in the 'Concerto for Piano
and Wind Instruments' (1924). There is no doubt about the
tremendous power of this work. The first movement is a thudding
concerto-allegro in A minor, framed by a stark and lugubrious
Largo. The Allegro is in ternary form, figs. 5–17 being repeated
almost exactly between figs. 27–38, and the continuous semi-
quaver patterning is replete with sequences in the Bach manner.
Still more Bach-like, or Vivaldi-like, is the unfolding cantilena of
the slow movement, while the finale is a fugue. The theme of the
fugue is harmonized from the start (its first two chords are
borrowed from the cadence of the preceding movement) and
undergoes several alterations during the course of the movement.
A new subject is introduced briefly as an A flat episode (fig. 80)
just before the beginning of the final 'tonic' section (fig. 84).
The movement is rounded off by a recollection of the opening of
the concerto (figs. 86–89) and a bouncing coda.

The fugue came into its own again in the 20th century, and it is
easy to understand its appeal (leaving aside the whole question of
neo-classical aesthetics); for fugal procedures can operate fairly
successfully without the aid of tonality, and traditional devices
such as stretto, inversion, augmentation and diminution offer
sleight-of-hand substitutes for development which composers
have found irresistible. Taking their model from Bach again—
this time 'the 48'—Paul Hindemith (1895–1963) composed his
Ludus Tonalis (1942), a series of fugues and interludes (aptly
called!), and Dmitri Shostakovich (b. 1906) his '24 Preludes and
Fugues' (1951). Both sets have the fugues arranged systematically,
though not according to Bach's order. Shostakovich's keys
ascend by fifths and alternate major with relative minor, like
Chopin's *Préludes*—thus: C major, A minor, G major, E minor,
D major, B minor, etc.—while Hindemith arranges his fugues
according to his own theory of tonal relationships based on the

harmonic series. Between each fugue is an interlude linking it to the next, and the opening 'Prelude' is turned upside-down and played in retrograde inverse motion at the end as a 'Postlude'.

One other baroque form should be mentioned in this context, since it provides something like the same sort of structural assistance as the fugue, namely the *passacaglia*. Hindemith's *Nobilissima Visione* (1938) ends with one and Benjamin Britten, no doubt following Purcell, has been drawn to it, notably in the finale of the second String Quartet (1945) and the fourth 'Interlude' in 'Peter Grimes'.

The composers we have just been dealing with have largely avoided the problem of form without tonality by borrowing a second-hand constructional logic from the past through parody. This has generally given rise to static non-developmental forms, as with Stravinsky—lengths of music pasted together; or forms where the development is an adjunct of contrapuntal manipulation, as with Hindemith. The ability to develop his material organically is one of the things which distinguishes Béla Bartók (1881–1945) from both these composers. As a composer his development followed its own course, assimilating external influences rather than being converted by them, and we may trace this development in his six string quartets. These represent him throughout his life, and taken together probably amount to the most significant works of this type since Beethoven. The first (1908) is a rather immature work in three movements, each quicker than the one previous and employing cyclic devices. The second Quartet (1917) is again in three movements, this time ending with the slow one, and showing the influence of Hungarian melodic and rhythmic folk-idioms, together with a more astringent harmonic style—particularly in the second movement, the scherzo.

But it is in the third Quartet (1927) that we find Bartók in his maturity; the Hungarian influences fully absorbed. It is in one movement, with four 'parts'—slow, fast, slow, fast—marked respectively *Prima parte*, *Seconda parte*, *Ricapitulazione della prima parte* and *Coda*. It is interesting to compare the first part with its '*ricapitulazione*'. At first sight they hardly seem to be related at all.

However, on closer inspection some correspondences are evident, most obviously between the *Lento* sections at fig. 11 (p. 7, Boosey and Hawkes miniature score), and fig. 7, p. 30. (Compare also the bars which lead up to these two sections). Even so, it is more a return to a similar type of movement and texture than a thematic recapitulation in the accepted sense. The *Seconda parte* is a type of rondo, though all the thematic material of this movement, episodes as well as refrains, is clearly inter-related, consisting essentially of ascending and descending scalic figures in one mode or another altered rhythmically. The opening section (*A*) contains a ternary thematic group, moving from clashing D minor and E flat minor (fig. 3) to clashing A minor and A major (fig. 5) and back again (fig. 7). The first episode (*B*) starts at fig. 10 (cello and viola) and continues contrapuntally with close canonic imitations between pairs of instruments (fig. 12) and by inverse movement as well (fig. 16). The refrain section (*A*) returns at fig. 23 (figs. 26 and 28 unmistakably corresponding with figs. 3 and 5, thematically and harmonically). At fig. 31 the second episode (*C*) commences; a double fugue with subject and answer at the conventional intervals and strettos and inversions to follow. This leads to highly abbreviated returns of *A* (fig. 36) and *B* (fig. 38) with a coda starting at fig. 41. Tension is built up in a passage characterized by glissandos and semi-tonal clashes only to dissolve into the *Ricapitulazione*. The coda of the work as a whole develops the material of the second part further, thus the overall shape of the work is $A_1 \ B_1 \ A_2 \ B_2$.

The last three quartets demonstrate the importance that Bartók attached to overall unity as clearly in their way as the interlocking 'parts' of the third. The fourth (1928) and fifth (1934) are both five-movement works which balance symmetrically on each side of a central movement—slow in the fourth, a scherzo in the fifth. The resulting arch or *bogen*-form is further underlined by the fact that the fourth movement of no. 4 is actually a free variation on the second movement, while the first and the last also have thematic material in common—thus we have the scheme $A_1, B_1,$ C, B_2, A_2. Similarly in no. 5, the first movement itself is arch-shaped, recapitulating the subjects of the exposition in reverse order (and upside-down) after the central development section. The procedure in no. 6 (1939) is somewhat different. Here the first three movements start with an introductory *Mesto* theme—a sort of motto, heard first as a solo leading into a straight-forward sonata-form movement, then in two parts leading into a *Marcia* in ternary form, then in three parts leading to a *Burletta* also in ternary form. The fourth movement begins similarly with the 'motto' in four parts, but this time it is no longer an introduction, it is the beginning of the slow-movement finale itself. It is as if, after three false starts, the finale can at last proceed to its conclusion, which it does with recollections from the first movement.

Bartók's use of a motto theme and thematic recall in his final quartet is quite consistent with his whole approach to structural thematicism, though it represents a radical simplification of cyclic ideas found in the fourth and fifth quartets, and widely elsewhere. The appeal of symmetry is everywhere obvious, most strikingly in his use of arch-forms, also in numerous ternary movements, and in the ternary aspect of his sonata form. Yet for all their symmetry there is no rigidity. Growth is continuous and organic; the very essence of the music.

In contrast to the self-conscious formalism of some of his contemporaries it is clear that Bartók had a natural feeling for form. Individual movements as well as complete works are thematically integrated by means of change and interchange of motives, and symmetrically balanced in an architecture of the emotions. He had the advantage of Arnold Schoenberg (1874–1951) in being able to free himself from the oppressiveness of the late 19th-century Teutonic tradition by, as it were, speaking his native language rather than inventing a new one. Schoenberg began as one would expect a *fin-de-siècle*, rather earnest Viennese of promise to begin. From this period we have the programmatic String Sextet *Verklärte Nacht* (1899), a single-movement work, and a mammoth tone poem *Pelleas und Melisande* (1903). Gradually his chromaticism crept away from tonality and his search for some other means of cohesion and unity led to the 'Chamber Symphony' (1906) which is continuous and articulated rather like

Liszt's Piano Sonata, with scherzo and slow movement intervening between the three sonata-form divisions of the principal material; thus:

Exp: Scherzo: Dev: Slow movt: Recap.

But as Schoenberg's musical language became more divorced from tonality, it became clear to him that something was needed to take the place of tonal cohesion. Aimless atonality might suffice in short or fragmentary works, as in *Pierrot Lunaire* (1912), but large-scale abstract musical construction needed a system. Not that—when it came to the point—he applied his 'system' to large-scale construction immediately. In fact, a glance at the titles of the movements in his *Suite* for piano—'Prelude', 'Gavotte', 'Musette', 'Intermezzo', 'Minuet', and 'Gigue'—and its date, 1924, might make one suspect neo-classical modishness at first. But Schoenberg's neo-classicism was never light-hearted, or light-headed, like that of '*les Six*'. He was led in this direction partly as a reaction against the unrestrained emotionalism of his early works, and partly because in this, the most thorough working out of his twelve-note method of composition to date, such simple forms would help to give his music a readily appreciable shape. It was an entirely reasonable precaution to use traditional forms here and in the 'Wind Quintet' of the same year, when in other respects the music was so revolutionary. The system of planned atonality had been maturing for more than a dozen years (since Wagner at least, Schoenberg would have said), and baldly stated it proposed that the melodic and harmonic ingredients of a piece should all derive from a basic set or series of twelve different notes; a 'note-row' comprising every degree of the chromatic scale arranged in order according to the choice of the composer. (If we refer back to the fugue subject in Strauss's *Also Sprach Zarathustra*—p. 156—we may observe that the last twelve notes form such a row.) This in itself would provide a greater unity than was possible now that the bonds of tonality had been cast off. Clearly it is a process akin to thematic metamorphosis, but instead of postulating an original theme, such a theme is itself regarded as a metamorphosis of something yet more basic;

the series of notes to which any theme might be reduced, and from which the thematic elements of a composition might be elaborated. Indeed, one could argue that this is just what happens consciously or unconsciously in composing. One could also argue that in Western music, melody and harmony are inseparably bound—as Wagner said 'melody is the surface of harmony'—and that Schoenberg coming directly in the main stream of late 19th-century chromaticism was bound to see the next step as total chromaticism, harmonic and melodic.

Having constructed the note-row there are several things that may be done with it. It may be inverted, retrograded, or both at once. Any note may be transposed up or down an octave, and the whole row in any form may be transposed. Notes may be superimposed to form chords, or the row broken up and distributed on different levels in the texture. Even so, in practical terms the composer does what he likes with the series. Composing starts where the system stops and in fact there are probably no works of any length and merit which are entirely serial in the strict sense. Berg's 'Lyric Suite' (1926) is a case in point. This is a String Quartet with six movements, in three contrasted pairs, the contrasts becoming more and more violent as the work progresses. Thus, I and II *Allegretto gioviale—Andante amoroso*, III and IV *Allegro misterioso—Adagio appassionato*, V and VI *Presto delirando—Largo desolato*. Emotionally then, the suite represents a gradual intensification of a manic-depressive trend, and it is in this drive towards the final opposition of the frenzied and the forlorn, that its emotional unity is realized; a unity which (when all is said and done) probably owes little or nothing to the thematic interconnections between movements. Thematic cross-references of this sort are nevertheless extensive and elaborate, not to mention borrowings which include the opening bars of 'Tristan' in the last movement (bb. 26–27). Formally most of the movements are fairly clear. There is no mistaking the ternary form of the *Allegro misterioso*—the trio is marked *Estatico*—or of the *Presto delirando* with its two trios marked *Tenebroso*.

Not all the movements of this work make use of strict twelve-note technique, which is mainly to be found in the first, third,

fifth and sixth movements. The opening page of the finale shows
the system in action. The underlying idea here is a rhythmic one
at first, and as each instrument enters in a sort of fugato the
number of notes to the beat increases from two, to three, to four,
to six, thus giving the impression of an acceleration in tempo.
This acceleration is accompanied by a crescendo from *pp* to
f molto. The cello (with its C string tuned down to B) announces
the note-row (Ex. 21 (i)—*A*)—used previously in the work—and
within the first six bars repeats it a further three times. The viola
is the second instrument to enter and it does so with a new version
of the row (Ex. 21 (ii)—*B*) in which we hear first the low notes
(F and below, though not the E flat for some reason or other)
then the high notes of *A*. Thus:

The first violin enters with *B* inverted (and diminished), and the
second violin with *A* (also inverted and further diminished), while
in bars 6–8 we find a transposed version of *B* (starting on A
instead of F) now spread over more than three octaves by means of
octave transposition and given to the first violin. In effect, these
eight bars are an epitome of the whole work. The quickening note
values combined with the gradual crescendo clearly parallels the
work's progress towards expressive extremes, and the separation
of the row *A* into high and low components in *B* reflects the same
evolution from comparative equability to emotional heights
and depths. This becomes explicit when transpositions expand

the row's original compass of a major 7th to over three octaves, and the dynamic range to *ff molto*. The rest of the movement treats this material more freely, in a kind of rhapsody of despair, dying away at last without even a double bar to give it decent burial. The whole work clearly demonstrates that the twelve-note system does not preclude a highly-charged emotionalism. Indeed, it would be strange if it did, considering its origins.

Before leaving the 'Lyric Suite' one other aspect of its construction should be remarked upon, namely, the importance which the number 23 and its simple multiples play in determining the length and speed of certain movements. It is more than a coincidence that I is 69 (23×3) bars long, III in 138 (23×6) bars long, IV is 69, V is 460 (23×20) and VI is 46 (23×2); and that, for example, the three sections of the third movement are articulated as follows: *Allegro misterioso* = 69 bars, *Trio estatico* = 23 bars, and *Tempo I* again = 46 bars. Further, an examination of the metronome markings of the last three movements reveals that in IV, $\quarternote = 69$; in V, $\dottedquarternote = 115$ (23×5); and in VI, $\quarternote = 69$ (*Tempo I*), $\quarternote = 46$ (*Tempo II*) and $\halfnote = 46$ (*Meno largo*). Nor is this all. The number 23 crops up more often than has been indicated here, though why it does is a mystery. The fact that the work was dedicated to Berg's friend Alexander von Zemlinsky strongly suggests that the figure has some alphabetical significance (A.Z. being the initials of the dedicatee). Whatever the explanation, clearly this number is of formal significance, since it influences both the length and the speed of certain movements, and in doing so interrelates them. Thus, in terms of pulse, VI recalls IV, so perhaps does V, though here the relationship is more complex (five beats of V equalling two beats of IV). But certainly the common pulse of IV and VI is easily sensed by the listener— more so than elaborate thematic metamorphoses might be— hence tempo relationship as a principle must be regarded as a valid integrating device. We shall return to this function of tempo later.

In spite of his adoption of his master's revolutionary technique Berg actually sounds like a traditional composer. In this respect he is unlike Schoenberg's other famous pupil, Anton Webern

(1883–1945). Webern may be said to have combined Schoenberg's system with Debussy's impressionistic use of colour. But whereas Debussy's most characterisic effects were produced by the orchestration (or pianistic placing) of chords with primary consideration to the 'colour' or 'atmosphere' thereby produced, Webern does the same with single notes or melodic fragments, so that the interest is neither harmonic nor melodic in the traditional sense, but lies in a 'melody of tone colours'. This technique of *Klangfarbenmelodie* can be traced back through Schoenberg to Mahler, where it appears as an occasional trait in his orchestration. But the comparison of Webern's *Klangfarbenmelodie* with what we might call Debussy's *'Klangfarbenharmonie'* does not take into account the fact that Debussy at his most impressionistic is also at his most improvisatory, while Webern (whose music may or may not be intelligible as a kind of abstract impressionism) organizes his colours according to strict serial procedures. Characteristically the row is split between instruments and spread over a wide range so that no melodic shape or continuity is discernible. The row then reproduces itself according to the principles already enumerated, but much more strictly and especially through various types of canon, including mirror inversion and retrograde movement. Throughout the exposition of the first movement of his 'Symphony' (1928) for example, the two horns are in mirror canon, so are the clarinet and bass clarinet. These and other canons are separate components of a note-row (A, F sharp, G, A flat, E, F, B, B flat, D, C sharp, C and E flat) presented forwards and backwards with both forms upsidedown at the same time—four strands which thread their way from instrument to instrument across the score, In the second and last movement, a set of variations on an eleven bar 'theme', each variation plays itself forward for five and a half bars, then backwards for five and a half bars, over and above profuse mirror canons. In this sort of writing not only are the pitches and time-values of the notes treated canonically, but also their dynamics, timbres and nuances. Schoenberg, in clarifying his ideas with regard to melody and harmony, had hardly touched upon rhythm, dynamics, tone-colour, etc., in so far as they enter into the formal unity of a work. Yet neither he nor his pupils were unaware of the important structural role these elements could play, and we have already observed Berg in the last movement of his 'Lyric Suite' using shorter note-durations combined with thickening texture and a gradual crescendo to shape the opening bars. Clearly there is some psychological and physiological response in the human to regular variation of these elements. At its most primitive, it is everyone's experience that we become more excited when the pulse of music quickens, when it gets louder, or higher. In Western music this is usually felt as an adjunct of melody and harmony; but we have examples of autonomous rhythm in the rhythmic modes of the *Ars antiqua*, and the isorhythmic techniques of the *Ars nova* as obvious precedents for arbitrarily fitting notes to predetermined rhythms. The possibility of using rhythms, and other elements such as dynamics and timbres, as independent entities, and controlling the way they will vary in themselves and in relation to each other, must be recognized as a means by which music may be shaped. As a structural device it can extend row-serialism to all the variables in music, a phenomenon which might be described as more or less total serialism.

Let us examine some examples of rhythm functioning independently and treated systematically. This is not really a modern idea as we have observed, but in the 20th-century Stravinsky in 'The Rite of Spring' (1913) and *Les Noces* (1923) spun out whole passages by means of rhythmic ostinatos in variable metres. Bartók, in his fourth Quartet, begins the fourth movement with the following 'series' in which single crotchets interject between groups of crotchets expanding from two, to five, and back again. Here are the first twelve bars of the cello part, expressed rhythmically and without bar lines.

I 2 I 3 I 4 I 5 I 3 I 2

The effect is of tension mounting and subsiding, and examples are fairly common in the works of Stravinsky and Bartók. More recently the idea has been taken up by Boris Blacher (b. 1903), but it is Olivier Messiaen (b. 1908) who has most fully explored these and other types of rhythmic systematization.

As early as 1940 we find chord and rhythmic series of unequal lengths permutated with each other in the first movement of his *Quatuor pour la fin du temps*. In his *Mode de valeurs et d'intensités* (1949) time values and dynamics are combined serially. His work for piano, *Cantéyodjayâ* (1953)[1] shows some of these effects. An episode marked 'Modéré *(mode de durées, de hauteurs et d'intensités)*' (pp. 8–10) starts in the right hand with a series in which the values of the notes increase by demisemiquavers from one to eight (i.e. a crotchet). The first four of these notes—D, C sharp, B flat and G sharp—are marked *pp*, the last four—A, E flat, F sharp and C—are marked *ff*. The rest of the passage uses only these notes, but in a different order with, on each occasion, their original time value and intensity. Thus D, whenever it occurs, is always a demisemiquaver and always pianissimo; C is always a crotchet and always fortissimo. (The other two staves are organized similarly, with their own notes, durations and intensities.) Elsewhere in the work we may observe:

pp. 6–7   'alba'—an ostinato of chords with the values of 2, 3, 4 and 8 semiquavers under a cantilena marked 'Modéré, *avec une nostalgie passionée*.'

pp. 13   'Modéré *(gamme chromatique des durées, droite et rétrograde)*' where the durations of the bass notes reduce progressively in value from 23 demisemiquavers to 1, while the treble increases from 1 to 23 (p. 18 also).

p. 17   'Presque vif, brutal' where the rhythm of the first 7½ bars is retrograded in the next 7½.

p. 19   'Vif *(interversions)*' where a four-note series, D, E, D sharp and A—respectively and consistently valued at 2, 3, 4 and 8 semiquavers—are permutated in the bass.

p. 22   'Vif *(rhythme non rétrogradable amplifié au centre)*' where a durational series is expanded through the insertion of new rhythmic groups. The resulting rhythmic and dynamic series always remains symmetrical about its centre (this is what Messiaen means by '*non rétrogradable*'—rhythms which have already been retrograded!).

[1] Universal Edition.

Such devices as these might seem to be little more than note-spinning. Nevertheless, they may be justified by the musical effects they produce; the intriguing way certain ideas fade in and out; the interesting and even beautiful accidents which result from the collision of these variables as they rotate.

The overall structure of this work is loose and episodic, but two main sections are apparent, which are combined and concluded in a summary recapitulation.

A (pp. 3–10) rondo with 5 returns of the opening *cantéyodjayâ* refrain; the last two episodes, the longest ones (pp. 6–7 and pp. 8–9) employing rhythms and intensities as described above.

B (pp. 10–24) an arrangement of short *Refrains* and lengthy *Couplets*, beginning with an exposition of the refrains and continuing with couplets and refrains alternating thus: *1r, 2r, 3r: 1c, 1r: 2c, 2r: 3r* leading into

C (pp. 25–27) a recapitulation of the first and third refrains, and finally the *cantéyodjayâ* with reminiscences of episodic material from *A*.

Messiaen's pupils have adopted his serial ideas more or less, but on the whole they have fought shy of his exotic and sumptuous textures, preferring to apply his lessons (usually) in the delicate *pointilliste* manner of Webern. Even Stravinsky has come under the spell of Webern in works written since 1952.

Perhaps the best known example of the post-Webern style is *Le Marteau sans Maître* (1954) by Pierre Boulez (b. 1925). This work is less strictly serial than some of his earlier compositions, but in any case we shall consider some of the overall formal elements rather than the detailed bar to bar construction of the music. It comprises nine movements, and is scored for alto voice and 6 instruments. The movements are as follows:

I   *avant 'l'artisanat furieux'* (flute, vibraphone, guitar, viola)
II *commentaire I de 'bourreaux de solitude'* (flute, xylorimba, percussion and viola)
III *'l'artisanat furieux'* (flute and voice)
IV *commentaire II de 'bourreaux de solitude'* (xylorimba, vibraphone, percussion, guitar and viola)
V   *'bel édifice et les pressentiments'* (flute, guitar, viola and voice)

VI   *'bourreaux de solitude'* (flute, xylorimba, vibraphone, percussion, guitar, viola and voice)

VII   *après 'l'artisanat furieux'* (flute, vibraphone and guitar)

VIII   *commentaire III de 'bourreaux de solitude'* (flute, xylorimba, vibraphone and percussion)

IX   *'bel édifice et les pressentiments' double* (flute, xylorimba, vibraphone, percussion, guitar, viola and voice).

The internal relationships are already hinted at in this list. Nos. II, IV, VI and VIII (group *A*) belong together as commentaries on some idea held in common, nos. I, III and VII (group *B*) are a kind of triptych centring round the actual setting of *'l'artisanat furieux'*, while V and IX are related by virtue of their common text. Each group possesses certain musical characteristics peculiar to itself. For example, the even numbered movements (group *A*) are marked by a tone-quality in which xylorimba and percussion figure prominently (also in IX which acts as a summary of the whole) while the others do not use percussion. Further, if we compare the tempo indications of the two groups we can see that they are purposely differentiated and internally related. It will be recalled that we have already observed tempo relationships used as an integrating device in Berg's 'Lyric Suite'.

> *A*   II   *Lent* ($\downarrow$ = 76)
>   IV   *Assez rapide* ($\downarrow$ = 132, i.e. 76 × 2)
>   VI   *Assez lent* ($\downarrow$ = 63)
>   VIII   *Assez lent* ($\downarrow$ = 76)
> *B*   I   *Rapide* ($\downarrow$ = 208)
>   III   *Modéré* ($\downarrow$ = 52, i.e. $\downarrow$ = 104, or 208 ÷ 2)
>   VII   *Rapide* ($\downarrow$ = 208)

A still closer look at *A* shows that they are interconnected by simple rhythmic ideas allotted to the percussion instruments, and that they are typified by a fluctuating tempo-structure, similar (though not the same) in each. If we can regard tempos here as one would themes in, say, Liszt, these four movements are seen to be inter-related. And undoubtedly it is a tempo-relationship that the composer intends us to be aware of, even unconsciously, and which, together with the characteristic tone-qualities of the ensembles and the reappearance of certain rhythmic features, provides the main unifying element. The movements of group *B* partake of the nature of linking movements, and to some extent they provide timbre and tempo contrasts with the movements of group *A* while showing a consistency in these matters within themselves. It will be observed that *rapide* and *modéré* are related to each other in the speed-ratio 2:1.

Nos. V and IX are perhaps the least similar movements despite the fact that they each set the same words—and this is the point. Boulez here allows himself musical diversity in the knowledge that the words, however dissimilar in treatment, will relate the two. No. IX also functions as a recapitulation of ideas from the other movements. The texture at bar 130 (*Tempo Modéré, sans rigueur*) unmistakably recalls III with its identical tempo marking. Earlier in this finale (bb. 9–11) there is even a reference to the actual notes of the opening of VI—compare the vibraphone and viola parts backwards and forwards. From bar 42 onwards we begin a recapitulation of the principal tempos characteristic of both groups, *A* and *B*. This section sums up the work as a whole and the ensemble is all but complete. The voice is wordless, finally drifting away on the sound of the flute and 'thumbed' cymbal.

Obviously the principal formal elements here, tempo and timbre, are new to Western music as structural entities in themselves. However, here they provide the basis of the formal cohesion of *Le Marteau sans Maître*, which may be illustrated as follows:

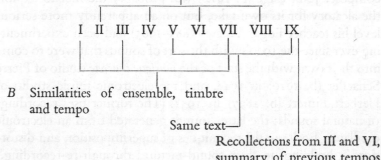

A Similarities of ensemble, timbre, tempo and tempo variation

I II III IV V VI VII VIII IX

B Similarities of ensemble, timbre and tempo

Same text—

Recollections from III and VI, summary of previous tempos and timbres

Serialism is, after all, a systematization of the repetition–variation principle which is the basis of traditional form. It would seem no more objectionable that a mathematical programme should be used than a literary one of the sort we are already familiar with in 'programme' music—the parallel between the two may be more exact than we realize at first. Paradoxically *Le Marteau sans Maître*, for all its order, appears to justify itself more by the delicate quality of its sounds, as do Debussy's most impressionistic pieces, than by any effect exceeding the sum of the parts—the evidence of form in action.

Radical as this work may appear in certain respects, it is formally comprehensible in traditional terms. In this it cannot be said to typify the most recent trends, which to a greater or lesser extent abrogate the controlling order of the composer (and even of the computer) in favour of the performer and the mechanical circumstances of performance. It is true that no piece of music has ever been heard exactly the same way in any two performances, for some link in the chain from composer to listener is always different. Further, in the case of classical cadenzas, soloistic ornamentation and continuo realization, the actual notes were left to the guided spontaneity of the performer, while the combined improvization of a group of soloists upon a predetermined sequence of chords is an important ingredient of Jazz. These, not to mention the indeterminate rhythm of the clavecin preludes of d'Anglebert,[1] are precedents for the reintroduction of the idea of leaving something to chance in modern music. The American composer John Cage (b. 1912) was probably the first to exploit the aleatory for its own sake, but on an apparently more serious level his teacher Edgar Varèse (1885–1965) had been experimenting ever since the 1920's with the sort of sounds that were to come into their own with the start of the *musique concrète* studio of Pierre Schaeffer (b. 1910) in 1948, and the electronic music studio of Herbert Eimert (b. 1897) in 1951. (The former uses recordings of natural sounds; the latter sounds generated from an electronic oscillator. Both use the techniques of superimposition and distortion in building up their sound-pictures through re-recording.)

[1] *HAM* 232.

In the case of *musique concrète* the typical effect might be described as surrealist, while electronic music lends itself ideally to abstract composition based on completely serial treatment. But electronic music did not long maintain its splendid isolation from the world of natural sound and human unpredictability. In his *Gesang der Jünglinge* (1956) Karlheinz Stockhausen (b. 1928) combined the human voice with electronic sounds, and has since gone on to taste the delights of 'chance music'. He introduced into his *Zeitmasse* (1956) certain sections in which accelerandos, ritardandos, and tempos are left to the judgement and ability of the five players, with the result that these free passages are unlikely to sound the same way twice. The work is primarily a study in speed relationships, as are many avant-garde works. Titles such as 'Prolation' (1958) by Peter Maxwell Davies (b. 1934) indicate the importance of this aspect in their structure. Stockhausen's next work, *Klavierstück XI* (1956), is printed on a single, large piece of paper, and gives 19 musical snippets which may be played in any order the performer desires. Each snippet is capable of numerous interpretations with regard to tempo and dynamics, and the work ends when each section has been played once, and one—any one—twice, thus closing the form with a recapitulation! The itinerary of this work is thus capable of infinite variation. In *Kontakte* (1960) Stockhausen writes for piano, percussion, tape recorder and three loud-speakers, thus combining chance effects (deriving from the impossibility of synchronizing the live performance and the pre-recorded tape) with electronic music, and the remarkable stereophonic effects he had achieved in his *Gruppen* (1957) for three orchestras. The exploitation of spatial effects has, of course, an honourable history, especially in the music for *cori spezzati* in the 16th and 17th centuries, and it was also an occasional factor in Berlioz's musical design—notably in the *Requiem* (1837) with its vast orchestra and brass bands placed at the compass points. Again, the titles of many avant-garde works illustrate their composers' interest in 'space' as an additional dimension to 'time' in which music might exist; see, for example, the *Perspectives* (1956) of Luciano Berio (b. 1925).

By forsaking an accepted musical vocabulary and syntax in

favour of something varying from a total serialization of the elements of pitch, duration, tempo, dynamics and timbre in musical construction, to their haphazard interaction through aleatory contrivances; by enlarging instrumental resources to include electronically produced and manipulated sounds; and by exploring the formal possibilities of time and space relationships, avant-garde composers seem to have left all but their devotees behind. It cannot be denied that such music communicates with fewer and fewer people, and sociologically this is probably an unhealthy state of affairs. Yet a composer like Luigi Nono (b. 1924) seems able to breathe life into Stockhausen's abstract techniques, and though his music is still limited in its appeal, nevertheless it makes its appeal in the same way that the music of the past does. But in any case, there are no absolute arguments that can dismiss this music, for it may be said that any and every human activity is (or may be) significant, and that for some there is pleasure and even edification of a kind to be gained from its most accidental and apparently nonsensical manifestations. In other words, there is no such thing as nonsense!

The implications of 'chance music' with regard to form are quite profound; they exaggerate the whole problem of form in modern music and should at least make us think again about what it means. Form is usually regarded analytically, as a breakdown and discovery of universal elements of structure—as it were, a highest common factor of harmonic, melodic and other emotion-shaping procedures as they appear in a group of works. But form—shape, arrangement of parts, visible aspect, mode in which a thing exists or manifests itself (to quote the dictionary)—is also a multiple of these things. Possibly the last and most salutary lesson the student learns is that the form of each piece of music is different. This is the very *raison d'être* of the newest music, in which the creation of a unique musical form is sought; unique not only with respect to each piece but to each performance as well.

Form as a multiple, as a resultant, seems at present to be the only way of applying the word to this new music. Undoubtedly it will provide a source of novel effects that the more sluggishly flowing main stream will convert to its own use in time, as has already happened with the twelve-note technique of Schoenberg. But assuming for the moment that it will prove viable in itself, it is not impossible that formal principles will in the end be revealed through familiar acquaintance and analysis. The mathematics and psychology of choice are areas in which they may well be discoverable. Some clear thinking in the matter of the space-time relationship—on a musical rather than a cosmological level—might also discover the order in seeming chaos.

Index